El Golpe

T0124344

Wildcat: Workers' Movements and Global Capitalism

Series Editors:
Immanuel Ness (City University of New York)
Peter Cole (Western Illinois University)
Raquel Varela (Instituto de História Contemporânea [IHC]
of Universidade Nova de Lisboa, Lisbon New University)
Tim Pringle (SOAS, University of London)

Also available:

The Cost of Free Shipping:
Amazon in the Global Economy
Edited by Jake Alimahomed-Wilson
and Ellen Reese

Choke Points:
Logistics Workers Disrupting the Global
Supply Chain
Edited by Jake Alimahomed-Wilson
and Immanuel Ness

Power Despite Precarity:
Strategies for the Contingent Faculty
Movement in Higher Education
Joe Berry and Helena Worthen

Dying for an iPhone:
Apple, Foxconn and the Lives of China's
Workers
Jenny Chan, Mark Selden and Pun Ngai

Just Work?
Migrant Workers' Struggles Today
Edited by Aziz Choudry and
Mondli Hlatshwayo

Wobblies of the World:
A Global History of the IWW
Edited by Peter Cole, David Struthers
and Kenyon Zimmer

Arise:
Power, Strategy and Union Resurgence
Jane Holgate

Augmented Exploitation:
Artificial Intelligence, Automation and
Work
Edited by Phoebe V. Moore and
Jamie Woodcock

Organizing Insurgency:
Workers' Movements in the Global South
Immanuel Ness

Southern Insurgency:
The Coming of the Global Working Class
Immanuel Ness

Amakomiti:
Grassroots Democracy in South African
Shack Settlements
Trevor Ngwane

Workers' Inquiry and Global Class Struggle:
Strategies, Tactics, Objectives
Edited by Robert Ovetz

The Spirit of Marikana:
The Rise of Insurgent Trade Unionism
in South Africa
Luke Sinwell with Siphiwe Mbatha

Solidarity:
Latin America and the US Left in
the Era of Human Rights
Steve Striffler

Working the Phones:
Control and Resistance in Call Centres
Jamie Woodcock

El Golpe

U.S. Labor, the CIA, and the Coup at Ford in Mexico

Rob McKenzie

With Patrick Dunne

PLUTO  PRESS

First published 2022 by Pluto Press
New Wing, Somerset House, Strand, London WC2R 1LA

www.plutobooks.com

British Library Cataloguing in Publication Data
A catalogue record for this book is available from the British Library

ISBN 978 0 7453 4563 5   Hardback
ISBN 978 0 7453 4562 8   Paperback
ISBN 978 0 7453 4566 6   PDF
ISBN 978 0 7453 4564 2   EPUB

This book is printed on paper suitable for recycling and made from fully managed and sustained forest sources. Logging, pulping and manufacturing processes are expected to conform to the environmental standards of the country of origin.

Typeset by Stanford DTP Services, Northampton, England

Simultaneously printed in the United Kingdom and United States of America

Contents

List of Photographs

Series Preface

Workers' movements are a common and recurring feature in contemporary capitalism. The same militancy that inspired the mass labor movements of the twentieth century continues to define worker struggles that proliferate throughout the world today.

For more than a century, labor unions have mobilized to represent the political-economic interests of workers by uncovering the abuses of capitalism, establishing wage standards, improving oppressive working conditions, and bargaining with employers and the state. Since the 1970s, organized labor has declined in size and influence as the global power and influence of capital has expanded dramatically. The world over, existing unions are in a condition of fracture and turbulence in response to neoliberalism, financialization, and the reappearance of rapacious forms of imperialism. New and modernized unions are adapting to conditions and creating class-conscious workers' movement rooted in militancy and solidarity. Ironically, while the power of organized labor contracts, working-class militancy and resistance persists and is growing in the Global South.

Wildcat publishes ambitious and innovative works on the history and political economy of workers' movements and is a forum for debate on pivotal movements and labor struggles. The series applies a broad definition of the labor movement to include workers in and out of unions, and seeks works that examine proletarianization and class formation; mass production; gender, affective and reproductive labor; imperialism and workers; syndicalism and independent unions, and labor and Leftist social and political movements.

Prologue

In the pre-dawn darkness outside Mexico City, in the dim light created by streetlamps, a group of about 300 thugs and tough guys prepare to enter the Ford Cuautitlán Assembly Plant. They are men willing to commit acts of violence for the right price and are armed with clubs and firearms. Many have been drinking or have strengthened their resolve with drugs. They are wearing ill-fitting Ford uniforms with company ID badges displayed on their chests. The government union officials and gangsters who have hurriedly pulled the group together wait for the final OK to enter the plant.

It is January 8, 1990. The events of the next few hours will shape the lives of workers at the plant irreversibly. Within a few months, hundreds will have lost their jobs, after protesting the violent attacks on them that were about to begin. Within a few days, one worker will be dead.

In isolation, the Golpe (meaning "coup" in Spanish) at Ford Cuautitlán is a gut-wrenching tale of a courageous struggle and its betrayal. Faced with the opposition and resources of one of the largest employers in Mexico, the dominant labor federation in the country, the ruling Mexican political party, and the U.S. government, workers fought valiantly for years against wage cuts and for elemental union democracy. But the Golpe cannot be viewed in isolation.

Domestically, a challenge to the authoritarian rule of the Partido Revolucionario Institucional, or Institutional Revolutionary Party (PRI), was brewing. In 1988, a coalition of left parties, the Frente Democrático Nacional, or National Democratic Front (FDN), had won the July election, vowing to reverse the free-market reforms the PRI was promoting. Only quick and decisive electoral fraud on the part of the PRI enabled it to hold on to power. Undeterred by the true vote against him, President Carlos Salinas, a Harvard-educated Ph.D., moved forward with his program of deregulation, privatization, austerity, and free trade that began in the wake of the 1982 economic crisis. The worker insurgency at the Ford Cuautitlán plant was the latest manifestation of rising militancy in the working class. As diplomatic cables detailed in this book demonstrate, Salinas and his government feared further industrial action would scare off foreign capital. They had to crush the workers—and in the form of the Confederación Trabajadores de México, or Confederation of Mexican Workers (CTM), they had a compliant union federation that they could turn to for support. When that proved to be insufficient, they found help from outside the country.

Some readers will be aware of the long history of intervention by the United States in South and Central America during the Cold War. The CIA was a critical agent of political change in the region, waging largely successful covert operations against the left-of-center governments in Guatemala, Cuba, British Guiana, the Dominican Republic, Brazil, and Chile. In 1981, U.S. President Reagan authorized the CIA to conduct covert operations against the Sandinista government in Nicaragua. Part of the Reagan administration's justification for this was based on the belief that if Nicaragua fell under the control of a leftist-leaning government, neighboring Mexico could be next. To protect the PRI, but more importantly to protect American capital investment into the country, the DoS looked to support the decades-old status quo forces that would stand in the way of democratic industrial action like that practiced in Cuautitlán.

Joining this anti-communist crusade was the foreign-policy leadership of the American Federation of Labor-Congress of Industrial Organizations (AFL-CIO), the largest labor federation in the United States. Since the end of World War II, many of the AFL-CIO's top officers and staff had worked hand-in-glove with U.S. intelligence services to fight communism in foreign trade unions. Latin America proved to be a crucible in which purported representatives of the U.S. labor movement organized, trained, and funded right-wing groups to wreak havoc on the social fabric of nations led by left-leaning governments. Most of this work was done by the American Institute for Free Labor Development, created in 1962, referred to in the text as AIFLD or the Institute. Although the Institute claimed to be a private organization, the U.S. government financed it, and,

1

The Birth of AIFLD and the Coup in British Guiana

As Kirkland has always done, and as I would always do and George Meany, vigorously deny that the CIA ever had anything to do with the AIFLD. I would be willing to swear on a Bible, and I'm a practicing Catholic, that the CIA did not finance the AIFLD. But, that doesn't do any good because even if they did, I would have to deny it.

William Doherty Jr., 1996

The American Institute for Free Labor Development (AIFLD) was incorporated as a non-profit organization in late 1961. Created as an immediate response to the success of the Cuban revolution, it was the product of over a decade of prior collaboration between the CIA and the American Federation of Labor-Congress of Industrial Organizations (AFL-CIO) in the Cold War struggle.[1]

As the ultimate defeat of Nazi Germany became evident in the final months of World War II, the Soviet Union and the U.S. began planning for a post-war confrontation. The devastation caused by the war and the pre-eminent role of communists and labor militants in the anti-Nazi resistance had helped put leftists in a strong position in post-war European unions. As early as 1944, the Office of Strategic Services (OSS), the forerunner to the Central Intelligence Agency (CIA), calculated that it would have to make significant efforts in foreign labor unions to meet the communist challenge. Serafino Romualdi, who later would become the first executive director of AIFLD, was assigned as an OSS Special Agent with the rank of Major, to work against the communists in labor unions in the liberated areas of Italy in 1944.[2]

In 1920, as a young man of 20, Romualdi joined the Italian Socialist Party in his native province of Perugia. Two months later, fascist squads from nearby Tuscany overran the region and began looking for socialist leaders. Romualdi fled, eventually landing in New York City in 1922. He got a job with an anti-fascist Italian-language newspaper associated with the International Ladies Garment Workers Union (ILGWU), eventually joining the editorial staff in 1933. With the entry of the U.S. into World War II in 1941, Romualdi began organizing anti-fascist groups among Italian communities in South America. In 1945, with the support of ILGWU President David Dubinsky, Romualdi was granted an earlier request to establish a Latin American operation under an American Federation of Labour (AFL)-affiliated organization.[3] After the end of the war, he would spend the rest of his career working with U.S. intelligence in Latin America.[4]

In 1944, the AFL also began a campaign against communist influence in foreign trade unions. At a convention that year, the AFL passed a resolution, drafted by Jay Lovestone, creating the Free Trade Union Committee (FTUC). Nominally independent from the AFL, it directed the foreign policy of the AFL throughout the 1940s and 1950s. Its members included George Meany, David Dubinsky, Mathew Woll, Irving Brown, and Jay Lovestone.[5] Lovestone would be the executive director of the FTUC and become the international affairs director of the AFL-CIO in 1963. The FTUC gave money to anti-communist unions and anti-communist political forces. Starting in 1948, it received most of the funds for doing this from the CIA or its component, the Office of Policy Coordination.[6] A proposed contract between the CIA and the FTUC clarifying their alliance and goals was found in the Hoover Institution Library Archives.[7]

With the Allied victory, the U.S. began the Marshall Plan for the reconstruction of Europe. The Soviet Union and the communist-dominated World Federation of Trade Unions (WFTU) opposed the plan. The American Congress of Industrial Organizations (CIO) ceded from the WFTU in protest, and, along with the AFL, which had never joined the WFTU, they helped initiate the International Confederation of Free Trade Unions (ICFTU) in 1949.[8] One of the organizers of the ICFTU was William C. Doherty Sr. Doherty had close links to the CIA and his son, William C. Doherty Jr., would be intimately connected with the conception, life, and ultimate end of AIFLD.

Doherty Sr.'s career fighting communism began at a young age. He joined the army in 1919 and was part of the U.S. Army's Expeditionary Force sent to Russia to support the White movement, a loose coalition of anti-communist forces who opposed the Bolsheviks in the Russian Civil War (1917–22). He spent three years in Vladivostok, Russia, and became a chief communications officer. On returning to the U.S., he got a job with the U.S. Postal Service and became the president of his local union. In 1941, he was elected president of the National Association of Letter Carriers (NALC). In 1941, Doherty Sr. also became the youngest person to be elected as vice-president of the national AFL-CIO. At the end of World War II, General Lucius B. Clay chose him to help the trade union movement re-establish itself in the Allied controlled areas of West Germany.[9] In addition to his work with the NALC and the ICFTU, Doherty Sr. was also involved in the post-war revival of the Postal, Telephone and Telegraph International (PTTI), an International Trade Secretariat (ITS).[10] The International Trade Secretariats were created around the turn of the century, but following World War II they became tiny and were quickly dominated by American affiliates, due to their dependence on CIA finances.[11] In 1962, Doherty Sr. was appointed ambassador to Jamaica, the first trade union leader selected for an ambassadorship.[12]

Much of what we know about the senior Doherty's CIA links comes via former CIA agents Paul Sakwa and Tom Braden, who remember Doherty Sr. parceling out cash to foreign union leaders.[13] The CIA hired Sakwa in 1952, and he served until 1962. He was sent to Paris to work in the French branch as a case officer. According to Sakwa, the CIA paid Doherty Sr.'s expenses.

Tom Braden was an assistant to Agency Director Allen Dulles and vigorously defended CIA activities after his retirement. In a phone interview conducted for Jonathan Kwitny's 1984 book *Endless Enemies: The Making of an Unfriendly World*, Doherty Sr. admitted to working with Braden "very closely." To the suggestion that he had funneled CIA money to foreign unions, he would only say he had "never been on a CIA payroll" or "I never supplied money to anybody except on behalf of the organization I represented."[14]

These earlier government-supported, anti-communist activities on the part of labor organizations would soon lead directly to the establishment of AIFLD. Perhaps the most important player in this episode was Joseph A. Beirne, President of the Communications Workers of America (CWA). According to AFL-CIO President Lane Kirkland, "The most significant thing, as I recall, about Beirne was his role in the creation of the American Institute for Free Labor Development (AIFLD). I think that Joe was the moving party in that."[15]

Serafino Romualdi claimed that the idea for the Institute came to Beirne in somewhat of an epiphany while flying over the Andes mountains on the western side of South America.[16] According to Romualdi, Beirne was contemplating the poverty of the region and decided that what these people needed to do was change their outlook and view of the world. Upon his return, Beirne inaugurated a training program for Latin American labor leaders, an effort for which he would rely on the assistance of a fellow Irish Catholic, William C. Doherty Jr.

In April 1958, Beirne arranged to have Doherty Jr. tour Latin America with Romualdi's deputy at the AFL-CIO, Andrew McLellan. McLellan was working at the Federation's International Affairs Department. The trip's goal was to select a group of anti-communist labor leaders who would undergo on-site training at a new PTTI school in Washington, DC.[17] Beirne brought 16 of these Latin American communications workers to the nearby CWA Training Center in Front Royal, Virginia, for a three-month stay in 1959.

William Doherty Jr. worked for the PTTI and supervised Beirne's 1959 training program.[18] On completion of the training course, the Latin American workers would return home and have their salaries paid for nine months while they organized anti-communist unions and did administrative work for those organizations.[19] When Beirne's Latin American communications workers went home, their wages were paid by the PTTI, according to Romualdi.[20] In a 1996 interview, William Doherty Jr. said that this funding came from the International Cooperation Agency (ICA), a forerunner of the U.S. Agency for International Development (AID).[21] The PTTI's member unions included Beirne's communications workers as well as the letter carriers of the NALC, of which William C. Doherty Sr. was president.[22] This training model would become the core activity of AIFLD in the coming decades.[23] (See Appendix.)

Beirne went on to play his critical role in the formation and development of AIFLD. In April 1961, he approached the National Institute of Labor Education (NILE), a small non-profit, with a one-page proposal to train around 250 trade union officers from Latin America. The training content would include "regular tool subjects, plus consideration for functioning of a free society and methods of dealing with Communist efforts to capture control of unions." On May 12, 1961, AFL-CIO President George Meany convened a "Policy Design Committee," with the idea of growing this original concept into a program that would encompass all of Latin America.[24] In July 1961, NILE sent Beirne's concept to the University of Chicago's labor education department, the University Research and Education Project (UREP), to develop an organization that could fulfill the plan.[25]

That year, the University of Chicago's UREP was contracted to develop an organizational blueprint for an institute that would train Latin American labor leaders. The AFL-CIO provided $20,000 for this. That model organization, which became known as the American Institute for Free Labor Development, would include business leaders as well as union officials. The UREP director was John McCollum, a young sociologist from the University of Chicago. McCollum was certain he would be the director of the new organization.[26]

Conflict arose early in the formative period of AIFLD. The parties hadn't clearly defined the role of government in the new organization, and Professor McCollum explained that he preferred a program that was "not dominated by the government." The question of government participation was still unresolved when McCollum presented his formal proposal to the AFL-CIO policy committee in September. The only major part of McCollum's proposal, which excluded the Federation's typical anti-communist, pro-free-enterprise rhetoric, that made it through Meany's Design Policy Committee was the new organization's name: "The American Institute for Free Labor Development."[27] McCollum and Beirne quickly got into another dispute about the size and scope of the initial AIFLD training program. McCollum was struggling to find enough foundation money to pay for the 25 trainees he envisioned. The much larger number of students Beirne wanted would require substantial government funds. The issue became a pretext for Beirne and Meany to force McCollum out. Beirne said McCollum's resignation would be a "sound alternative" and there was "a very sharp difference between you and me." In November 1961, McCollum finally got the message and offered his resignation to Meany, which was accepted in January 1962.[28] But the reality of his departure, according to AIFLD donors in the Rockefeller family, was that McCollum "did not resign but got fired— 'out and out fired'—by George Meany."[29]

In his autobiography, Romualdi wrote that McCollum resigned for "personal reasons." Romualdi recounts that he was then offered the AIFLD director job by George Weaver, Assistant Secretary of Labor for International Labor Affairs, during a plane trip from Texas to Washington, DC. In March 1962, Romualdi replaced McCollum and became executive director of AIFLD.[30]

The Beirne–PTTI–CIA model for AIFLD, which was developed at the beginning of the 1950s, was thereby adopted over an alternative economic development "Alliance for Progress" model advocated by McCollum and others, including Walter and Victor Reuther of the United Automobile Union (UAW). The McCollum faction envisioned an organization controlled by labor, which would provide economic assistance focused on workers as the best method to fight communism. This was not a foregone conclusion. By mid-1961, the failed Bay of Pigs invasion of Cuba had soured the CIA's relationship with U.S. President John F. Kennedy. The new president blamed the CIA for the fiasco. By early 1962, he had fired Agency Director Allen Dulles and two other high-ranking officials. Meany's advocacy with the Kennedy administration for the CIA's preferred AIFLD model was no doubt instrumental to its ascendancy. With the approval of the training program version, laced with some "social projects," AIFLD was now poised to be an active combatant in the Cold War.

AIFLD's formal unveiling was timed with its first training course at Front Royal in June 1962, according to minutes from the Labor Advisory Committee on Foreign Policy.[31] President Dwight D. Eisenhower established the Advisory Committee as a result of a study on international labor activities conducted during the administration's second term. That study called for increased coordination between organizations involved in international labor affairs: the Departments of State, Labor, and Defense, the CIA, the U.S. AID, and the U.S. Information Agency. The Advisory Committee's second meeting was in March 1962, and those attending included George Meany, Serafino Romualdi, Joseph Beirne, Director of CIA Thomas McCone, AID Administrator Fowler Hamilton, Secretary of State Dean Rusk, and Secretary of Labor Arthur Goldberg.[32] The organization voted to charter AIFLD as a member of the Committee and fund it with $350,000 of government money. Arthur Goldberg, Secretary of Labor, personally delivered $100,000 of that to Romualdi to begin operations in June.[33]

According to Romualdi, the first meeting of the AIFLD board of trustees took place in the Commodore Hotel in New York in October 1961.[34] The president of the new organization would be AFL-CIO President George Meany and the chairman of the board would be J. Peter Grace, president and CEO of W.R. Grace and Company, a diversified industrial company with extensive holdings in Latin America. Grace was a leader of the U.S. Council of the International Chamber of Commerce and was president of the 1,000 member branch of the Catholic religious order the Knights of Malta, which traced its origins back to medieval Knights Hospitaller. He had long served as a liaison for CIA-financed religious missions in Latin America.[35] Romualdi has said that Grace and Meany were very close, and probably had daily contact during the 1960s.[36] Charles Brinckerhoff of the Anaconda Company and Juan Trippe of Pan American World Airways were also recruited to serve on the board of directors.[37] The secretary-treasurer would be Joseph Beirne of the CWA. The director of the Social Projects Department would be William C. Doherty Jr., William C. Doherty Sr.'s son.[38] Doherty Jr. (often called Bill), after Romualdi's retirement, became AIFLD executive director in 1965 and held that job for 30 years.[39] (Romualdi would later die of a heart attack while attending a Confederation of Mexican Workers (CTM) conference in Mexico City in 1967. Rumors circulated within AIFLD that he had been assassinated, as he was embittered over not getting an ambassadorship. Exploding a cyanide tablet near someone was reported to produce heart attack symptoms.[40])

After graduating from high school in the Washington, DC, area, Doherty Jr. had attended the Catholic University of America. He enlisted in the Army Air Corps in 1944 during World War II. With the war's conclusion, he went to Germany to support the reorganization of the German trade unions into what came to be called the Confederation of German Trade Unions (Deutscher Gewerteschaftsbund, DGB) which was being organized in the Allied occupied areas. His father was also involved with the union effort under the U.S. occupation. The FDGB, a rival confederation, was organized in the Soviet-occupied areas.

Doherty Jr. returned to the U.S., completing his philosophy degree at Catholic University where he also played football. He married in 1949 and started working part time as a Capitol Hill policeman. Doherty Jr. somehow parleyed that into becoming the president in 1950, at age 24, of a local branch (#32) of the American Federation of Government Employees (AFGE) union, with 1,000 members.[41] At this time, his father was the president of the Public Employees Department of the AFL and would have known the president of the AFGE, also a member of the Department, who might have played a role in this. The younger Doherty quickly moved on to Georgetown University, where he attended the School of Linguistics and Georgetown Law School (as well as the School of Foreign Service, according to his AIFLD biography). Georgetown University Law Center records show him enrolled from 1951 until April 1953, when he withdrew. Returning to Europe in 1953, at the age of 26, Doherty Jr. got a job as an assistant director of the Regional Activities Department of the ICFTU and was stationed in Brussels, Belgium. He stayed until 1955 and then began working for the PTTI in Mexico. In a 1996 interview with the Association for Diplomatic Studies and Training (ADST), Doherty Jr. claims to have been the first American trade unionist to establish a presence in Latin America. He worked for the PTTI until 1962 and then began working for AIFLD. At AIFLD, he held the top position of executive director at the Washington, DC, headquarters from 1965 until it was disbanded in 1996.[42] As journalist Jonathan Kwitny sardonically noted about William Jr.'s rise to union power: "Long and arduous it wasn't."[43]

In 1994, President Clinton nominated William Doherty Jr. to be ambassador to Guyana, the former colony British Guiana. In an ironic twist of fate, the government of Guyana rejected him. Perhaps unknown to Clinton, the newly elected president of Guyana already had a history with Doherty Jr. and AIFLD.

AFL/CIA in Guyana

In 1953, British Guiana, an English-speaking British colony populated by the descendants of slaves and workers from Africa and India, elected its first native-born prime minister, Dr. Cheddi Jagan. Jagan's father had been a cane cutter on a sugar plantation.[44] While studying dentistry at Northwestern University, Jagan married an American nursing student who was active in the Young Communists. He came to support immediate independence for Guiana and the nationalization of the sugar industry.[45] The Jagans returned to Guiana in 1943, and in 1948 Jagan led a huge funeral march for five workers shot and killed at a sugar plantation strike.[46] He won election as chief minister in 1953. UK Prime Minister Winston Churchill believed Jagan to be too leftist, suspended the constitution and jailed him. After being released from jail, Jagan won re-election as prime minister in 1957 and again in 1961.

Like Churchill, U.S. President Kennedy also determined that Jagan was a socialist threat and, after meeting with his National Security Officers, ordered him to be unseated.[47] Suddenly, things started going badly for British Guiana. Previously unheard-of radio stations began to broadcast in the capital criticizing Jagan. Newspapers printed false stories about approaching Cuban warships. Race riots took the lives of more than 100 people. A massive fire started in the center of the capital. Operatives of the CIA, working under cover of an American labor union, helped organize strikes in British Guiana against Dr. Jagan's government in 1962 and 1963.

These general strikes focused on a proposed change to the national labor law. The International Affairs Department of the American Federation of State County and Municipal Employees (AFSCME) was reportedly run by two intelligence agency aides who operated out of the union's headquarters in Washington with the knowledge of the union's leadership.[48] In 1959, the CIA had begun funding AFSCME, through its President Arnold Zander, to set up an education program for government workers in Latin America according to a *New York Times* article written in 1967. AFSCME was part of an ITS, the Public Service International (PSI). With the CIA money, operatives allegedly persuaded some British Guiana public employees and dockworkers to organize strikes. At one point, one of the agents served on the bargaining committee for the dockworkers' union. Intervention in the strike was called "Operation Flypast," and was a joint operation of the CIA and the AFL-CIO, or, as a British Foreign Office official, J.C. Stackpoole, called them, "the AFL/CIA."[49] The strikes lasted long enough to disrupt the national economy.[50]

Jagan believed that the CIA, AIFLD, Serafino Romualdi, and William C. Doherty Jr. were primarily responsible for the actions against his government. In July 1963, Jagan wrote a letter to the *New York Times* saying, "local trade unionists known to be hostile to the Government—and none others—have been trained by the American Institute for Free Labor Development to overthrow my government."[51] Following the fall of Jagan's government in 1963, free and fair elections for prime minister were not held until 1992, when Jagan was again elected.[52] After refusing Doherty's diplomatic credentials, Jagan told the *New York Times*, "Maybe President Clinton doesn't know our history but the people who advise him should at least know their own history."[53] He thus blocked Doherty's nomination as ambassador to the now independent Guyana.[54] Further evidencing the AIFLD–CIA relationship and their joint role in Guyana specifically, in 1999 the CIA acknowledged that it had been the "executive agent of policy" and the "action arm of covert operations" in British Guiana.[55]

When asked in 1996 about his relationship with Irving Brown, an AFL-CIO international affairs director with career-long links to the CIA, Doherty explained some of how AIFLD worked:

> As long as I stayed within the policy guidelines of the AFL-CIO and its political, economic, and social objectives, we had a very large degree of autonomy to go out and to do our thing. We had the staff and the money to do it…. AID financing went to the regions; it didn't go to the AFL-CIO or go to a central body. Capital and money is what runs things.[56]

In 1996, retired AFL-CIO President Lane Kirkland was also asked a question in an interview about the management of AIFLD and its sibling organizations, the Asian American Free Labor Institute (AAFLI) and the African American Labor Center (AALC), and how the AFL-CIO International Department fit into the chain of command of these. He responded, "Well, the institutes were set up as independent bodies." Kirkland's response raises a question here as to who was managing AIFLD.[57]

When asked about what percentage of funding AID or later the National Endowment for Democracy (NED) provided for AIFLD, Doherty replied, "I'd say the percentage never got below 80. I'm just guessing that off the top of my head." Doherty recalls that AIFLD received $18 to $20 million in a "better" year from U.S. government sources.[58] In fact, the U.S. government almost entirely funded AIFLD. Between 1962 and 1974, AIFLD received a total of $58.2 million from AID while the AFL-CIO contributed $2.46 million, and during that time span U.S. businesses added $1.6 million.[59] By 1985, the $19.4 million yearly budget was about 98 percent furnished by federal money.[60] With massive government funding, AIFLD went on to establish 13 national training centers across Latin America. Romualdi claimed that by 1966–7 the Institute was running schools in every country in the region except Haiti, Paraguay, and Cuba.[61] And according to Perry Fellwock, a former National Security Agency employee turned whistleblower, writing in 1973, "a CIA case officer is undercover in almost every AIFLD office abroad."[62]

In a remarkably detailed account of daily life as a CIA agent in Latin America during the 1960s, Philip Agee, in his book *Inside The Company: CIA Diary*, lists many organizations and individuals involved with the CIA. Agee spent twelve years in the CIA before becoming disillusioned. After going public with his story, he spent the rest of his life in virtual exile. His glossary of names includes the following entries:

AMERICAN INSTITUTE for FREE LABOR DEVELOP-MENT (AIFLD). CIA-controlled labor center financed through AID. Programs in adult education and social projects used as front for covering trade union activity.

POST, TELEGRAPH and TELEPHONE WORKERS INTER-NATIONAL (PTTI). Used by the CIA in labor operations: principle agents in PTTI, Joseph Beirne, President of the Communications Workers of America and William Doherty.

BEIRNE, JOSEPH. President of the Communications Workers of America (CWA) and Director of the American Institute for Free Labor Development. Important collaborator in CIA labor operations through AIFLD and the Post, Telegraph and Telephone Workers International (PTTI).

ROMUALDI, SERAFINO. AFL representative in Latin America and principal CIA agent for labor operations in Latin America.

DOHERTY, WILLIAM. Inter-American representative for PTTI and CIA agent in labor operations. Executive Director of AIFLD.

BROWN, IRVING. European representative of the American Federation of Labor and principal CIA agent for control of the International Confederation of Free Trade Unions (ICFTU).[63]

Agee recounts working directly with Doherty on a CIA project in Ecuador in 1960 when he was assigned there.[64]

In 1978, the Agency prepared a Memorandum for the Record for U.S. Senator Lloyd Bentson, assessing the damage done to it by Agee's disclosures. The CIA wrote to Bentson:

Agee's first book [*Inside the Company: CIA Diary*] exposed 170 Agency personnel and numerous agents and operations in Latin America known to him during his years of service there. These exposures resulted in the retirement of more than 100 active foreign agents. As of June 1977, the monetary cost of Agee's exposures were estimated to be more than $2,000,000. The Agency continues to incur other costs—both direct and indirect.[65]

Inside The Company has stood up in almost every detail over time. A CIA analysis, obtained by *Wall Street Journal* reporter Jonathan Kwitny, calls the reporting "complete" and "accurate."[66] In interviews with Kwitny, five former CIA operatives corroborated Agee's assertions about AIFLD and the CIA.[67]

Kwitny was able to arrange an interview with Doherty Jr. in the fall of 1981 for his book *Endless Enemies*. He wanted to ask him about Agee's assertion that Doherty was a CIA agent, the CIA analysis of the book, and other links between the Agency and AIFLD. The interview did not go well. There was an exchange of letters between Doherty and Kwitny following the incident. These two letters are in the George Meany Memorial Archives (GMMA) at the University of Maryland. Kwitny writes that Doherty had contacted his *Wall Street Journal* editor to complain about the interview, saying he didn't get a full chance to air his views. In his letter of response, Kwitny goes on to say:

This seems a strange contention to me from someone who showed up 45 minutes late for a scheduled interview that I went all the way to Washington for, hollered at me almost the whole time I was in your office cutting me off before I could ask full questions or present detailed assertions by former CIA officers and others that I wanted to discuss with you, then raced out of the room 20 minutes into the interview…[68]

Determined to get the last word, Doherty replies in part, "I must repeat for the record that there has never been any involvement between AIFLD and the CIA."[69]

But, in another interview, when asked what the business community contributed to AIFLD, Doherty veered off topic and said:

As Kirkland has always done, and as I would always do and George Meany, vigorously deny that the CIA ever had anything to do with the AIFLD. I would be willing to swear on a Bible, and I'm a practicing Catholic, that the CIA did not finance the AIFLD. But that doesn't do any good because even if they did, I would have to deny it. And therefore, the denial will never be accepted anyhow, so I don't bother going around denying it.[70]

When the CIA hires agents, they must sign a secrecy agreement as a prior condition of employment. It requires that they disclose no classified information. The fact that the executive director of AIFLD was an agent certainly was classified then and would be now.

George Meany and his successor Lane Kirkland would vigorously deny CIA involvement in AIFLD and the AFL-CIO for three decades.[71]

2

Labor's Foreign Policy Contested and the Military Takeover in Brazil

I did my best to try and lift the lid on it. And someday it will all come out.

Victor Reuther, 1967

In April 1966, the small circulation magazine *Ramparts* printed a story on the Michigan State University Group, a technical assistance program in South Vietnam. The *Ramparts* exposé quoted a former project director, who said that it was a front for CIA covert operations. The *Ramparts* piece unleashed a series of other articles detailing CIA involvement in U.S. civilian organizations and changed how Americans would view the CIA.[1]

One of the pieces that followed was an interview in May 1966 with Victor Reuther, brother of UAW President Walter Reuther and the head of that organization's International Affairs Department. In that *LA Times* interview, Reuther suggested there were ties between AFL-CIO foreign policy, AIFLD, and the CIA.[2]

The Reuther brothers, Walter, Victor, and Roy, were sons of a German immigrant, Valentine Reuther, who settled in the Midwest. He was a union activist and socialist. When Walter and Victor were children, Valentine brought them to visit Eugene Debs, a socialist candidate for president, then imprisoned for his opposition to World War I. In the 1930s, Walter and Victor visited the newly created Soviet Union and worked in an auto plant there. Upon their return, they began working to organize the fledgling UAW.[3] Following the successful strike and occupation of General Motors (GM) plants in Flint, Michigan, in 1936–7 and a decade of fierce factional fighting, Walter would become the international president of the new union, and appoint Victor to be director of the UAW Education Department and then director of international affairs.[4]

During the 1950s, the CIO assigned Victor Reuther as European director. The CIO was a union federation composed of unions representing mainly unskilled workers in mass production industries, which often put it at odds with the American Federation of Labor (AFL), a federation composed mostly of unions based along craft lines. While every bit as anti-communist as the AFL leaders, the Reuthers had differing ideas on what "free unions" should be doing. While sometimes working together and often in opposition to the AFL-affiliated FTUC, Victor learned of the vast amounts of money being distributed by the FTUC to the service of anti-communist causes, primarily by AFL European Director Irving Brown.[5] This money was far more than could be accounted for from union funds. Revelations in the 1960s that many dummy foundations funded by the CIA had contributed large amounts of money to U.S. labor unions and their international labor affiliates proved that his concerns were valid. Victor Reuther claimed that the unions later shown to have received the CIA-sourced distributions included the Oil Chemical and Atomic Workers Union (OCAW), AFSCME, and the Newspaper Guild.[6]

In 1955, the CIO and its UAW affiliate merged with its former rival the AFL to form the AFL-CIO. The new conglomerate was headed by George Meany. Meany was a New Yorker who dropped out of school at the age of 16 and became a plumber, after serving a five-year apprenticeship. At 22, in 1922, he became a full-time business agent for his local union. He worked in a full-time union position for the rest of his career. In 1952, he became the national AFL president and, after it merged with the CIO, he remained in that office until 1979, when he retired at the age of 86. Meany embraced "business unionism." Meany's brand of unionism focused on the immediate workplace needs of its members and the sale of their labor, rejecting broader social goals. Shortly after the AFL and CIO merger, he told an employer's group that he "had never been involved in a strike and had never belonged to a union that had called one."[7] Walter found working with Meany to be a frustrating experience and the two leaders had significant disagreements on issues like union organizing and civil rights. At the core, they held opposing views about the mission and purpose of the trade union movement. At the forefront of those differences were foreign affairs and relationships with international labor organizations.[8]

During the 1950s, Meany and his chief lieutenant in foreign affairs, Jay Lovestone, had created a worldwide network in the FTUC funded by CIA cash. In Victor Reuther's view, this made them vulnerable to control by the donor.[9] When AIFLD began operations in 1962, it opened the door to the infusion of government funds on a still more substantial basis. The UAW had initially supported the creation of AIFLD, and Walter agreed to serve on the board with the understanding it was to be a joint effort with academic institutions. Subsequent events would change the UAW position on AIFLD.

In March 1961, President Kennedy announced his economic and social development program in Latin America called the Alliance for Progress. He hoped to raise the masses in Latin America out of poverty and stop the spread of Castro-inspired socialism. Four weeks after the Alliance was announced, the failed Bay of Pigs invasion moved the Reuthers to call for an even more radical economic development program for Latin America based on the International Trade Secretariats and embracing the Peace Corps. The UAW called this the Council for Social Progress. As we saw in the previous chapter, Beirne, Doherty, and Romualdi were at the same time developing a rival trade union initiative with Meany's support, which led to the creation of AIFLD in 1962. The Kennedy administration decided to support the AFL-CIO backed AIFLD model over the UAW's program. Walter Reuther stayed away from the 1961 AIFLD meeting, where George Meany and Peter Grace were elected as president and chairman of the board, but he retained a nominal membership on the board of trustees.[10]

His brother Victor had viewed AIFLD with suspicion since its inception. In the fall of 1961, Victor wrote to Walter expressing concern about the nine months' pay the AIFLD training graduates would receive on returning home, saying, "Each of them will not only be open to the charge by our opposition that they are agents of the U.S., but they clearly will be in the pay of a U.S. institution which includes employers and government in what is presumably a 'labor training' program."[11] Since AIFLD became the only U.S. government-backed labor program in Latin America, Victor believed it to be "very nearly a private, unregulated, and irresponsible monopoly."[12]

Overthrow of Goulart in Brazil

AIFLD established training centers in Brazil at the end of 1962. The first group of 33 Brazilian labor leaders arrived at Front Royal for training in January 1963. Their six-month course included classes in U.S. labor history, economics, and techniques for fighting communists and fascists. Follow-up surveys found that many of the Brazilian leaders were largely unimpressed, and U.S. officials, impatient with the training, were eager to embrace a long-planned coup d'état.[13] In April 1964, the democratically elected president of Brazil, João Goulart, was overthrown by a CIA-backed military coup. Serafino Romualdi, AIFLD Executive Director, had known about the planning for the coup.[14]

The deposed President Goulart was a member of the Brazilian Labor Party and enjoyed widespread support from workers and the trade union movement in Brazil.[15] When the coup began, the Brazilian Communist Party called for a general strike. AIFLD-trained unionists were in place to effectively split labor, exhorting the communications workers to stay on the job. Their directives kept communications systems operating, allowing the military to coordinate and seize power.[16]

Workers were at the center of conflicts in the Goulart government, and it would be accurate to characterize the coup as one staged against workers.[17] When the military seized control in Brazil, they put army officers in charge of unions; they abolished the right to strike, and opposition dissidents were imprisoned and, in some cases, tortured. Following the takeover, communist-led unions were put into trusteeship and purged of leftists and Goulart supporters. Labor contracts negotiated during the Goulart government were allowed to be terminated by employers. In the aftermath of the coup, AIFLD representatives began advocating for a wage freeze proposed by the military regime. The AFL-CIO embraced the new regime and bragged about bringing it to power.[18]

Victor Reuther attended the first meeting of the Labor Advisory Committee (composed of representatives of the Departments of State, Labor, and Defense, the CIA, the U.S. AID, the U.S. Information Agency, and the AFL-CIO) held in May 1964, after the coup. He raised questions about the ethics of labor's role in the events in Brazil. Although he was at the meeting in an unofficial capacity, he heard reports about AIFLD doubling their activities and coordinating with officials from the Department of State (DoS). Andrew McClellan, the AFL-CIO Inter-American Regional Organization of Workers (ORIT) representative, defended the new Brazilian government's practice of intervening in unions as "necessary to provide continuity in legal counseling and social welfare services."[19]

In *On Company Business*, the 1980 documentary film about the CIA, an American worker named Richard Martinez says he was recruited in 1962 to help build unions in Brazil. A union member from a Latino working-class background, he was hired by Tom Robles. Robles had been active in the New Mexico State AFL-CIO, and Martinez identified him as the AFL-CIO state secretary. Robles was also the labor attaché at the U.S. Embassy in Peru from 1962 to 1964 when he recruited Martinez. Following his tenure with the DoS, Robles would work for the International Affairs Department of the AFL-CIO under Jay Lovestone.[20] The author Jonathan Kwitny interviewed Martinez for his book *Endless Enemies* and found him consistent in his claims. Martinez also provided Kwitny with corroborating documents and photos.[21] In the film, Martinez says, "my position was to be administrator and organizer for the Postal Telephone and Telegraph International, which was, I later learned, one of the phony organizations under the CIA. My boss was Wallace Leahy, one of John McCone's [Director of the CIA, 1961–5] top hands." Martinez's work would consist entirely of helping to foment the 1964 coup against Goulart.[22]

William Doherty Jr., then AIFLD director of the Social Projects Division, three months after the coup, gave an interview on an AFL-CIO-sponsored radio program. When asked, "What happened to these individuals who learned the techniques and programs of Free Trade Unionism [the AIFLD training program] in recent developments?" He replied:

Well, very frankly, within the limits placed on them by the administration of João Goulart, when they returned to their respective countries they were very active in organizing workers and helping unions introduce systems of labor-management relations. As a matter of fact, some of them were so active that they became intimately involved in some of the clandestine operations of the revolution before it took place on April first. What happened in Brazil on April first did not just happen—it was planned—and planned months in advance. Many of the trade union leaders— some of whom were actually trained in our institute—were involved in the revolution and in the overthrow of the Goulart regime.[23]

A Split in American Labor Goes Public

Victor was irate over AIFLD's participation in the Brazilian coup.[24] After similar events in the Dominican Republic in 1965, he advocated with Walter that the UAW leave the AFL-CIO. Walter agreed with Victor that the CIA was using the trade union movement to cover for covert activity. Still, he did not believe that Victor would be able to provide enough documentation to stand up to the barrage of fabricated documents and lies that the CIA could produce. Walter opposed forcing a split with the AFL-CIO on foreign policy instead of domestic issues. The conservative craft unionism of the AFL and the CIO liberalism of the Reuthers were often in conflict, and he believed a better opportunity would come.[25]

In 1965, the UAW was involved in a union organizing drive at Airmold Products in Tonawanda, New York, owned by the Grace Company, whose CEO, Peter Grace, had recently become chairman of the AIFLD board. The company mounted an all-out attack against the UAW and the concept of unionism. Their anti-union literature included criticism of unions' funds being spent to help international unions. The Grace Company leaflets said, "Do you want to pay dues to help finance foreign unions in foreign countries? Ask the paid organizer about this private foreign aid program."

Walter objected strenuously to the participation of corporate executives in AIFLD, and the Tonawanda incident gave him a chance to move against AIFLD. Although he knew government money was also involved, he limited his attack to corporate funding. He resigned from the AIFLD board that year.[26]

Victor had been pondering what to do about AFL-CIO, AIFLD, and the CIA for quite some time before the *LA Times* interview in May 1966. In the article, he gave as an example of CIA meddling eight individuals in Panama who were posing as representatives of the International Union of Food and Allied Workers, an ITS. They did this without the knowledge of that organization's general secretary, who was forced to abolish their Panama office and its entire Latin American operations as a result. Andrew McClellan hired these mysterious "representatives." Reuther asserted that the AFL-CIO International Affairs Department was "involved" with the CIA, and they had not reported much of that activity to the executive council.[27]

Reaction to the 1966 *LA Times* article was immediate. Joseph Beirne of the CWA, who had run the pre-AIFLD training prototype and was the AIFLD secretary-treasurer, along with Meany, labeled Victor's remarks "a damned lie."[28] After a contentious June executive council meeting, Walter was promised a complete discussion of the AFL-CIO's Latin American operations at the August executive council meeting.[29] However, before that meeting, Walter received phone calls from both Vice-President Hubert Humphrey and former Attorney General Robert Kennedy, who urged him to cease the warfare over AIFLD. Walter criticized Victor for speaking publicly about the CIA. He thought he had worked out an agreement with Meany through his top aide, Lane Kirkland, to keep AIFLD off the agenda in the interests of national security and that Meany had agreed to this in a face-to-face meeting.[30]

Walter prepared for the August executive council meeting by having his staff investigate AIFLD. In July, UAW General Counsel Joe Rauh wrote to Walter Reuther and reported the conclusions of the research:

> Since I know you are mulling over the CIA matter, you are entitled to have this thought before you. We can demonstrate, all apart from George Meany's admissions to you personally, that there is a massive CIA involvement in the foreign affairs operations of the AFL-CIO and vice versa.... [M]y personal assessment, based on what we have learned to date [is] that Vic's statement was mild indeed and that you can lead from strength, not weakness.[31]

When Walter got to the August meeting, in the first item on the agenda, Beirne commenced an attack on Victor, whose words he compared to the "slanderous line of the Commies."[32] Beirne made a motion to denounce the "campaign of vilification that has been waged against AIFLD." The resolution passed with a 23–2 vote, with only Walter and Joe Curran of the Maritime Union opposed. The resolution declared:

> The Executive Council commends the American Institute for Free Labor Development for their work in carrying out the policies of the AFL-CIO in the international field and rejects out of hand the campaign of vilification that has been conducted against the AIFLD.[33]

In 1975, Philip Agee would name Beirne as an important CIA collaborator in the labor movement.[34]

It was probably this meeting that brought about Walter's decision to have the UAW leave the AFL-CIO.[35] In February 1967, he resigned from the AFL-CIO executive council. In May 1968, the UAW was suspended from participation in AFL-CIO affairs for non-payment of dues.[36]

The attacks on Victor for exposing the role of the CIA in AIFLD were not limited to labor. In a May 1967 edition of the *Saturday*

Evening Post, Tom Braden, a retired CIA official who was a top assistant to CIA Director Allen Dulles between 1951 and 1954, wrote an article entitled "Why I'm Glad the CIA Is 'Immoral.'" It appeared to be a defense of CIA operations in private U.S. organizations. Braden also seemed to cross a line by discussing CIA agents operating in a cultural organization and a journalistic publication. However, his article contained new information: as chief of the International Division of the CIA, he had given Walter Reuther $50,000 in 1951 which, he, in turn, provided to Victor to spend on behalf of anti-communist unions in West Germany. The article caused Victor much embarrassment and further criticism. Victor admitted to doing it, but also recounted Braden's effort to recruit him as a CIA agent who would play the same role Irving Brown was doing for the AFL-affiliated FTUC. He declined the offer.[37]

While Braden's article gave the impression of unauthorized action by a partisan, it is more likely that he proceeded with the foreknowledge of the CIA, who were aware of the impending publication and had ample time to invoke Braden's secrecy oath. The Johnson administration had prior knowledge about the article before publication. It was a common tactic for the CIA to expose covert operators who were no longer useful. The Reuthers' actions against AIFLD had put them in that category.[38]

In his 1966 interview with the *LA Times*, Victor called the foreign policy of the AFL-CIO "a vest pocket operation run by Jay Lovestone."[39] The deep animosity between Lovestone and the Reuthers stretched back three decades.

Jay Lovestone first arrived in New York City with his Russian immigrant family in 1906. As a young man, he became immersed in the radical politics of the time. Using a talent for factional maneuvering and working behind the scenes, he rose to become the head (general secretary) of the American Communist Party by the end of the 1920s. During the 1930s, the general secretary and other American communists became engulfed in the infighting that enveloped the Soviet Communist Party. Lovestone had aligned himself with Nikolai Bukharin, the head of the international communist organization the Comintern. Bukharin was also the last central figure who stood in Stalin's path to complete power in Soviet Russia. Stalin's fight against Bukharin was eventually successful, and it resulted in Bukharin's execution in 1938.[40]

Lovestone and ten other Americans received orders to go to Russia for meetings in 1929 during the fight that was raging between Stalin and Bukharin. There, Stalin removed Lovestone as general secretary of the American Party. He allowed the other Americans to leave but forced Lovestone to stay. With the help of a friend, Lovestone was able to escape Russia with his life.[41] Upon returning to the U.S., he organized the American Communist Party Opposition (Lovestonites), but by the middle of the 1930s, he had become intensely and personally anti-communist.[42]

Lovestone continued his mission to organize American workers. He focused on the ILGWU where one of his party sympathizers ran for union office. In 1933, with Lovestone's help, that Lovestonite became the president of the largest local in the ILGWU and one of the largest local unions in the U.S. The International President of the ILGWU, David Dubinsky, recognized Lovestone's talents and his potential for fighting communists. In 1937, Dubinsky, a relative conservative in the newly organized CIO, sent Lovestone $100,000 to help Homer Martin, president of the second largest union in the CIO, the UAW, fight the communist influence there.[43]

Lovestone became Martin's chief of staff for two years and wholly controlled him as a union trial of four expelled UAW executive board members would later prove. Following Lovestone's directions, Martin began a purge of UAW communists and their allies, who had become the most powerful faction in the union. The communists had gained this position due to success in union organizing and then in the sit-down strikes that had spread across the auto industry.[44] Martin fired dozens of staff people in addition to the four suspended international executive board members. He replaced them with loyalists.[45]

Another dominant UAW faction was the Reuthers. Although the alliance would be short-lived, the Reuthers sided with the communists against Martin and Lovestone. Martin fired Victor Reuther and his wife, Sophie. Martin had risen to the presidency of the new union based on his oratory skills developed as a Baptist minister, but as an administrator, he was an incompetent bungler. Despite Lovestone's best efforts, Martin proved to be no match for the communists, the Reuthers, and John L. Lewis, the president of the CIO, who also intervened. At the next UAW convention, delegates elected R.J. Thomas president, and Martin and Lovestone were gone. The Reuthers would never forget or forgive Lovestone.[46]

Following his failure to take over the UAW, Lovestone would disband his party and turn entirely against the Soviet Union and communism. In 1944, with Dubinsky and Meany's support, he would become the FTUC executive secretary and begin working closely with the forerunner of the CIA. For 30 years, he would direct the foreign-affairs activities of the AFL and become one of the most influential players in the Cold War.[47]

Lovestone's war with the Reuthers would rage on. In 1954, while negotiating the merger of the AFL and the CIO, the UAW leaders hoped to have Lovestone fired from the FTUC. In December 1954, Lovestone wrote to Irving Brown that "Victor Reuther, that self-inflated character," was conducting a campaign of "vicious slander" and that "Victor and his like have a notion they will demand your head and mine as a price for unity with the AFL."[48] In 1956, Lovestone's lover and a CIA contact, Page Morris, wrote, "Jay is obsessed with destroying Reuther. He can think and talk of nothing else. Everything else is at a standstill."[49]

In 1954, Lovestone began reporting to James Angleton, the counterintelligence head of the CIA.[50] Angleton was one of the more sinister figures to emerge during the Cold War. Among Angleton's more noteworthy activities were Operation CHAOS and HT/LINGUAL. HT/LINGUAL was a CIA program that intercepted the mail of American citizens, opened it, copied it, and then sent it on. It was in effect from 1955 to 1973. During that time agents opened 215,000 pieces of mail. One of those whose mail was intercepted was Victor Reuther.[51] In 1967, Angleton began Operation CHAOS in response to the anti-Vietnam War movement. During the six years of its existence, it spied on the 300,000 individual Americans and over 100 organizations opposed to the war in Vietnam. The CIA sent 5,000 reports to the FBI.[52] Both programs were illegal.

Angleton became obsessed with the idea that a Soviet mole had penetrated the Agency in 1960. In pursuit of the effort to uncover this phantom individual, Angleton and his office tracked Lee Harvey Oswald, Kennedy's accused killer, four years before the J.F.K. assassination. Angleton supervised Oswald's CIA file from October 1959 to November 1963. He was involved in covering up this and other CIA connections to the Kennedy assassination events for the rest of his life.[53]

Early on, Angleton saw that labor unions were central to communist strategy and a crucial battleground in the Cold War. He needed sources of intelligence in this arena.[54] Angleton developed a close personal relationship with Lovestone, who became a virtual member of Angleton's family. They would have communications almost every day for 20 years. Before 1963, Lovestone would send intelligence reports from his FTUC operators to Angleton. When he became the director of international affairs for the AFL-CIO in 1963, he would report on news and rumors concerning the labor movement. Angleton was able to keep the Lovestone operation off the books and secret within the Agency until the early 1970s.[55] Upon learning of the Lovestone operation when he became a new CIA director in the 1970s, William Colby assigned a trusted officer, Horace Feldman, to look into Angleton's activities. Feldman told Colby:

> Here we have a senior officer in the labor movement, a domestic organization outside our mandate, and he is in our pay. And he publishes a newspaper, the *Free Trade Union News*. This is a clear violation of our charter. Lovestone is collecting information on U.S. citizens.[56]

By 1967, the AIFLD yearly budget was over $6 million, three times as much as the annual AFL-CIO budget.[57] Victor Reuther would go on to make several other public comments linking the CIA and AFL-CIO. In February 1967, in an interview with the *New York Post*, Reuther referenced Lovestone and his communist past. Victor reported on the CIA's past involvement in Federation operations in Latin America. He also asserted that the Agency had been involved in U.S. union elections. He went on to say, "I did my best to try and lift the lid on it. And someday it will all come out."[58]

The Day That Never Came: The End of the Reuther Threat

After the publication of the 1966 *LA Times* Reuther article, Cord Meyer, the CIA's officer in charge of operations in the international trade union movement, told a UAW official, "Something has to be done to stop this. It's doing a lot of damage." Within weeks, both a U.S. vice-president and a former U.S. attorney general would call Walter and ask him to stop the attacks on AIFLD.[59] Meany got the AFL-CIO executive council to circle the wagons around his lies and condemn Victor. However, by the end of 1968, the restraints that could be used against the Reuthers were gone. Walter had been a staunch supporter of President Lyndon Johnson, but Johnson declined to run for re-election under the weight of the Vietnam War debacle. Robert Kennedy was assassinated. Hubert Humphrey would lose the 1968 election, and Richard Nixon, a Reuther enemy, would become president. The UAW, its largest union affiliate, left the AFL-CIO.

In October 1968, Victor and Walter took a leased Executive Aviation Inc. private jet plane to Washington, DC. It was raining and 11:35 p.m. when they began their descent to Dulles Airport. A few hundred feet above the ground, the pilots went to visual control of the plane. They suddenly realized the aircraft was much too low. Victor described the impact at landing:

> As the pilot leveled, there was a jolt, the plane shuddered, and when the wheels touched there was a loud dragging and scraping sound…. The plane whipped from side to side, nearly capsizing, but the pilots held it to the runway until it had slowed sufficiently to allow them to maneuver it onto the soft surface of an open field…. We could see that we had struck a steel girder as we

landed: some four feet of it were rammed into the tail section and another six feet projected from the tail section to the ground.

In his memoir, *The Brothers Reuther*, Victor mentions that the altimeter was set to 29.96. An altimeter, or an altitude meter, is an instrument used to measure the altitude of an object above a fixed level. On the drive into Washington, DC, from the airport Walter said, "I guess this wasn't intended to be our time."[60]

On September 28, 1969, the Lear Jet which would carry Walter Reuther on its final flight several months later was found to have the pilot's altimeter in an out-of-tolerance condition. The altimeter was sent in for an overhaul.[61]

On May 9, 1970, Walter, his wife, two companions and two pilots flew from Detroit Metro Airport to the Pellston, Michigan, airstrip near the new UAW Education Center under construction. The leased Executive Aviation Inc. Lear Jet approached the runway and the dark area around it in low clouds and light rain. The plane was too low, and at 9:33 p.m., it slammed into some trees and burst into flames killing everyone onboard.

The National Transportation Safety Board (NTSB) did an extensive investigation of the crash. In its conclusions, the NTSB found the probable cause to be the pilot's inability to visually recognize how low the plane was because of the darkness and—yet again—a faulty altimeter that was likely to have been reading 200–250 feet higher than the aircraft actually was. In its opening synopsis, the NTSB report pointed to the "lack of visual cues" as a major cause of the accident.

But the summary is somewhat misleading in the latter regard. The pilots chose the only lit approach, Runway 5, but it lacked both Runway and Identifier Lights and a Visual Approach Path Indicator (VAPI). VAPIs give pilots their proper flight angle and help determine altitude. The primary approach, Runway 23, had a VAPI, but one of the runway lights was broken out so they used the runway without the complete set of lights. The pilots were not notified of this fault, as is customary, suggesting that the light broke near to landing time.[62] In the dark approach, the pilot would have had to rely on the altimeter to determine the aircraft's altitude.

The investigation of the altimeter revealed that a set screw was loose, one that would have held the vital calibration arm assembly in place had it been properly seated. The NTSB report went on to further describe this and a test that it conducted:

> During the disassembly of the altimeter it was observed that a brass screw may have fallen out and was lying loose in the case…. Considering that the screw may have loosened because of heat, a similar calibration arm mechanism was placed in an oven and heated for two hours at 1100 degrees Fahrenheit. This screw was found to be tight when examined.[63]

The report goes on to detail more problems with the altimeter.

> Further examination of the altimeter revealed that an incorrect pivot was installed in one end of the rocking shaft. At the opposite end of the rocking shaft, an end stone was missing. A ring jewel within the mechanism was installed off center. A second rocking shaft rear support pivot was incorrect. An incorrect link pin, which holds a spring clip in place at the pneumatic capsule was installed. An end stone which supports a shaft within the mechanism, was installed upside down.[64]

The manufacturer of the altimeter, Kollsman Instruments, reported about the altimeter:

> No identification was present to trace the specific instrument type and date of manufacture. The mechanism construction isolated the unit to one of three major types, each of which had numerous variations, none of which were TSO [Technical Standards Orders] certified.[65] All of these types were essentially military.[66]

The NTSB did not find conclusive evidence that altimeter problems were due to sabotage and did not make a determination about that. But some of the Reuther family did not believe that the crash was an accident. Walter's daughter, Elisabeth, hired a private detective to do an independent investigation.[67]

Victor, too, in a 1993 interview with A.J. Weberman, said:

> I've had very strong suspicions from the day the accident occurred. I'm convinced there was tampering with the altimeter and, although the plane was on the ground for only a short time, it was enough time. The full story was not told. When I wrote my book, I had not seen these files [Kollsman on the altimeter]. I relied on the then-General Counsel of the UAW, Steve Schlossberg, who I know from later experience was not too eager to make the investigation terribly thorough…. He was more interested in passing the reins of power to the new president, Leonard Woodcock, and getting the Reuther years behind him, so I felt he was too quick to accept the findings…. [H]e is now in Washington as the official representative of the ILO [International Labor Organization]…[68]

In the Weberman interview, Reuther said he did not believe the CIA was responsible and suspected old enemies like the U.S. Communist Party.[69] But, in a 1992 interview, Victor had also discussed motives for an assassination of Walter:

> …also I had exposed some CIA elements inside labor, and this was also associated with Walter. Although Walter knew I was right, he felt that I had put him in an impossible position. He said, "You're taking on an agency that can forge any document to prove we are liars."[70]

New research on the CIA's role in the U.S. labor movement since the Pellston crash requires another look at the Reuther death. Did anyone have a motive, the means, and an opportunity to assassinate Walter Reuther?

With the front lines in the Cold War moving from Europe to a developing world emerging from a colonial past, the CIA needed an instrument to confront the Soviet Union and its leftist and anti-colonial allies in that part of the world on the issues and in organizations involving workers. The Agency had already worked for over a decade to establish AIFLD at the time of Reuther's death. The AIFLD project was so successful that the CIA, with AFL-CIO participation, organized two similar entities: the AAFLI and the AALC.

Would AIFLD be able to survive under constant attack from the UAW, the largest industrial union in the free world, for being a CIA front organization? The UAW had much better international relations with other labor organizations than the AFL-CIO did. The latter had withdrawn from the ICFTU, which it had helped create, when the ICFTU wouldn't rubber stamp AFL-CIO positions. Then the Federation withdrew from the International Labor Organization when the ILO elected a Polish trade unionist as general secretary. During the 1960s, the AFL-CIO's foreign operations retreated into AIFLD, AAFLI, AALC, and ORIT, a regional organization of the ICFTU which it still controlled. The UAW would have continued to collect evidence about AIFLD-CIA activities, and they had shown they were willing to make that public.

The Reuthers threatened the CIA's decade-long investment in AIFLD, and there was no backup organization. Because of Reuther's attacks, the cover of many agents and assets in Latin America was endangered, with lives hanging in the balance. The relationship between the AFL-CIO and the UAW showed no signs of improvement. The animosity between Walter and Meany, if anything, had gotten worse. At the time of his death, Walter had just organized a rival labor federation with the Teamsters, the Chemical Workers and one other small organization called the Alliance for Labor Action.[71] The 30-year hatred between the international affairs directors of the two organizations, Lovestone and Victor Reuther, showed no signs of abating. By 1969, the Cold War had gotten hot. During this time, the CIA was involved in the Phoenix Program in South Vietnam, which was responsible for the assassination of between 25,000 and 40,000 National Liberation Front political cadres. How far would the elements in the Agency be willing to go to protect AIFLD and its sibling organizations?

Would the CIA have the means to put together an altimeter that would read several hundred feet higher than it should on a dark, rainy night? In the CIA's declassified electronic reading room, a search of documents containing the word "altimeter" returns over 150 items. While most of these concern topics like high-altitude spy planes or Soviet military aircraft capabilities, the Agency was very familiar with altimeters. Of interest is one document labeled "Air America Inc. Vientiane, Laos, Facilities and Capabilities." Air America was a CIA-operated airline. The document, written in March 1973, details the size of the Laotian facility, 1,615 employees, and explains they operate a fleet of 58 aircraft. They could completely disassemble, inspect, and overhaul those aircraft. The Avionics Shop could overhaul and test most electronic equipment in the plane, including altimeters, and those were tested, repaired, and maintained regularly.[72] It would have been well within CIA capabilities to assemble an altimeter so it would incorrectly read altitude.

Would it have been possible to replace an altimeter in the Lear Jet carrying Reuther on May 9? Much was made in the ensuing investigations that the flight list for the private Lear Jet was not publicly available, and no one could have known Reuther would be on that plane. As some pointed out, Reuther was traveling to the new site for the UAW Education Center almost every weekend at this time. The private investigator, retained at Walter Reuther's daughter's request, found a journalist who knew in advance that Reuther would be on the flight that night.[73] A bigger question regarding opportunity is, was it possible to install an altimeter onboard the plane during the 20 minutes it was on the ground at the Detroit Metro Airport? The NTSB did not do any testing of the feasibility of that.

In 2018, the NTSB responded to my own Freedom of Information Act (FOIA) request concerning the altimeter onboard the plane carrying Reuther, stating that the only information available was a summary of a report that indicated pilot error, due to lack of visible cues, and possible altimeter error were the causes of the crash. The NTSB found its full report on the accident in its records when I filed a new FOIA request in 2021 and sent them a copy of that report.[74] By 1992, the FBI had still not released over 200 pages of documents concerning Reuther's death, including correspondence between the field offices and FBI Director Hoover concerning the crash. The documents that had been released were so heavily redacted it was impossible to get any information from them.[75] A careful reading of the NTSB report points to "foul play" as the most likely explanation for the crash, and a sophisticated sabotage investigation was beyond their capabilities. They would have likely contacted the FBI for assistance, and this would account for the 200 pages of documents in the Bureau's possession. These 200 pages were part of an 8,400 page file on Reuther compiled by Hoover between 1935 and 1970.[76]

If Reuther's death was not an assassination, then the crash was an incredibly fortunate coincidence from the perspective of the CIA and the AFL-CIO foreign-policy leadership. AIFLD could now proceed with its work without the withering criticism and exposure it had received until then from the Reuthers.

With Walter's death, the UAW that was built by the communists and the Reuthers began a long slow death. The old union would be replaced by something much more compatible with George Meany's view of trade unionism. While the UAW drifted aimlessly for many years, in 2015, federal authorities began a corruption investigation that by 2020 had resulted in convictions or guilty pleas of eleven high-ranking union officials, including two international presidents, two international vice-presidents, and a regional director. That group did not include another international vice-president who died before he could have joined his wife in prison.[77] In March 2020, the international executive board hired a New York law firm to enter into negotiations over reforms with the U.S. attorney in an attempt to avert a Justice Department move to seize control of the union.[78] Later in the year, a tentative agreement was reached that called for a vote on direct membership election of international officers and six years of federal oversight.

The debate over AIFLD in the U.S. labor movement ended abruptly in 1970. Victor retired in 1972, and although they would at times disagree with the AFL-CIO on foreign policy, no other high-ranking UAW official would ever publicly link the CIA and AIFLD. In 1981, the UAW reaffiliated with the AFL-CIO with no significant changes made to the Institute. Following the reaffiliation, a UAW president joined the AIFLD board of directors. In 1985, Victor came out of retirement to support a dissident reform movement in the UAW. That effort ultimately proved unsuccessful. In 1988, the UAW united with the AFL-CIO in a cross-border organizing committee with the CTM, and participated in a conference in Texas and Mexico. The meeting participants would agree to form another organization. UAW President Owen Bieber would be co-chair of the auto section of this group, and Hector Uriarte, the general secretary of the Ford CTM, would be the Mexican co-chair.

3

AIFLD and the Battle of Chile

More important for us in the labor movement, we must discover as exactly as possible just what the role of U.S. labor has been in clearing the brush for advancing corporations, the State Department and the CIA. That we have played such a role is a fact, only the extent of that role is in question.... Has such a thing happened through the democratic processes we boast, or has our power and representation been hijacked by the CIA?

Fred Hirsch, 1974

Exactly what Salvador Allende Gossens was feeling throughout the morning of September 11, 1973, will never be known. Under siege in Chile's 168-year-old presidential palace *La Moneda*, as bombs rained down from Hawker Hunter jets, Allende was able to address his supporters over the airwaves, in which he declared to repay "the people's loyalty with my life." The Chilean president, who, three years before, was the first Marxist elected to the role in the nation's history, had seen the armed forces and a majority of the political establishment, with the backing of the United States and much of the international economic community, revolt against him. Facing almost certain death, he still had time in his broadcast to castigate the traitors who were toppling him "to defend the advantages that a capitalist society grants to a few." One group in particular stood out. "The sedition sponsored by the professional unions" had been a defining feature of the final eleven months of his presidency.[1] Strikes by truck owners, shopkeepers, mine supervisors, government employees, and other white-collar sectors had created not only a political deadlock between the government and opposition, but a bitter social chasm between those who supported or opposed Allende. By the end of the day, Allende was dead, and a military junta ruled the country.

Lt. Col. Patrick Ryan, head of the navy section of the U.S. military group in Chile, was less somber. He believed that September 11 was "our D-Day," and a "day of destiny" for Chileans. Ryan's attitude was reflective of the covert policy that the U.S. government practiced, a policy which sought to make Allende's position untenable.[2] In 1975, the Church Committee, which investigated CIA abuses, published a report on U.S. government plans to prevent Allende from obtaining and consolidating power, and revealed how covert funding had been given to opposition parties and groups as early as 1958.[3] It was not until the Chilean Declassification Project, launched in 1999 and leading to Peter Kornbluh's seminal 2003 book *The Pinochet Files*, that the specifics of the plans to topple Allende were revealed. Initial plans to bribe Chilean congressmen to vote against Allende's constitutional right to assume the premiership, and the plan to assassinate the head of the armed forces, were followed by an order to inflict as much economic suffering as necessary to remove the president. Most damning of all was that these plans were traced back to the Oval Office, and to Richard Nixon and National Security Advisor Henry Kissinger.

Through this whole process, the AIFLD served a critical role in the U.S. foreign-policy apparatus that sought the overthrow of Allende. Through a combination of educational programs and social development projects provided for South American labor unions, the Institute claimed to promote and defend "free trade unionism" throughout the continent. In reality, it fomented, funded, and organized anti-communist agitation. Dependent on the finances of the AID, AIFLD functioned as an arm of U.S. foreign policy, serving at the behest of the DoS and the CIA. In Chile, it sought to weaken the communist-dominated National Union federation before the election of Allende in 1970. After this point, its objectives morphed into promoting anti-government dissension among Chilean workers and small business owners that would result in the economic and social chaos which precipitated the coup d'état.

The role of AIFLD as an agent of social and political change in Cold War Latin America has not yet been sufficiently exhumed, either within a broader framework of U.S. intervention in the continent or in a specific focus on the coup against Allende in 1973. By focusing on U.S. intervention in Chile, this chapter provides perhaps the most damning example of the AFL-CIO's Cold War role, primarily due to the void of democracy, trade union protection, and basic human rights that resulted from the coup. It also hopes to re-center the role of organized labor as a powerful historical actor, a role that has come under question in the more presentist post-Reagan, Third Way-era historiography.

AIFLD appears most prominently in two accounts of U.S. policy toward Allende's government. The more recent, by Jonathan Haslam in 2005, offers a comprehensive discussion of the Institute. He links the organization's activities to both the truck owners' strikes of October 1972 and the summer of 1973, and the copper industry strikes throughout 1973. Haslam's conclusion that AIFLD's penetrative activities "paid off when tensions increased" outlines the Institute's intentions of causing economic chaos in Chile.[4] Edy Kaufman, in his 1988 work *Crisis in Allende's Chile*, is the only other historian to give a similarly serious level of agency to AIFLD in fomenting economic disruption. Describing the Institute as the "most interesting channel of foreign support for the opposition," Kaufman emphasized the significant number of opposition supporters who were "trained" as evidence for AIFLD's impact on the Chilean labor scene.[5] Kaufman's analysis of AIFLD is briefer than Haslam's, presumably due to having less access to the relevant archival material. Haslam was writing after both the Chilean Declassification Project had taken place, and after the AFL-CIO archives had opened, perhaps explaining why he writes in more detail on the Institute.

The analyses in those two works provide the most comprehensive coverage of AIFLD in the mainstream foreign-policy historiography. In Hal Brands' *Latin America's Cold War*, despite his desire to integrate perspectives "from several diverse realms—from the highest echelons of superpower diplomacy to the everyday negotiation of social and political relationships," he omits AIFLD altogether. His conclusion that Allende's "most critical economic wounds were self-inflicted" is therefore undermined. Discussing the role of

AIFLD in fomenting strikes would have enabled him to recognize that the "everyday" rupture of socio-political relations was touched by foreign influence. He instead relies on the testimony of Robert McNamara, then president of the World Bank, as evidence that "the whole damned economy is being destroyed" by Allende's policies.[6] Tanya Harmer's triangulated analysis of relations between the United States, Cuba, and Chile similarly emphasizes the agency of Chilean political forces at the expense of uncovering the full extent of U.S. influence into opposition groups. Harmer believes "it was Chileans who had let this [the resulting junta] happen.... Chilean truckers and miners had staged strikes in the hope of bringing their country to a standstill, with funding from outside but with a will of their own nevertheless."[7]

Where Brands and Harmer have more credibility in assessing the impact U.S. foreign policy had on Allende's opposition is their access to Spanish-language primary sources. Due to a lack of such primary sources here, pronouncements on the significance of AIFLD's impact in Chile have to be measured. Claims that the very existence of a Chilean opposition to the Popular Unity government was dependent on U.S. instruments such as AIFLD, without sufficient evidence from Chilean sources, would be as weak historically as they are patronizing to Chileans. A desire to recognize the agency of Global South actors should not, however, preclude an acknowledgment of the existence and indeed forcefulness of organizations such as AIFLD. Judgments such as that of Kristian Gustafson, who claims the CIA "was involved in the funding but was not the main motivator behind the crippling strikes," are therefore weaker for not considering AIFLD, who were important in not only funding but also in educating and organizing opposition groups.[8] The relationship between the Institute's activities and the opposition's motivation, which arose from long-standing Chilean class divides, was not mutually exclusive, as AIFLD was able to give significant help to sectors that were naturally inclined to oppose the government. There is evidence, however, to demonstrate the Institute's capacity to change minds, or at least to foment a fervent anti-communism where none had existed before, underlining the duality of the Institute as a reinforcer but also a creator of opposition to Allende.

On November 12, 1970, two months after being entertained at a White House dinner for Labor leaders, George Meany found himself in conversation with DoS officials once again. In an "off-the-record briefing," along with leaders of businesses such as the Anaconda Company, Meany heard about National Security Decision Memorandum (NSDM) 93, the Nixon administration's response to the election of Salvador Allende to the Chilean presidency. Here, Meany and AIFLD were given the go-ahead from the highest point in the U.S. foreign-policy-making apparatus to "maximize pressures on the Allende government to prevent its consolidation," or as Nixon privately declared to Kissinger, to "make the economy scream." After three years of economic and social crisis, a violent coup d'état, and the imposition of an ultra-right-wing military junta, Nixon's demand had been met.[9]

There is significant evidence that AIFLD served as an important instrument of the DoS and the CIA in their quest to rid Chile of Allende's socialism. Concluding this in part requires trusting the testimony of U.S. labor activists who, in well-intentioned efforts to hold the AFL-CIO to account for its foreign policy, might claim that the Institute was a more nefarious and important influence in Chile than it actually was. Despite public derision of such claims, AIFLD representatives privately welcomed a reputation of importance. Correspondence in the Institute's archives reveals how the representatives saw themselves as active participants in the Cold War, obsessed with how many Chilean union leaders they trained, compared to how many the "Marxist-Leninists" were reaching.[10] Concern over "the enemy" was coupled with near paranoia over AIFLD's image in Chile, which was tested in September 1971. Panic arose when an article appearing in the popular Chilean newspaper *El Siglo* claimed the Institute was serving the aims of the CIA. Lamenting that "it is obvious that we've had a leak somewhere," a memorandum was sent to Executive Director William Doherty warning of an "all-out attack on AIFLD and other US instrumentalities still in Chile," which "could make recruitment of representative candidates that much more difficult." Interestingly, this was followed by a criticism of the Nixon administration's "policy of low profile" in Chile, which, through its hostile nature, fueled greater suspicion of U.S. underground activities. AIFLD believed "a more dynamic policy on the part of our government would allow us to open more schools and start a full-scale program until we are thrown out of Chile."[11]

Missing from this warning memo was any denial of the points made by *El Siglo*. Of course, this is because they were probably true. A CIA report on "Communism in the Latin American Labor" from 1967 highlights how even before Allende came to power the Institute was serving the government. Praising AIFLD's contribution to the anti-communist gains made in South American labor movements, the report also cites the numerical strength of communist and anti-communist unions, information that correlates closely to the detailed reports on membership figures collected by the Institute. Information gathering was a crucial function that AIFLD served, and went far beyond a mere count of union membership. Detailed tracking of the political persuasion of both union leaders and members enabled estimates to be made on the overall political leanings of a national labor movement, allowing the CIA to discover that in "The Present Situation," "communists play a dominant role in the labor movement of Chile."[12]

Breaking the communist dominance of Chilean labor was AIFLD's original aim, and this naturally transformed into a more holistic effort to undermine the Popular Unity government after the 1970 election. As early as 1962, AIFLD Executive Director Serafino Romualdi had accepted that the "only way to defeat a Communist CUT [Central Unitaria de Trabajadores de Chile, the Chilean equivalent of the AFL-CIO] is through a breakaway."[13] While failing to achieve this goal over the course of the following decade, AIFLD made important friends during their efforts, which would enable them to create the economic turbulence that ensued during Allende's presidency. Robert O'Neill was one of them. O'Neill was serving as U.S. labor attaché to Chile, and given his prominence among the sources found in the Institute's archives, was also one of the most important AIFLD employees based on the ground in

Santiago. He believed as late as 1972 that a break-up of the CUT was still possible, if only workers in copper, LAN-Chile (the national airline), maritime unions, communications, and banks could form a block.[14] During her speech at the World Peace Conference at Yale in 1975, the Chilean leader's widow Hortensia Allende Bussi accused O'Neill of involvement in clandestine activities to promote economic sabotage during her husband's presidency.[15] The archival evidence available, and the parallel role O'Neill served as AIFLD employee and U.S. attaché, suggests that this accusation contained some truth.

AIFLD targeted several sectors of the Chilean labor movement: the maritime unions, the copper unions, and the *gremios*—these were guilds, rather than traditional unions, which incorporated small businessmen, such as truck owners, shopkeepers, or more white-collar industries, such as government employees. The importance of these sectors in fomenting the social unrest during the Allende presidency, and their strong ties to the Institute, are not coincidental. Through its role on the ground in collecting information on the political leanings of workers, and by providing training, organization, and finance to those unions who opposed Allende, AIFLD served an important function in the U.S. foreign-policy machine that was set in motion after NSDM 93. And, much to its delight, the Institute could claim that it helped cause devastating economic chaos in Chile during the months leading up to the military coup in September 1973.

AIFLD's longest and most trusted ally in the battle to win over the Chilean trade union movement from communism was the Maritime Federation of Chile [Confederación Marítima de Chile] (COMACH). With over 30,000 members it was one of the largest unions in Chile, and given the country's abundance of coastline, served one of the most important sectors in the economy. In Wenceslao Moreno, it had a leader that AIFLD deemed to be one of the most powerful union figures in the nation. While COMACH was not responsible for the most devastating strike action during Allende's presidency, and despite its failure to instigate a break-up of the communist-dominated CUT, the union gave AIFLD an important footing in Chile and may have played an important role on the day of the coup itself.

Moreno's own story underlines the closeness of AIFLD's relationship with COMACH. Having led maritime workers since 1950, he helped found the ICFTU in 1949, and served on the AIFLD board of trustees throughout the 1960s.[16] Working for the Institute had seen Moreno and COMACH used as central agitators for a break-up of the CUT, but attempts to create a rival National Confederation of Workers had failed to win sufficient support from other sectors. Even before Allende's election, Moreno appeared to be becoming weary of the anti-communist struggle. He complained to a board meeting in 1970 of how he had constantly been under attack from the Chilean press "for receiving payments in US dollars in exchange for defending the imperialist position," and "constantly being in contact with [Chairman of the AIFLD Board] Peter Grace and the CIA," perhaps explaining his decision to step down in 1972 from frontline trade union politics.[17] Moreno's relationships with Chilean labor and with the United States did not end here however. He returned after the coup, serving as the Pinochet regime's labor attaché to the United States. In this role he helped end a boycott organized by ORIT of Chilean goods in 1979 that had been formed in response to the persecution of trade unionists by the military government, believing that in allowing a very limited form of collective bargaining the junta had made sufficient concessions for the boycott to be cancelled.[18]

In 1972, however, Moreno's decision to step down from the COMACH leadership panicked AIFLD, who feared that years of buttering up the maritime union might go to waste. O'Neill pointed out how the support of new leader, ex-communist Martin Bustos, was "essential to keep the Federation democratic," but accepted that he would probably be "less understanding" of AIFLD's objectives. It appears that the U.S. chief of missions to Chile, Harry Shlaudeman, was consulted on the issue of maintaining COMACH support. Shlaudeman warned that publicity of this consultation (which was held with O'Neill and the AFL-CIO's Inter-American Representative Andrew McLellan) could damage any action taken. As chief of missions, Shlaudeman held a diplomatic role in the U.S. Embassy, but he also sat in on CIA meetings in which plans were discussed to fund Allende's opposition. News that he consulted with AIFLD on how to create opposition to the Popular Unity government was best avoided for both parties.[19]

Fear of losing influence in COMACH was understandable given the extensive financial efforts AIFLD had made to win its favor. This had generally been through loans for building projects, which helped transform the union's headquarters in the port city Valparaiso. In 1965, the building of a library, for example, was supposedly to enable the union's "sophisticated and democratically oriented leadership to strengthen its collective bargaining capacity, service the worker and his family, and enhance its influence amongst sister unions in Chile."[20] The library and a grant of $4,000 for earthquake relief was given in part to make up for the failure of a planned $5 million housing project that COMACH had been promised in 1964, but which failed to get off the ground. Moreno appeared to be forgiving however, as a renovated headquarters, complete with an AIFLD-funded ship-to-shore radio system, reinforced his own power among the maritime sector.[21] In 1971, AIFLD had started using the Deak Company to transfer U.S. dollars into Chilean escudos, to "take advantage of the black-market rate." This meant that rather than receiving 15.36 escudos to the dollar, COMACH and other unions funded would receive 35 escudos, "a premium of 100 percent compared with the official exchange rate." Headed by former Office for Strategic Services employee Nicholas Deak, the company was regularly used by the CIA for funneling money into U.S.-backed political groups, and it appears that COMACH was no exception.[22]

On the morning of September 11, 1973, the Institute's obsession with the goings on in Valparaiso appeared to be justified. The coup that day which led to the fall of the Popular Unity government began in the city, with the capturing of ports by the Chilean navy. There is no "smoking gun" evidence for either COMACH's or AIFLD's direct assistance in the navy's actions. It is certainly plausible, however, that AIFLD's activities indirectly supported them. The presence of four U.S. ships off the Chilean coast that morning has been cited as evidence for the Nixon administration's role in helping the Chilean military plan "Operation Unitas."[23] In this context, AIFLD had served a useful function. They had collected information about the political leanings of the port workers, which was then passed on to the CIA, and had subdued support for Allende among port workers, through educational programs and financial incentives, such as the building of homes and a library. Despite their lack of resistance to the coup, it is difficult to actually prove that any COMACH figures were themselves involved in the naval takeover of the ports. An AIFLD "Progress Report" from 1974 does introduce an affiliate union of COMACH (the Union of Merchant Marine Professionals, based in Valparaiso), which appeared to be made up of men trained by the navy, and retired navy officers. The subsequent political comeback of Moreno under the military junta, and the promotion of his former deputy at COMACH, Eduardo Rios, to president of the new National Confederation of Workers, again unveil a strong relationship between the junta and leading COMACH figures.[24]

In a packed outdoor amphitheater near the El Teniente mine in Cachapoal Province, crowds of copper workers put a clever spin on the anthem of Chilean socialism. Chanting "El Teniente, United, Will Never Be Defeated!" (as opposed to "The People United..."), they displayed their commitment to a strike that would wreak havoc on the economic strength of the Allende government.[25] Despite projecting this image of unity, the strikers did not command hegemony over their fellow workers, many of whom went back to work or, indeed, had never stopped. Lurking behind the strike, and enabling it to be as effective as possible despite a lack of widespread support, was AIFLD. As Chile's richest natural resource, copper accounted for the majority of the nation's foreign exchange earnings, with El Teniente itself producing up to 20 percent of this figure. Nationalization of the industry had broken the stronghold which saw Kennecott and Anaconda corporations own 80 percent of production, an egregious act in the eyes of AIFLD board member and Anaconda chairman Charles Brinckerhoff.[26] The expropriation of

American business was a decisive motivation behind NSDM 93, and AIFLD responded to the DoS's call accordingly.

Attempts to undermine support for Allende among copper workers formed an integral part of the Institute's Chilean program. Copper's position as Chile's principal export meant that mine workers were relatively more comfortable than those in other sectors, allowing AIFLD a potentially more receptive audience to their anti-communist, pro-market message. This opportunity did not go unnoticed; O'Neill stated clearly that "AIFLD will continue to stress contacts [in the copper sector], utilizing union-to-union trips and Front Royal course for younger leaders." The aim of these contacts was to create "internal dissension" within the copper unions. O'Neill hoped for "a reinforced effort by the International Trade Secretariats and US unions along these lines," to "add to the unrest."[27] Visits by copper leaders were quickly put in motion, with one taking place in the summer of 1971 dubbed "a great success." AIFLD's regional director, Jesse Friedman (Serafino Romualdi's stepson), emphasized the importance of making these trips available to Allende-supporting union leaders, to "show these influential leaders, through exposure to our unions, that they have been misled in the formation of their concept of the United States."[28] Despite the relative economic security of copper workers, many supported the Popular Unity government, forcing AIFLD to develop their tactics beyond haranguing students about the evils of communism. Aside from an emphasis on collective bargaining, Chilean copper workers were able to attend a U.S. Workers Congress in Las Vegas, where they were allowed to address the audience and then live with leaders of American copper unions for "a number of days." The trip was intended to offer "them an insight of the US family way of life which is so often distorted in the leftist Chilean press." American trade unionism, which rested on "bread and butter" solutions rather than ideological rigidity, was used to convince Chilean copper leaders that they owed no loyalty to the Workers' government, and that their members' concerns over pay were more important than the nation's foreign exchange earnings.[29]

In April 1973, this strategy paid off. AIFLD had sufficiently influenced enough copper leaders to cause a nationwide copper strike, directed against the government. Lasting 76 days, the strike was originally called at the El Teniente mine in an attempt to force the government to follow through and implement a policy of salary readjustment that had been promised. After spreading to other prominent mines based in the towns of Rancagua, El Salvador, and Chuquicamata, the strike began to lose support among the wider membership, and by May 7, 61 percent of the El Teniente workforce were back at work (and on May 16 workers in both Chuquicamata and El Salvador voted to go back to work completely). The absence of prominent union leadership in this return to work was telling, however. By creating enough leaders and supervisors committed to frustrating the Allende government, copper production was seriously weakened despite a large proportion of workers returning to the mines. Chilean filmmaker Patricio Guzman uncovered this often ugly friction between workers and union leaders in his three-part documentary *The Battle of Chile*. Footage of workers explaining why they had returned to the mines sees an emphasis on "duty" and putting the "benefit of all Chileans" above personal benefits. One worker bemoaned that "we've got a lot of comrades who still don't know why they stopped. They're fighting with the police because some guy sets himself up as leader, and he puts on a show for them, and they follow him like Christ." As late as June, however, 25 percent of the mining workforce was still on strike, and demonstrating in Santiago. One prominent copper leader even became the first labor leader to give a speech at the Catholic University of Santiago, whose predominantly middle-class student population was firmly against Allende. While the strike had by no means won widespread support in the country, or even majority support in the workforce, considerable "dissension" had been created.[30]

AIFLD stood back and admired its work, with Andrew McLellan gleefully reporting back to Jay Lovestone at the AFL-CIO that Allende was now "facing a crisis of heretofore unequalled portent for the future operations" of his government.[31] The Popular Unity government managed to spin the end of the conflict quite effectively, with up to 500,000 pro-government workers marching on Santiago as the strike petered out portraying a victorious finale. The stoppage had seriously undermined Chile's foreign exchange reserves however, which Jonathan Haslam has estimated to have cost the country at least $30 million.[32] While causing similar economic suffering to that which the Nixon administration enforced through reducing global copper prices, the strike had a much greater political and symbolic impact.[33] Not only did it amplify the social chaos and unrest caused by a deteriorating economic situation, it portrayed Allende as unable to govern even those workers he supposedly represented.

Yet, on September 11, when Allende was in his office in La Moneda, his presidential palace, under siege from the Chilean Air Force, it was "the revolt led by the professional unions" that he chose to castigate. By "professional unions," he was referring to groups of workers, predominantly from the transport and communications sectors, who had grouped together in 1971 as the National Command for Gremio Defense. *Gremio* in Spanish refers to a "guild" rather than a "union," and often refers to small business owners rather than blue-collar workers. One of the groups affiliated to the National Command was the Confederation of Chilean Professionals [Confederación Única de Profesionales de Chile] (CUPROCH), to which prominent mine supervisors belonged. Another, the Confederation of Truck Owners of Chile, were responsible for calling the devastating truck strikes in October 1972 and July 1973. Behind these organizations' creation, planning, and funding, was AIFLD.[34]

Historians of the coup now agree that the CIA effectively funded the truck owners' strike. To suggest that this was the extent of U.S. involvement, however, overlooks the importance of AIFLD, which can be said to have both created the institutions that called the strike, and to have trained those who led it. The first of these came in 1971, with the creation of CUPROCH. Correspondence in April 1971 between O'Neill and McLellan reveals a concern that the professional unions would receive printing machines. O'Neill suggested that the International Transport Federation might be interested in undertaking the project, "but then if the press is used against government policies it could affect relations with LAN-Chile [the national airline], which is pro-Government." The ITF were one of the key International Trade Secretariats that AIFLD used in Chile to create the professional unions, along with FIET (International Federation of Commercial, Clerical, Technical, and Professional Employees) and PTTI. The ITSs went far beyond supplying printing machines. These were the organizations through which the CIA "funneled" money to opposition groups, which the *New York Times* estimated to be near to $8 million over the last 18 months of the Allende presidency.[35] According to American labor activist, scholar, and journalist Professor Ruth Needleman, who interviewed both leaders of the Chilean professional unions and representatives of ITSs while working in Chile, AIFLD and the ITSs were critical in channeling this funding to the groups who could do most damage to Allende. By diverting U.S. government funds through an international trade union federation, payments were less easily traceable, and could appear more legitimate, under the guise of international solidarity between workers in the same sector. Needleman's claims were based on extensive interviews with relevant figures, such as the leader of the truck owners' strike Leon Vilarín, and Head of the PTTI Walter Legge. They provide the best explanation given thus far of how the CIA actually distributed their covert funds to the *gremios*, and suggest that their organizations depended on AIFLD and ITS support for their very existence.[36]

AIFLD's responsibility for precipitating the strikes did not stop at funding. Leaders of the National Command for Gremio Defense, of the truck owners' strikes, and the public employees' strike were all trained by the Institute. Many of these were trained by AIFLD at the Front Royal Institute, explaining why the number of Chileans trained in Virginia rose during Allende's presidency, to reach over 140 by 1973. Vilarín was one of these, who, despite being a former militant of the Socialist Party and friend of Allende himself, had been swayed by the allure of Front Royal.[37] Shortly after the October Strike, a group from the Government Employee Union [Agrupación Nacional de Empleados Fiscales] (ANEF) visited the U.S., including Milenko Milovanovic, who would go on to lead the government employees' walkout in the summer of 1973. Mihovilovic was described by the AIFLD report as a "very alert individual" who had "real possibilities in continued leadership in union work." This was after the Chilean received a standing ovation at the graduation banquet, which could have seen him dine with businessmen such as J. Peter Grace or Charles Brinckerhoff of the Anaconda Company.[38] Presumably the "real possibilities" AIFLD believed lay before him included the ability to organize a crippling public sector strike. Other key leaders of the National Command for Gremio Defense, such as Jorge Guerrero, Manuel Valdez, and Orlando Saenz, were reportedly trained in the U.S. by AIFLD. Correspondence after the coup between the former National Command for Gremio Defense leaders and AIFLD reveals quite a comradely relationship, however, insinuating that the Institute built useful contacts with the small business leaders who created social chaos.[39]

The *gremio* revolt came in two bouts, and served a dual purpose of causing economic sabotage, and creating enough social chaos to justify a military intervention. The first of these began at midnight on October 10, 1972. Twelve-thousand truck owners refused to drive after the announcement that the government would pilot a scheme for a nationalized road haulage system in Aysén. Solidarity with the strikers in other sectors quickly increased. Within a week, students, doctors, technicians, bank employees, merchant seamen, lawyers, and even dentists were striking. Mass walkouts across sectors exacerbated the economic damage from the stoppage, but the most critical losses came from the truck owners. Chile's reliance on road haulage for its economic activity, given its geographical predisposition to motorways rather than railways, meant that by November 11, 1972, the economy had lost $170 million.[40]

After Allende celebrated the end of the miners' strike in June 1973, a second wave of *gremio* strikes delivered a decisive blow to what remained of economic and social stability in the country. In the last few days of July, the sight of thousands of empty trucks, often left together at strategic points to block roads, was broadcast to the nation on opposition-backed television channels. This included government attempts to bring trucks back to Santiago for redeployment, a move met with fierce resistance from the truck owners. A political crisis ensued, in which the Senate accused the government of acting illegally to steal private property. Strikes by shopkeepers and government employees added to the chaos. Increasingly desperate, especially given the mobilization of far-right terrorist cells such as Patria y Libertad (Homeland and Freedom), Allende brought members of the armed forces into his cabinet. This included bringing Army Commander General Prats into the Ministry of Defense. Taking over from Prats as head of the Chilean Armed Forces was General Augusto Pinochet, considered by many to be a constitutionalist. It was a miscalculation that proved fatal for Allende.[41]

Noting that if you "kill the bitch" you "eliminate the litter," Pinochet did not mince his words.[42] A year to the day after the second truck owners' strike began, he declared that "the date has special importance for the history of the country, as the day on which the Gremio movement started, imposing the rejection of Marxist tyranny from Chile."[43] In Pinochet's assessment, the strikes that had been funded and organized by AIFLD had been the catalyst for the coup. With its principal aim of fighting communism in Latin American labor movements, the Institute had apparently achieved its goal in Chile.

The cost of this, however, was horrific. In October, the CIA Station in Santiago was given access to a "highly sensitive" summary on post-coup repression prepared for the new military junta. Information made its way back to the White House that more than 13,500 citizens had been rounded up in mass arrests. Made up of prominently left-wing activists, trade unionists, and workers, they were being held in 20 concentration camps around the country, such as the National Stadium in Santiago, and many were subject to torture. Approximately 1,500 civilians had already been massacred by mid-October, a number that would rise to 3,197 confirmed cases during the 17-year dictatorship. The manner of the executions, by firing squads into unmarked, secret mass graves, or disfigured bodies dropped into the ocean out of helicopters, leaves families ignorant of missing relatives' fates even today.[44] As if purging the country of left-wing workers and activists was not sufficient for the junta, the legal suppression of trade unionism was the next step, with a banning of collective bargaining and abolishing the CUT.[45]

The junta's crimes did not deter AIFLD from maintaining a working relationship with them. It is unlikely that this was due to a lack of information regarding the persecution. AFL-CIO leaders appeared to be aware to some extent of the information the CIA was receiving from Santiago, with Meany sending a number of cables to Pinochet throughout the 1970s, urging the General to intervene personally when trade unionists were arrested. The junta permitted the Institute to continue working with trade unions who had inflicted much of the anti-Allende action, even if much of AIFLD's work was complete.[46] Joseph Beirne articulated AIFLD's disapproving but ultimately tolerant stance toward the Chilean regime. He expressed concern in a report "that if the right-wing military regimes of Brazil and Argentina and several other South and Central American countries should collapse, the pendulum might swing to an even more reprehensible totalitarian left." To him this proved "in the long run that authoritarianism does not constitute a better shield than democracy against leftist extremism."[47] Far-right authoritarianism was not the Institute's preferred solution to replacing left-wing governments, but it was deemed acceptable if necessary in the short-run.

Acceptance of far-right military rule, to prevent consolidation of left-wing governments in the Global South, demonstrated how closely AIFLD aligned ideologically to the U.S. government. From Brazil, the Dominican Republic, or Argentina, to Indonesia, the Congo, or Iran, the United States assisted the overthrow of democratically elected governments by authoritarian regimes, who could be trusted to suffocate political forces hostile to America's Cold War aims. In Latin America, through their Institute for Free Labor Development, the American labor movement contributed to its government's foreign policy, collaborating with the DoS to organize, fund, and educate political forces who supported U.S. goals in the region, and collaborating with the CIA to collect information about the workers of the Global South. These efforts were supported by business leaders, whose concerns over their own capital harmonized with the concerns of the U.S. government, whenever left-wing economic nationalism surfaced.

Chile was yet another casualty in the pantheon of twentieth-century U.S. intervention, but one in which the nefarious role of American labor can clearly be proven.[48] Efforts to prove this have been led in a large part by American workers, seeking to uncover the exact role their union federation played in undermining not only the Chilean workers' government, but enabling the persecution that followed. Historians of American foreign policy should recognize these efforts, and incorporate the actions of American labor into their analyses when documenting U.S. interventionism during the Cold War.

In December 1973, the Emergency Committee to Defend Democracy in Chile held a conference of 300 diverse individuals. A report was published for the group by Fred Hirsch, a member of the Plumbers and Steamfitters Local 393 in San Jose, California. His paper was entitled, "An Analysis of Our AFL-CIO Role in Latin America or Under the Covers with the CIA." Hirsch's copyrighted paper was the first attempt by an American trade unionist to document AIFLD's efforts to disrupt and divide the leftist-leaning labor unions in Latin America. His work now resides in the CIA's declassified files and the General Libraries of the University of Texas, Austin.

The Hirsch paper begins by explaining the stakes for organized labor:

> More important for us in the labor movement, we must discover as exactly as possible just what the role of U.S. labor has been in clearing the brush for advancing corporations, the State Department and the CIA. That we have played such a role is a fact, only the extent of that role is in question. Has the U.S. labor movement allowed itself to be shanghaied into the service as the aide of the junta executioners of Latin America? Has such a thing happened through the democratic processes we boast, or has our power and representation been hijacked by the CIA?[49]

The document concludes with a call to abolish AIFLD. Hirsh presented a sample resolution for use at union meetings:

SAMPLE RESOLUTION 1

WHEREAS there is abundant evidence that the AFL-CIO has been involved in Latin America and the Caribbean in actions that violate basic labor principles and Latin America; and

WHEREAS it appears that U.S. labor actions have been instrumental in precipitating governmental takeovers and violence against unionists and working people abroad; and

WHEREAS the AFL-CIO, through the AIFLD, has involved the labor movement in questionable relations with multinational corporations, the U.S. State Department and the CIA;

THEREFORE, unless the AFL-CIO Executive Council can provide contrary evidence,

BE IT RESOLVED that this Labor Council disassociate itself from any further actions of the AIFLD and demand the dissolution of the Institute and complete disentanglement of the AFL-CIO International Relations Department with government and business strategies abroad.[50]

The Hirsch pamphlet led to a formal resolution that passed the Santa Clara County, California Central Labor Council (which includes San Francisco) by an overwhelming vote on March 4, 1974. The resolution specifically asked the AFL-CIO to "provide information that will enable this Council to reaffirm the integrity and high purpose of the AFL-CIO in foreign as well as in domestic affairs on behalf of all working people, here and abroad." The adopted resolution was a substitute to the one appended to the "An Analysis of Our AFL-CIO Role in Latin America" proposed by a local Teachers Union.[51]

The Santa Clara resolution garnered attention at the national AFL-CIO. Bill Doherty left Washington, DC, to visit the errant California labor body. He denied AIFLD involvement in the Brazilian coup and claimed that the Institute had no "in country programs" in Chile during the 1973 coup. He laughed off the question of CIA connections. The Santa Clara Central Labor Council stood its ground and sent Doherty away.[52] A few years later this action was followed by efforts of some substitute teachers in Chicago to expose the links between the American Federation of Teachers and its President Albert Shankar and the CIA.[53] The trip to California marked a new turn in Doherty's career. From this point on he was assigned with administering AIFLD and also tasked with managing internal dissent over AFL-CIO foreign policy in the U.S.

Several courageous national union leaders spoke out against the junta whose rise to power had been supported by the AFL-CIO leadership. They included: Pat Gorman, Amalgamated Meat Cutters and Butcher Workmen of North America; Ralph Helstein, United Packinghouse Workers; Leonard Woodcock, UAW; Floyd Smith of the International Association of Machinists and Aerospace Workers; and Harry Bridges, International Longshore and Warehouse Union.[54] These actions would lay the basis for a more significant rebellion against AFL-CIO foreign policy in the 1980s.

In 1974, Jay Lovestone was forced out as director of the AFL-CIO International Affairs Department. George Meany learned that Lovestone had been maintaining his relationship with James Angleton and the CIA seven years after being instructed to end it. Meany had discovered a letter and a check made out to Lovestone's long-time paramour, Page Morris, from Angleton.[55] Meany appointed his son-in-law, Ernie Lee, to be international affairs director.

Chile would go on to become the first and most extreme experiment in what is now called neoliberalism. Assuming top economic positions during the junta's 17 years of dictatorship were a group of 25 Chileans dubbed the "Chicago Boys," who had returned to Chile after studying "monetarism" under Milton Friedman at the University of Chicago in the 1950s in a DoS-funded exchange program.

The theory of monetarism calls for the government to refrain from regulating the market except for the money supply. The junta gave the Chicago Boys free rein to implement Friedman's theories. They reduced government spending, implemented free trade agreements, privatized dozens of state companies, removed most governmental controls on private economic activities, and privatized the government pension system. The junta repressed all political opposition to this. Milton Friedman himself visited Chile and met with Pinochet in 1975. He praised the economic measures the military junta was taking.[56]

As with much of the AFL-CIO foreign policy during the Cold War, its actions in Chile would have unintended consequences. The junta's economic program became a field test for the same monetarist economic policies that would later be put in place by Ronald Reagan and adopted in principle by many of the elites of both major U.S. political parties. Free trade agreements, like the North American Free Trade Agreement (NAFTA), would devastate the highly unionized manufacturing economy in the U.S. Privatization of government services would be a constant threat to the newly organized public employee sector. The building trades' unions would be forced into defensive battles to protect prevailing wage laws that regulate wages in government construction projects. The neoliberal agenda, first put into place in Chile, would come back home to haunt the AFL-CIO.

4

El Salvador, Nicaragua, and AIFLD's Agenda for Central America

The days are over when a small group of right-wing staffers in Washington develops foreign policy for the AFL-CIO and get a rubber stamp from the executive council.

Edward Clark, International Vice-President,
Amalgamated Clothing and Textile Workers Union, 1985

On the night of January 3, 1981, two American AIFLD employees, Michael Hammer and Mark Pearlman, were having a late-night dinner with a Salvadoran, José Rodolfo Viera, at the Sheraton Hotel in San Salvador. Viera was the general secretary of a peasant workers' union and El Salvador's land reform agency director. AIFLD was renting a suite at the Sheraton for him.[1] The hotel was located in a stylish neighborhood, and they might have heard music from the disco in the building. While they talked at a table in the hotel restaurant, the Salon de las Americas, a right-wing businessman, Hans Christ, some witnesses claim, led two Salvadoran soldiers to the restaurant's entrance. They opened fire, one with a .45 caliber submachine gun and the other with a 9 mm submachine gun, killing all three men at the table.[2] These murders and the subsequent failure of the Salvadoran government to prosecute those who ordered the killings would lead to political problems for the Reagan administration and the AFL-CIO, which supported the administration's policies in Central America.

El Salvador had long been considered a breeding ground for revolution by the U.S. before Michael Hammer opened AIFLD's first country office there in 1966.[3] Throughout the late twentieth century, El Salvador had the most unequal distribution of income in all of Latin America. Between 60 and 70 percent of the population were rural peasants living in extreme poverty on subsistence farms. As a country without a significant industrial base and few exportable resources outside of agricultural products, land was the critical component of wealth and survival. Most of that land, almost 80 percent, was owned by just 10 percent of the population.[4]

During the 1960s, these subsistence peasants were being forced off the land by large farmers expanding sugar, cotton, and coffee production for export.[5] With so much farmland devoted to export crops, food production dwindled, resulting in hunger, malnutrition, and an infant mortality rate of 10 percent, four times higher than that of Cuba at the time.[6]

The percentage of landless peasants increased from 20 percent of the population in 1960 to 30 percent in 1970. By 1974, it stood at 41 percent.[7] Unions were illegal in the countryside, but the Catholic church began to organize peasant cooperatives in the 1960s, and by 1965 these had come together to form the Christian Peasants Federation known by its Spanish initials FEC-CAS. Priests in the countryside, inspired by liberation theology, encouraged peasants to join FEC-CAS, which advocated for land redistribution, and better wages and working conditions for agriculture workers. FEC-CAS began to move to the left politically in the face of resistance from the landed oligarchs and the military.[8]

In most Latin American countries, AIFLD built or supported anti-leftist, pro-American unions among urban and industrial workers. In El Salvador, AIFLD would pursue a similar strategy among rural agricultural workers and peasants.[9] In 1966, with the support of the El Salvadoran government, Michael Hammer, with AIFLD money, began to fund infrastructure projects in the countryside, hold training seminars for sharecroppers, and pay for land purchases for some of the landless peasants. He continued the peasant association FEC-CAS's work of organizing cooperatives, attracting many of its supporters. In 1968, Hammer formed this AIFLD-created network into the Salvadoran Communal Union (UCS).[10] Being a union, it was not technically legal, but the government supported it as an alternative to the more militant and political organizations sprouting up.[11]

While Chile had a long history of democratic governance before the 1973 coup, El Salvador had been under military control longer than any other country in Latin America. Arturo Araújo, a reformer, was elected in 1931 in the last actual democratic presidential election before the Civil War of the 1980s. He was ousted in a military coup a few months later. Military participation in politics would become institutionalized with the National Party of Conciliation (PCN) founded in the early 1960s.[12]

An opposition coalition headed by a charismatic Christian Democrat, José Napoleón Duarte, challenged the PCN in the 1972 presidential election. Duarte's alliance included socialists and communists. With the Duarte coalition ahead in the early returns, the government simply stopped announcing the count and proclaimed as victor the PCN candidate, Colonel Arturo Molina, by 10,000 votes out of a total of 650,000 cast. Another colonel, who had backed the Duarte coalition, initiated a coup to prevent Molina from taking power. The military quickly crushed the coup, and Duarte was arrested, severely beaten, and forced into exile.[13]

By 1972, it was apparent that the organized peasant movement was gaining momentum, and it was seen as communist subversion by the oligarchs and the military. In July 1973, the Molina government told AIFLD to leave the country. The junta could have destroyed the UCS, but it allowed it to survive. The UCS stayed in communication with AIFLD and sent members to AIFLD's training seminars in Guatemala.[14] Before it left El Salvador, AIFLD arranged to fund the UCS via the Inter-American Foundation (IAF), an independent U.S. government agency that became its chief funding source.[15] One of the principal leaders of the UCS during the 1970s was José Rodolfo Viera, who became its undisputed leader in 1978. Hammer and Viera had a long relationship stretching back to AIFLD's earliest Salvadoran leadership training in the mid-1960s.[16] After leaving El Salvador, AIFLD assigned Hammer to be its country director in Brazil.[17]

The 1972 election convinced many Salvadorans that peaceful change in El Salvador was impossible. The left continued to grow throughout the decade.[18] Robert White was ambassador to El Salvador between 1980 and 1981 and said he was fired from the foreign service by Ronald Reagan for refusing to cover up the Salvadoran military's involvement in the murder of four American churchwomen there in 1980. He described the left in El Salvador to a congressional subcommittee as follows:

> The guerrilla groups, the revolutionary groups, almost without exception began as associations of teachers, associations of labor unions, campesino unions, or parish organizations which were organized for the definite purpose of getting a schoolhouse up on the market road. When they tried to use their power of association to gain their ends, first they were warned and then they were persecuted and tortured and shot.[19]

In the fall of 1980, five leftist armed guerrilla groups formed the Farabundo Martí National Liberation Front (FMLN) after the personal intervention of Fidel Castro tampered down the divisions that had prevented the various socialists and revolutionaries from uniting. That same year, political opposition groups with diverse ideologies formed the Democratic Revolutionary Front (FDR).[20] The FMLN/FDR would remain at war with the U.S.-backed Salvadoran governments until 1992 when they signed a peace accord, and the FMLN/FDR became a legal political party.[21]

In 1979, with El Salvador on the brink of civil war following the Sandinista victory in Nicaragua, a group of young reformist military officers instigated a successful coup to remove Molina as President. The post-coup government initially supported land reform, civilian control of the military, and an end to corruption and human rights abuses. The cabinet was composed of a political cross-section of El Salvador. A few months later, it was subverted by more conservative military officers, who formed a new government with Duarte, who returned to El Salvador, and the Christian Democratic Party (PDC).[22]

Land reform was going to be central to the program of the new junta. They called on the UCS to provide support for the effort. However, internal splits and financial scandals had weakened it during the 1970s.[23] AIFLD and Michael Hammer were invited back into the country to give technical assistance to the land reform initiative and help organize political support for the Duarte–PDC–military government.[24] When AIFLD returned in mid-1979, they got involved with the UCS again, hiring 400 of its members as full-time organizers in the countryside. The Institute quickly reasserted its control of the peasant workers union.[25] Almost the entire $2 million annual UCS budget was paid for by AIFLD. The UCS had become little more than a front for AIFLD and U.S. policy.[26]

The Christian Democrats approached José Rodolfo Viera and offered him the presidency of the Salvadoran Institute of Agrarian Transformation (ISTA) if he would back the new Christian Democrat/military government. ISTA would be in charge of the new land reform program. Afraid of losing influence over Viera, AIFLD representatives tried to persuade him not to take the ISTA position and instead offered him an AIFLD job at $1,000 a month (a lot of money in El Salvador at the time).[27] After consulting with Archbishop Óscar Romero, Viera took the ISTA job.[28] On March 6, 1980, the government enacted the land reform law.[29]

The original 1979 coup government had designed Phase I and Phase II of the new agrarian reform law. Under Phase I, farms over 1,235 acres would be expropriated with compensation and turned over to the peasants who worked them. Under Phase II, farms between 247 and 1,235 acres would be appropriated. The coffee-growing elites owned many of these. The hostility from the landowning elites to Phase I was so intense that the government indefinitely postponed Phase II.[30] AIFLD was responsible for designing Phase III, which would redistribute the smaller parcels of land. The Institute contracted with Dr. Roy Prosterman to administer the Phase III program. He had created a land reform program intended to thwart a guerrilla insurrection in South Vietnam. Phase III was called the land-to-the-tiller law, and it began on April 28, 1980, after Phase II had stalled.[31] The law was forced onto El

Salvador with nearly universal Salvadoran government, civilian, and military opposition. Soon the Phase III land reform program bogged down due to this opposition. AIFLD's El Salvador office hired one of Prosterman's former students and an expert on agricultural law, Mark David Pearlman, to be a full-time staffer advising the reform's ongoing implementation.[32]

Rodolfo Viera was now officially responsible for the land reform program.[33] Many problems beset it. If Phase I had been fully implemented, it would have affected 7.2 percent of farm families, but it never got that far. The only actual beneficiaries of the program by late 1980 were UCS peasant union members, and now they were also becoming victims of rural terror. Opponents of land reform killed dozens of UCS members and organizers. An assistant to Viera, Leonel Gomez, testified to a U.S. congressional subcommittee that between January and March 1980, 240 leaders of UCS peasant cooperatives were murdered. He blamed the Duarte–military government security forces for 80 percent of them, while guerrillas and others unknown had killed two.[34]

According to his aide Gomez, after taking over the ISTA, Viera had discovered large-scale corruption in the land reform program. He found that the government had overvalued the original land purchases for Phase I by $40 million and paid twice for some of the farms. Viera had taken the evidence of the corruption to Duarte and the government, but they did nothing. He began making the charge of fraud publicly on television.[35]

AIFLD had reassigned Michael Hammer to the Washington, DC, AIFLD headquarters, directing technical assistance programs related to peasants and peasant organizations. He was living in Potomac, Maryland, when contacted by Viera requesting a meeting. Viera indicated that he was in "hot water."[36] Hammer flew to San Salvador on an emergency mission after learning the land reform effort was in jeopardy and Viera might resign.[37] He went to confer with Viera and had just arrived on the morning of January 3.[38] Viera met with Hammer and Pearlman for dinner at the Sheraton Hotel later that night, shortly after going public with the land reform corruption charge. Perhaps this was the subject of their conversation on

January 3, 1981. No one will ever know, as none of them survived the evening.

That same Saturday evening, a wedding party was taking place in the Sheraton Hotel's coffee shop. The party included right-wing oligarchs, military officers, and Hans Christ, a wealthy landowner and right-wing businessman. Christ was the son of a German immigrant who came to El Salvador shortly after World War II. Christ spotted Viera and told the group that he wished Viera was dead. A short time later, Christ met with Lieutenant Rodolfo Isidro López Sibrián and Captain Eduardo Ernesto Alfonso Ávila Ávila in the hotel parking lot. The officers allegedly ordered two low-ranking guardsmen to kill Viera and the two others at the table. The soldiers followed Christ into the restaurant and killed all three men—Viera, Hammer, and Pearlman.[39]

Michael Hammer had likely been a CIA officer, although there is no direct evidence of this.[40] Born in Paris in 1938 to German parents who fled Nazi Germany in 1933, he spent his youth in Ecuador. When the family moved to the U.S. in 1950, he became a U.S. citizen. After serving four years in the U.S. Air Force, he studied in Switzerland then enrolled at Georgetown University's School of Foreign Service. He spoke five languages.[41]

The Georgetown School of Foreign Service, located in Washington, DC, has a history with the CIA. A 2018 article, appearing on the *CNBC* website, announced, "The CIA is hunting for its next generation of talent." That year the CIA was looking to fill more than 100 jobs. According to the article, the Agency recruits in veterans' groups, military bases, and schools that run the gamut from local colleges to Ivy League universities. It goes on to explain that foremost among these is the Georgetown University School of Foreign Service.[42] These recruitment efforts didn't just begin in 2018. A 1969 CIA document announces "AGENCY-SPONSORED TRAINING AT LOCAL SCHOOLS. 1969 Fall Semester." The memo explains the procedure for acquiring tuition advances for Agency sponsorship at ten DC-area schools. Georgetown University is in this group.[43] In 1985, the Agency began the Officer-in-Residence (OIR) program, which would:

Assist Agency staff recruiting efforts by placing in selected schools experienced officers who can spot promising career candidates, can counsel students as to career opportunities, and can use their knowledge and experience to address questions or concerns students may have regarding the Agency. Encourage the study and knowledge of the intelligence profession through participating in seminars, courses and research. Afford senior officers a year or two to recharge their intellectual batteries in an academic setting by teaching in an area of academic or work-related expertise.[44]

The CIA pioneered an OIR program at Georgetown University. The first OIR, Harold Bean, who also taught an undergraduate class at Georgetown, hung framed CIA memorabilia bearing the Agency's name on the walls of his office, clearly indicating affiliation.[45]

While still a student at Georgetown in 1964, Hammer began working part time in AIFLD's Washington, DC, office as a messenger. Jesse Friedman, an AIFLD deputy director in the 1980s, claimed that Serafino Romualdi, AIFLD executive director in 1964 and Friedman's stepfather, told Hammer to resign as aide and come back at a professional level. Hammer took a "couple more courses" and returned as a program officer in 1965. After being sent to Israel to train in agricultural cooperatives, he founded the agrarian component of AIFLD. It was in this capacity that he was assigned to El Salvador in 1966.[46]

Two weeks after the Sheraton murders, an article by Reed Irvine, a conspiracy-oriented conservative, appeared in *Accuracy in Media* attempting to blame the Hammer–Pearlman–Viera killings on Philip Agee and two pieces written about El Salvador that appeared in a publication associated with him, *Counterspy*. The Irvine article said that the Marxist left carried out the murders and that they resulted from the articles in *Counterspy* linking the CIA and AIFLD and criticizing both Hammer and Viera.[47] As the facts of the killings came out, they discredited the Irvine version of events, but the article appeared again in *Human Events* a month later.[48]

At the same time the Irvine article appeared, the U.S. solicitor general, Wade McCree, was making a presentation before the

Supreme Court arguing that the government had the power to revoke Philip Agee's passport. In response to a question, McCree blurted out, "Just recently two Americans have been killed in Salvador. Apparently, they were some kind of undercover persons, working under the cover of a labor organization." McCree later said his remarks were intended to be "hypothetical." The CIA declined to comment, and AIFLD said they did not know about any relationship between the murdered AIFLD men and the CIA.[49]

Hammer was given a hero's burial in Arlington National Cemetery on the specific authorization of President Carter. Classified DoS documents show that an unusual effort was made to make sure high-level Carter administration officials attended the funeral. Vice-President Walter Mondale and Secretary of State Edmund Muskie made remarks at the funeral service.[50] The president-elect, Ronald Reagan, sent his newly appointed national security advisor Richard Allen to the funeral as well.[51] The U.S. government did not make the same effort for Pearlman, or the four American church-women killed in El Salvador just two weeks before the Sheraton murders.[52] Jeane Kirkpatrick, designated by Reagan to be ambassador to the United Nations, said she knew Hammer as "a very brave man.... I shared a lot of views and values and some common activities with him and with others at the AIFLD and the AFL-CIO."[53]

AIFLD in El Salvador did not confine itself solely to working with agricultural workers. In the summer of 1980, a new labor coalition was formed with their financial assistance called Popular Democratic Unity (UPD). The UPD's base was in a Christian Democratic regional labor organization, and with AIFLD funding, it grew quickly, as the leftist unions had been driven underground by repression and violence. By 1982, the UPD was the largest labor federation in El Salvador. It was composed of five labor organizations; the mostly rural UCS, FESINCONSTRANS, composed primarily of construction trade workers, the Salvadoran Workers Central (CTS), made up of public employees, and two smaller peasant worker bodies that had split off from the UCS in the 1970s. AIFLD paid 80 percent of the operating budget of these groups except for the CTS, which was financed independently of AIFLD.[54]

In the 1982 Constituent Assembly elections, the UPD made an all-out effort to get out the vote for Christian Democratic candidates. They never openly endorsed the party, as workers and peasants had realized few gains during the previous administration. They did see the elections as progress for democracy under the Duarte–military junta. However, as the 1984 presidential election drew near, the UPD was no longer prepared to lend full support to the PDC and conditioned this support on specific promises and government influence. For this, they would learn the political price required for AIFLD financial support.[55]

In 1979, faced with relentless criticism of AIFLD both internationally and domestically, a decision was made to scrap the business component of the Institute, which Walter Reuther had first objected to in the 1960s. The new AFL-CIO president, Lane Kirkland, and Bill Doherty met with the AIFLD chairman of the board to inform him his services were no longer needed. They traveled to New York to have lunch with Peter Grace in the W.R. Grace Company's corporate dining room. After several drinks, the conversation turned to the equine sport of polo. Grace had been the captain of the 1933 U.S. Olympic polo team, and Kirkland was a big fan of the game, having cleaned out horse stalls for polo teams as a boy. For two hours, they didn't discuss labor or Latin America but spent the entire time discussing the minutiae of polo. Finally, late in the afternoon, Grace turned to Kirkland and said, "Lane, I understand you came up here to fire me. Don't you think that's it's time that we get that over with?" And Lane says, "Peter you're perfectly right and you are fired."[56]

By this time, the AFL-CIO Cold War consensus on foreign policy was unraveling. Some manufacturing unions had concluded that involvement overseas in the anti-communist crusade led to the rise of right-wing authoritarian regimes that suppressed unions and workers' wages, making those countries desirable places for American companies to relocate. Public employee unions found themselves in competition for tax dollars with defense appropriations and military aid budgets. The AFL-CIO union membership had also been affected by the social movements of the 1960s and many had opposed the war in Vietnam.[57] Some of the affiliate unions had supported the candidacy of George McGovern, whom Meany and the AFL-CIO had refused to endorse for president in 1972. These trends would merge around opposition to U.S. policy in El Salvador.

In September 1981, Jack Sheinkman, the Amalgamated Clothing and Textile Workers Union (ACTWU) secretary-treasurer, organized the National Labor Committee in Support of Democracy and Human Rights in El Salvador (NLC). He enlisted union presidents Doug Fraser of the UAW and William Winpisinger of the International Association of Machinists as co-chairs. Within a few years, they had recruited the heads of 23 national unions as NLC members and supported the creation of 27 local committees. Sheinkman, Fraser, and Winpisinger limited the NLC membership to international presidents to avoid the red-baiting they expected from President Kirkland's faction. The interventionist faction did not hesitate to red-bait the local committees but held off until 1987 before red-baiting the NLC.[58]

Over the coming decade, the NLC was active in preventing U.S. military intervention in El Salvador. It opposed military aid to El Salvador and promoted a U.S. policy of negotiations between the FMLN/FDR rebels and the Salvadoran government to end the conflict. The NLC defended imprisoned and kidnapped trade union leaders in Central America, sent U.S. trade union leaders for visits to Central America, and sponsored a speaking tour of El Salvadoran union leaders in the U.S. The NLC lobbied the U.S. Congress toward its goals and coordinated with other non-labor groups in the Central American peace movement. It eventually worked on stopping military aid to the Contras in Nicaragua.[59] To achieve its objectives, the NLC began organizing for the national 1983 AFL-CIO convention in Florida.

Following the murders of Pearlman, Hammer, and Viera and the resulting union and national attention they brought, AIFLD began an effort to pressure the government of El Salvador to apprehend and prosecute those responsible. It hired investigators, brought witnesses to the United States to give testimony, and turned the evidence they collected over to the U.S. Embassy. The U.S. pressure resulted in El Salvador getting confessions from the two corporals who committed the murders. They identified two officers as having given them the orders and the guns on January 3, 1981. Those officers, Lieutenant Rodolfo López Sibrián and Captain Eduardo Ávila Ávila, had their first court hearing in October 1982. Sibrián had changed his appearance, making it hard for witnesses to identify him, while Ávila's uncle was on the Supreme Court and was in attendance at the hearing. Perhaps unsurprisingly, the court dismissed the charges against them.[60] Between 1982 and 1985, a succession of Salvadoran courts threw out all charges against López Sibrián and Ávila based on "insufficient evidence." El Salvador's Supreme Court upheld these decisions.[61]

By 1983, Clarence D. Long, Democrat congressman of Maryland, added foreign-aid appropriations legislation that would condition 30 percent of the $64.8 million requested for El Salvador for that year be suspended unless the killers of the four American churchwomen, Pearlman, and Hammer, were brought to trial. The Reagan administration opposed the condition regarding the AIFLD workers because they knew the highest levels of the Salvadoran military were linked to the AIFLD murders. A congressional aide sent two memos and made five calls to Doherty asking for AIFLD support for Long's condition. Doherty did not return those calls. The proviso relating to Hammer and Pearlman was removed from the bill that was passed by Congress. AIFLD said their inaction was due to a "lack of human resources." AIFLD had two lobbyists working with Congress at the time. The Catholic church was active in supporting the churchwomen conditions being added to the legislation, and Congress approved those.[62]

While El Salvador refused to prosecute the alleged murderers of Pearlman, Hammer, and Viera, the AFL-CIO continued to support the military aid that the Reagan administration was giving to the country. That aid amounted to $354 million between 1980 and 1982.[63] Their position on this changed in 1983, not long after the case against the officers broke down. Bill Doherty announced the reversal, outlining that support was suspended "until there is justice in this case, as well, of course, as in the cases of other U.S. citizens."[64] The AFL-CIO policy change was the opening the NLC had needed to advance its case for an end to military aid to El Salvador.

At the 1983 AFL-CIO convention, the NLC delegates pushed through this broad compromise resolution:

> The AFL-CIO reiterates its insistence that aid to the government of El Salvador is made contingent upon its progress in implementing the land reform program, protecting trade union rights, establishing a just judicial system, and bringing the right-wing "death squads" under control. Until we are satisfied that progress is being made in these areas, the AFL-CIO will not support military aid to the government of El Salvador.[65]

The AIFLD-financed labor federation, the UPD, was unwilling to give Duarte and the Christian Democrats their unconditional support in the 1984 presidential election. The leadership met at the AIFLD center in Honduras in July 1983 to agree on a list of demands to present to Duarte. These included human rights improvements, wage increases, and direct labor participation in the government, including high-level appointments. They also called for direct negotiations with the FMLN/FDR to end the war. The Christian Democrats agreed with most of the demands. They promised to incorporate labor participation in the agrarian reform and other labor relations matters in exchange for UPD support in the election.[66]

Duarte and the Christian Democrats won the 1984 election with significant UPD support that included door-to-door canvassing by almost 1,000 activists and financial contributions of at least $500,000–$800,000.[67] A DoS source said at least $50,000 in cash was carried into the country by AIFLD reps to assist Duarte in the 1984 election.[68] The Reagan administration considered the 1984 election a great victory. Still, the NLC believed Duarte was merely a front to justify U.S. military aid. The real power was held by the far right that controlled the legislature, the judiciary, and, most importantly, the military.[69] Following Duarte's election victory, the U.S.

began putting pressure on him to move to the right to appease the real power in the country, the business sector. The U.S. saw the UPD as an obstacle to this.

In a few months, the UPD union federation came to believe that Duarte's government had not lived up to the pre-election agreement and threatened to break their alliance. The leftist unions had begun to recover from years of terror, and challenged the Popular Democratic Unity's dominance as a labor federation.[70] Ignoring ominous warnings from AIFLD Country Director Bernard Packer and the U.S. Embassy, in August 1984, the UPD held a press conference criticizing Duarte for the state of the economy and for failing to open negotiations with the FMLN/FDR. They also made some objections to U.S. military aid. Packer told UPD leaders their actions were an insult to AIFLD, which had been paying 80 percent of the expenses of four of the five UPD federation's unions.[71] The Institute proceeded to attempt to force the UPD unions to join another labor federation, the Confederation of Democratic Workers (CTD), which they believed they could more easily control. Many of the UPD leaders resisted, and some of the union affiliates were in open rebellion. Those would lose AIFLD funding. Bill Doherty traveled to El Salvador in January 1985 after getting a letter from some of the UPD unions refusing contact with Packer. A battle between opponents of the new Federation and AIFLD loyalists erupted in some unions, with AIFLD intervening in the inter-union conflicts or entirely cutting off funding for some organizations.[72] In April 1985, Ramón Mendoza, the general secretary of the UPD, said, "AIFLD is organizing dummy conventions, buying off labor leaders and using anti-democratic and destabilizing methods and blackmail against [El Salvador's] democratic trade unions."[73] When the March 1985 election took place, one of the Christian Democrat's central pillars of support, the UPD, was divided and disarrayed.

Never having diverged far from U.S. foreign policy for long, the AIFLD/AFL-CIO reversed its position on military aid in early 1984 and supported the latest Reagan administration request for $70 million. It claimed El Salvador had made progress with the Duarte election.[74] Doherty, relentless in his determination to adhere to the

Reagan administration position, supported continued military aid based on the army's discharge of Sibrián and modest PDC gains made in the 1985 legislative elections.[75] The NLC objected to Kirkland's reversal of the position adopted at the 1983 convention, and a new debate about how the AFL-CIO should make foreign policy began. When the Salvadoran Supreme Court dropped all charges against Sibrián and Ávila in November 1984, it strengthened the NLC's position. These events set the table for a major confrontation over foreign policy at the October 1985 AFL-CIO convention.[76]

The NLC organized a fact-finding mission to El Salvador in February 1985. The delegation included ACTWU secretary-treasurer Jack Sheinkman; American Federation of Government Employees (AFGE) President Ken Blaylock; American Federation of State County and Municipal Employees (AFSCME) International Vice-President Victor Gotbaum; Keith Johnson, President of the Woodworkers Union; and five other officers. Joining these national labor leaders on the trip was Frank Hammer, the slain AIFLD agent Michael Hammer's brother. Frank had just won election as the bargaining committee chairman at a 4,000 member UAW GM local (UAW 909) in Michigan. He was also an activist on the left. Frank had written an opinion piece published in the *New York Times* in December 1984 criticizing support in the U.S. for Duarte's decision to dismiss López Sibrián from the army, and calling for a reduction in military aid until justice was served. In the *Times* opinion piece, he wrote:

> The DoS can't call for justice on one hand and then indirectly support the death squads with the other. Congress should do what they did in the case of the four churchwomen murdered in El Salvador in December 1980: put conditions on the aid that we send to El Salvador. In the nuns' case, 30 per cent of one year's appropriations was held up until a verdict was reached.[77]

When the American unionists arrived in El Salvador, AIFLD staff refused to meet with the delegation because of Hammer's presence, this on orders from Washington. In a contemporaneous note,

Hammer wrote, "I was told that the guy who's the current AIFLD director [Bill Doherty] turned seven shades of purple when he heard I was on the trip."[78]

Upon returning to the U.S., the NLC delegation issued a comprehensive 27-page report of their findings, "The Search for Peace in Central America." A flurry of activity followed. Some local unions passed resolutions opposing U.S. military assistance to El Salvador and supported an April 20 national demonstration for "Jobs, Peace and Justice." Articles on El Salvador appeared in national and local union newspapers, and speaking engagements were held. On May 17, Frank Hammer testified before the House Appropriations Subcommittee on Foreign Relations about the Sheraton murders, highlighting three years of inaction and demanding that Congress withhold military aid to get justice.[79]

In the period leading up to the October 1985 AFL-CIO convention, the NLC was at peak strength with 23 unions, containing a majority of the AFL-CIO total membership.[80] The AFL-CIO leadership and the government-funded institutes became increasingly active domestically. AIFLD hired David Jessup to commence a counterattack on the critics of the Federation's foreign policy. Jessup had previously founded the Institute for Religion and Democracy to provide an alternative voice to those of Protestant denominations who he believed were providing moral and financial support for leftist movements in Central America and other parts of the world. He became a controversial figure in the Central America debate after alleging that the Methodist Church was engaged in collaborative projects with communist governments and movements.[81] Jessup's labor strategy included a focus on countering the NLC's activities by organizing a base of support among international presidents and lower-ranking officials for the AFL-CIO's policies. He utilized the directors of the institutes; AIFLD (Latin America), AAFLI (Asia), AALC (Africa), and the Free Trade Union Committee (FTUC) (Europe), the director of international affairs, Irving Brown, and AFL-CIO President Lane Kirkland. A memo sent in May 1985 by Jessup details the AFL-CIO leadership's plans to hold conferences in New York and Michigan in late September 1985 (a few weeks

before the October convention) to mobilize support for their pro-
interventionist foreign-policy agenda. The stated purpose of the
meeting was:

1. To <u>inform</u> State labor leaders about AFL-CIO policy and procedures for state and local central bodies to follow regarding
international affairs, and to hear their concerns and expectations
regarding the International Affairs Department.
2. To <u>mobilize</u> state labor leaders for follow-up actions on certain
issues, such as (examples only):
  a. Campaign for free South African trade unionists....
  b. Sponsor local international affairs educational events....
  c. Raise funds to send equipment to Central American
     unionists.[82]

The participants in this conference were to be by invitation
only and included state federation officers, state federation executive boards, central body officers, AFL-CIO Staff, Committee on
Political Education (COPE) staff, international union representatives, international affairs directors of international unions, support
groups, and others. This grouping encompassed almost everyone
who had any leadership connection whatsoever with the AFL-CIO.
There are several topics, but the first listed is "Overview, plus explanation of International Affairs organizations such as ICFTU, ILO,
OECD, OECD, ORIT, AIFLD, AALC, AAFLI, etc."[83]

The conference featured Bill Doherty as a speaker on Central
America. Doherty had been the executive director of AIFLD for
over 20 years at the time of the conferences. He had long-time links
to the CIA, and there is no reason to believe that he wasn't a "CIA
agent with full benefits, tenure, and pension," as Philip Agee said to
Fred Hirsch about Doherty in 1975.[84]

Morris Paladino was on the agenda to speak for an hour on the
Philippines. Paladino was executive director of the AAFLI. Before
that, Paladino had studied at the City College of New York. He
was appointed a staff person for the ILGWU in 1941, working
under its president, David Dubinsky. He served in various capacities

there until 1959. While employed by the ILGWU, he was awarded a one-year fellowship at Harvard. In 1960, he was made the assistant secretary general of the ORIT. In 1964, Paladino became the deputy executive director of AIFLD. George Meany appointed him executive director of AAFLI in 1970.[85] Agee listed Paladino as the principal CIA agent for control of ORIT in *Inside The Company*.[86]

At the end of the second day, the conference attendees were to be addressed by Lane Kirkland, AFL-CIO president. Kirkland was born in Camden, South Carolina, and raised in the heart of the Jim Crow South. Kershaw County, where Camden is located, produced six Confederate generals during the Civil War. Kirkland's great-grandfather, William Lennox Kirkland, joined the Charleston Light Dragoons and was killed in the war in 1864. He was a prosperous member of the South Carolina planter aristocracy, who, according to the 1860 census, owned 156 slaves. When General Sherman and his Union army moved through the area, the freedom fighter Harriet Tubman arrived with a convoy of five steamships and took the liberated former slaves away from the Kirkland plantation after which some of them joined the union army. His great-grandmother's father, T.J. Withers, was a senator in the Provisional Confederate Government and a signer of the articles of secession.[87] Lane Kirkland referred to the Civil War as the "War of Northern Aggression" throughout his life.[88] Kirkland's father attempted to establish himself as a cotton broker in the 1920s, but when the Depression came his business collapsed and he became a cotton buyer, a middle-class profession. As a boy, Lane was sent for a time to live with an uncle, Marion Adickes, a manager of a local textile mill and a firm enemy of trade unions, who boasted of keeping his mills union free.[89] In 1940, the 18-year-old joined a special New Deal program to train merchant ship officers and became a deck cadet. Upon graduation in 1942, he became a member of the Masters, Mates and Pilots union and served as a deck officer onboard merchant ships throughout World War II.[90]

When the war ended, Kirkland found employment in the Naval Hydrological Office and went to school at night. He went to Georgetown University where he enrolled in a special program for students who aspired to careers in the foreign service. Kirkland's biographer, Arch Puddington, said it wasn't clear why he chose this program.[91] Fellow alumni would include Bill Doherty and Michael Hammer. After earning a bachelor's degree in 1948, he went directly to work for the AFL Research Department, specializing in international relations. At that time, the Central Intelligence Group was beginning to funnel large amounts of money to the AFL-created FTUC in Europe.[92]

In 1960, Kirkland became President Meany's chief assistant, and, in 1969, Meany anointed Kirkland to become his future successor when he supported him for the office of AFL-CIO secretary-treasurer.[93] Kirkland replaced the 85-year-old Meany as the Federation president in 1979. His succession was managed behind closed doors by Meany, who chaired the 1979 convention, making the nomination himself. The new president, like his predecessor, was an ardent anti-communist throughout his career. He strongly supported U.S. involvement in the Vietnam War and was instrumental in the AFL-CIO's refusal to support the anti-war Democratic nominee Senator George McGovern for president in 1972.[94] In 1976, Kirkland became a founding member of the Committee on the Present Danger, which called for larger military budgets to confront the Soviet Union.[95] He worked tirelessly to support the Solidarity Union in its effort to topple the Polish communist government and "surreptitiously" channeled money to it through the FTUC. Henry A. Kissinger, a close friend of Kirkland, said, "The success of Solidarity owes a lot to Lane. He supported it with funds and organizers, and he had a big effect on American policymakers."[96]

Irving Brown, who had previously been the director of the African American Labor Center (AALC), was slated to begin the 1985 two-day foreign-policy conference with an overview. Irving Brown had been linked to the CIA for four decades, and more evidence exists for Brown being a CIA operative than for any other individual in organized labor.[97] Brown had been a disciple of Jay Lovestone while Lovestone was the head of the American Communist Party (Opposition).[98] He ran the FTUC operations in Europe during the 1950s. In early 1982, when AFL-CIO foreign policy came under scrutiny by the NLC unions, AFL-CIO President Kirkland appointed Brown to be AFL-CIO international affairs director, replacing Ernie Lee, Meany's son-in-law.[99] On the AFL-CIO International Affairs Department staff, Mark Anderson soon came into conflict with the new director over which unions the Federation should support in Africa. In South Africa, then still an Apartheid state, Brown supported a Zulu chief who cooperated with the South African government, while Anderson advocated for unions who supported the anti-Apartheid African National Congress of Nelson Mandela. The conflict became so intense that Anderson left the International Affairs Department believing Brown wanted to fire him.[100]

The planning memo also raised the issue of "who pays" for the conference. David Jessup signed the document and sent it to seven individuals, including Brown, Doherty, and Paladino. Eugenia Kimble, director of the Free Trade Union Institute (FTUI), was also sent a copy. The FTUI was set up in the months following the Reagan administration's creation of the NED in 1983. The FTUI would receive money from the NED and pass it on in the form of grants to the AIFLD, the AAFLI, the AALC, and the FTUC. The only reason Kimble would have received this memo was that the organizers were looking for Endowment funding to pay for this conference.[101] Individuals with long-time links to the CIA, likely using government money which originated in a United States Congressional budget, organized these conferences to reach a political goal in a domestic labor organization. Jessup notified the memo recipients of a meeting on conference planning to be held May 10, 1985, at the AAFLI office in Washington, DC.[102]

The initial conference concept grew into an eight-city tour with AIFLD staffers addressing invited union officials in New York, Detroit, Philadelphia, Boston, Providence, Milwaukee, Chicago, and Dallas. Accompanying the AFL-CIO officials were three Central American unionists affiliated with AIFLD-aligned unions. The first meeting held in New York September 13–14 was defensive in tone. Speakers complained about "those within our movement whose intentions are good but who are grossly uninformed."[103] At the Detroit meeting, Frank Hammer challenged AFL-CIO policy. This meeting was also enlivened by a disagreement between Brown and Doherty over whether the Federation had taken a position on military aid for the U.S.-supported right-wing rebel Contras in Nicaragua. Doherty said that the AFL-CIO had taken no position but that the executive council might do so in a few weeks. Brown argued that the AFL-CIO *did* have a position which was to oppose U.S aid to the Contras but encourage the Nicaraguan government to enter a dialogue with them.[104] Heading into the 1985 convention, the AFL-CIO foreign-policy leadership appeared to be off balance.

On May 12, an article appeared in the *Boston Globe* entitled "AFL-CIO split on Latin America," written by Lynda Gorov. The article describes George Meany's successful efforts to keep U.S. unions solidly behind the Vietnam War. It explains that Kirkland was attempting to do the same thing with the Reagan administration policies on Central America. Still, union workers and union leaders were refusing to go along this time. Gorov interviewed several area labor leaders involved in a regional union affiliate of the NLC. These labor leaders linked AFL-CIO foreign policy to declining union membership, cuts to social programs, and repression of workers in Latin America. Edward W. Clark, an international vice-president of the ACTWU in New England, is quoted as saying "The days are over when a small group of right-wing staffers in Washington develops foreign policy for the AFL-CIO and get a rubber stamp from the executive council." Bill Doherty downplayed the dispute and told the *Globe* that it continues only because the dissidents were "ill-informed."[105]

When the 1985 AFL-CIO convention began in Anaheim, California, on October 3, the National Labor Committee unions had a combined membership of just under 7.2 million, a majority of U.S. unionized workers. Many of the NLC unions were pushing for a clear denunciation of the Reagan administration's support for the Nicaraguan Contras. The Federation's top foreign-policy staffers hoped to avoid mentioning the undeclared war against Nicaragua and instead focus criticism on the Sandinista government. The factions reached a backroom agreement that would call for a negotiated settlement rather than a military solution in Nicaragua but would also denounce the Sandinistas. The foreign-policy conservatives had managed to stop an explicit anti-Contra resolution but had to concede on general anti-war language for the first time. Both sides assumed that the fight was over, and this compromise resolution would pass without an acrimonious floor fight. They turned out to be wrong.[106]

As soon as the resolution was read to the 1,000 assembled delegates, a rush to the microphones began. The first delegate Kirkland called on was Kenneth Blaylock, president of the AFGE. He had been on the NLC trip with Frank Hammer that visited El Salvador earlier in the year and AIFLD had refused a meeting with them. Blaylock's union had suffered one of the first waves of job losses resulting from Reagan's privatizations and cuts to government programs. After relating his experiences visiting the war-torn areas in Nicaragua and of hearing mothers' tales of atrocities committed against their children by the Contras, he said:

> ...Now I don't know about the rest of you people here, but when I look at Iran, I look at Vietnam, I look at Nicaragua, I look at El Salvador, Guatemala, I would like for one time for my government to be on the side of the people, not on the side of rich dictators living behind high walls.[107]

When Blaylock finished, some tentative clapping began, which turned to sustained applause and then erupted into cheering and whistling. For the next 90 minutes, speakers took turns denouncing the Reagan administration or condemning the Sandinistas. What had happened was extraordinary, the first floor debate on foreign policy in AFL-CIO history. While the debate surprised almost everyone, it also revealed the depth of angst felt by many about the future of organized labor.

While the compromise resolution passed easily, the split in labor became obvious. The Federation's foreign-policy leadership successfully defeated the efforts to pass a resolution in favor of halting military aid to the Contras. Still, the NLC delegates forced them

into a compromise resolution tying military assistance to human
rights improvements and calling for negotiations between the
Salvadoran government and the FDR/FMLN rebels.[108] These resolutions allowed the NLC unions to lobby Congress for reductions in
military assistance when disagreements arose over human rights, and,
in 1987, the NLC was successful in passing a resolution opposing
Contra aid.[109] The resolution, which represented a major shift in
national AFL-CIO policy away from U.S. intervention, also called
for the withdrawal of Soviet and Cuban military assistance to the
Sandinista government of Nicaragua. The resolution read in part:

> We urge the Reagan Administration to pursue in good faith a dip-
> lomatic rather than a military solution to the conflict within the
> framework of the Guatemala Plan, that will provide for guaran-
> tees of democratic freedoms along with a halt to outside aid to all
> armed opposition groups.[110]

The battle over AFL-CIO foreign policy took place on the local
level too. In the run-up to the 1985 convention, a memo was written
by Samuel Haddad, an AIFLD deputy director, to Bill Doherty
on AIFLD letterhead with the subject of "Labor Groups Working
Against AFL-CIO Labor Policy." In the memo, Haddad states:

> The really big problem that we face is the creation of all kinds of
> fronts in support of the Sandinistas and the Guerrilla movement
> in El Salvador and the support of these groups with CPUSTAL
> [Permanent Congress of Trade Union Unity of Latin America],
> WFTU [World Federation of Trade Unions] affiliates in general
> in the hemisphere as opposed to the AFL-CIO working with
> ICFTU affiliates.[111]

The memo goes on to list twelve organizations engaging in
these actions, including the NLC. One of these is the Minnesota
Labor Conference on Central America. The Minnesota group organized rallies and opposition to U.S Central American policy within
unions. Another such rank and file union group was the Minnesota

Trade Unionists for Peace, a group formed by concerned individuals from various locals throughout the Minneapolis/St. Paul metropolitan area. They began a campaign called "Not One Penny for the Contras." Its spokesman was Wayne Wittman, a Korean veteran, grandfather, church deacon, and AFSCME member.[112] Sue Mauren, a Teamster and the vice-president of the Twin Cities Coalition of Labor Union Women (CLUW) reported in a story covered by the labor press that, after two months of living and studying in Nicaragua, she thought it was a mistake for the United States to continue giving aid to Contra rebels who were attempting to overthrow the Sandinista government. Mauren stated that conditions have improved since the Sandinistas overthrew the Somoza government.[113]

An opposing view was taken by Dan Gustafson, the president of the Minnesota AFL-CIO, who was working in support of AIFLD and AFL-CIO foreign policy. Part of David Jessup's strategy for winning support for Federation foreign policy was to arrange exchange visits between U.S. union officials and their AIFLD-aligned counterparts in Central America.[114] Gustafson took such an AIFLD-sponsored trip to Central America in 1985. During the 14 days of the journey, the majority of the time was spent in Nicaragua. The *Union Advocate* newspaper reported, "That image of a deteriorating country was a pervasive one for Gustafson. It stuck with him throughout his tour of that country. 'The (Nicaraguan) state is literally collapsing,' Gustafson said."[115] The labor group spent only two days in El Salvador and believed that they were in danger there. They were greeted at the airport in San Salvador by two Chevrolet armored vans. Each carried an armed driver and guard. The union leaders were free to go anywhere they wished in the city, but they could do so only in a group accompanied by guards. The American trade union delegation appears to have seen little of El Salvador. Gustafson would later speak in favor of continuing aid to the Contras during the debate at the 1985 national convention.[116]

The battle over these differing positions was fought out at the 1987 Minnesota State AFL-CIO convention. Betty Thomas, a delegate from the Oil Chemical and Atomic Workers, presented a resolution on the third day of the convention as part of the report of the Human Rights and Services Committee:

> WHEREAS: During the past six years, the Reagan Administration has attempted to impose a policy of military and economic intervention on Central America despite historic evidence that such policies have not brought peace to the area;
>
> and WHEREAS : The hypocrisy of the Reagan Administration is demonstrated by its opposition to boycotts and intervention in South Africa while at the same time it urges support for the Contras in Nicaragua and imposes a boycott on trade;
>
> now; therefore, be it RESOLVED: That the 30th Constitutional Convention of the Minnesota AFL-CIO recommend that the national AFL-CIO support the Guatemala City peace plan in Central America and call on the U.S. administration to demonstrate its support for the achievement of peace and non-intervention in the region;
>
> and, be it further RESOLVED: That the Minnesota AFL-CIO recommend that the national AFL-CIO urge congress to reject the administration's request for aid to the Contras in Nicaragua and instead press the administration to seek peaceful resolution of the conflict in that country;
>
> and, be it finally RESOLVED: That the Minnesota AFL-CIO recommend that the national AFL-CIO pledge support to the democratic unions in El Salvador in their opposition to President Duarte's violations of trade union and human rights.[117]

Gustafson, who was chairing the session, ruled the anti-Contra motion out of order, saying, "The resolution as it is before us does not meet the policy standards of the national AFL-CIO." Gustafson tabled the resolution then went on to tell the delegates that the AFL-CIO did not support an end to U.S. aid to the Contras unless the Soviet Union and Cuba ended their aid to the Sandinista government in Nicaragua. An AFSCME delegate, Eliot Seide, rose to challenge Gustafson's ruling, and then his challenge and the resolution were both passed by a voice vote. It may have been the first such measure ever passed by any state AFL-CIO.[118]

Who recruited Gustafson and others to take the AIFLD trip to Nicaragua? The NED likely funded these trips and the money probably originated in a congressional budget. Did someone ask Gustafson to speak at the 1985 convention in opposition to the NLC effort to end aid to the Contras? Was Gustafson encouraged to rule the resolution at the 1987 Minnesota convention out of order? Were Irving Brown or Bill Doherty involved with this? Was the CIA working outside of its mandate inside the U.S., organizing support for administration foreign policy? These questions might be answered if the Minnesota AFL-CIO executive board minutes or AFL-CIO convention transcripts were open to researchers. They remain closed along with the bulk of the Federation Cold War records. AFL-CIO President Richard Trumka did not respond to my request to view these records.[119]

PART II

El Golpe

5

Mexico in the 1980s

Recalcitrant workers are expelled from their locals and, because of strict union shop requirements, lose their jobs. Dissident victories in shop elections are voided. Union thugs exert physical "persuasion" when necessary.

Central Intelligence Agency description of the Confederation of Mexican Workers' (CTM) tactics, December 1983

Mexico has had a long and sometimes troubled relationship with the United States. It lost to the U.S. perhaps the two wealthiest provinces in the western hemisphere in terms of natural resources and agriculture, California and Texas, in the Mexican–American War (1846–8). A number of U.S. employers have since been located in Mexico, forming social relationships that have at times also been difficult.

Some historians trace the beginning of the Mexican Revolution (1910–20) to a strike and accompanying violence that took place at a U.S.-owned copper mine in Cananea, Sonora, in 1906.[1] The Greene Consolidated Copper Company employed over 5,000 Mexican workers and paid them around 70 percent of what the company's 2,000 American employees received for doing the same jobs. The unequal pay, as well as other poor conditions, led to a strike that had the support of the local population. During a demonstration in support of the workers, Cananea mine managers shot and killed three people. The angry mob responded by killing the two American managers responsible. In response, a posse of 275 from Arizona, led by an Arizona ranger, responding to a call for help from the company, entered Mexico illegally and came to Cananea. Other workers were killed in the ensuing violence before the government sent in Mexican state and federal troops, who expelled the interventionists and restored order. According to the company representative

Colonel William Greene, "trouble was incited by a Socialistic organization that has been formed by malcontents opposed to the
Díaz [President of Mexico] government."[2] That would not be the
only time that a U.S. employer blamed socialist agitators for labor
problems in Mexico.

American intelligence services have conducted extensive operations in Mexico over the years. Philip Agee, the former CIA agent,
was assigned to Mexico in the late 1960s. He worked for the CIA in
Mexico City under the cover of the U.S. Olympic Committee and
later wrote that in the 1970s the Agency had 50 people working in
Mexico, 15 who were working under cover of the DoS. While being
trained for the Mexico assignment, he observed that CIA policy was,
"We prop up the good guys, our friends, while we monitor carefully the bad guys, our enemies, and beat them down as often as
possible."[3]Agee recalled that "Because of the strategic importance
of Mexico to the U.S., its size and proximity, and the abundance
of enemy activities, the Mexico City station is the largest in the
hemisphere."[4]

In 1981, the newly elected U.S. president, Ronald Reagan, took
office and appointed William Casey to be his Director of Central
Intelligence (DCI). Casey had experience working with the OSS in
World War II and had been Reagan's campaign manager during the
1980 presidential campaign. Casey became the first DCI to take a
place at the White House as a fully participating cabinet member.
He also became the first DCI in 16 years to stay on from one presidential term to the next. So important did the CIA prove to be to
Reagan that its appropriations grew by 50 percent over the administration's first three budgets.[5]

Casey came into office with the outlook that Central America was
in grave danger from leftist revolutionaries. One of his first actions
was to hire 500 mercenaries who were trained by Argentinians to
launch attacks on Nicaragua, where the Sandinistas had taken power
following a revolution in 1979. This grouping would later become
the Contras, funded and directed by the Agency.[6]

Reagan's DCI held the view that Nicaragua and El Salvador, which
was being assailed by a guerilla insurrection, were like dominoes aimed

toward Mexico. Throughout Casey's tenure, he would maintain that Mexico was dangerously unstable, with a 50–50 chance of undergoing a significant political destabilization. He came into conflict with some CIA intelligence professionals on the issue of Mexico during his time as DCI. These career intelligence experts believed Casey over-estimated the potential for chaos in Mexico. Those disputes would spill into the press. However, Reagan and his foreign-policy advisors would support Casey and his appraisal.[7]

Casey hired Dr. Constantine Menges to be his first national intelligence officer for Latin America. In that capacity, he would represent Casey to other agencies and head a monthly meeting on potential threats then recommend the response. Menges was a foreign-policy conservative who had recently written an op-ed piece for the *New York Times* entitled "Mexico: The Iran Next Door." Iran had descended into chaos during the preceding administration and was considered an intelligence failure on the part of the CIA. In his first meeting with Casey, Menges brought a two-page paper which argued that communists in partnership with others were involved in what he called the "Destabilization Coalition." The paper identified Latin America as one focus of this coalition. The countries that Menges identified as targets of the coalition in that region were Colombia, Venezuela, Central America, Panama, Belize, and Mexico. He characterized Mexico as the main prize in the area. Menges had also written an article in 1979, before the Sandinistas had overthrown the Somoza regime, in which he predicted, "Success [of the Sandinistas] would create the political base and momentum for beginning revolutionary warfare against Mexico during the early 1980s."[8]

One measure of CIA interest in Mexico during the 1980s is the number of research papers in the CIA's declassified files on the topic. There are many such papers on Mexico in those files which assess labor unions, politics, its government, and its economy in the 1980s. Besides appearing to be well written and objective, with hindsight, they seem to have been highly accurate. They also give a picture of CIA thinking on Mexico during the period. Their analyses of Mexico would have guided and propelled CIA covert activities, which of course were not declassified. These papers contain some redactions.

By 1984, Casey had shuttled the ultra-conservative Menges off to the National Security Council and replaced him as national intelligence officer for Latin America with a career professional, John Horton. Casey pushed for a National Intelligence Estimate (NIE) on Mexico to be completed by the CIA, which would reflect both his and the Reagan administration's views. This NIE became a source of conflict with Horton, who resigned after the Agency published it. He would go public with his disagreements on Mexico, believing that it posed much less danger than Casey purported.[9]

The Outlook for Mexico

The NIE paper, entitled "The Outlook for Mexico," was published for the intelligence community in April 1984, and covers what it expected for Mexico through the rest of the 1980s. It begins by saying, "The Mexican political system is under greater stress today than at any time in the last 30 years."[10] The authors judged it was likely that the Mexican political system would probably remain intact but that there was a 20 percent chance that political opposition and centrifugal forces would result in political destabilization. The 20 percent figure was a compromise between Casey's 50 percent position and Horton, who thought destabilization likely to be at less than 20 percent. Five intelligence professionals are listed as opposing the 20 percent figure as excessive: the Director of Intelligence and Research, DoS; the Director of the Defense Intelligence Agency; the Assistant Chief of Staff for Intelligence, Department of the Army; the Assistant Chief of Staff for Intelligence, Department of the Air Force; Director of Intelligence, Headquarters, Marine Corps. Casey's view would prevail.[11]

"The Outlook for Mexico" describes the Mexican political system as one of the most complex and inscrutable in the developing world. It had allowed the ruling Institutional Revolutionary Party (PRI) to monopolize repressive power for over five decades. Government leaders and party bosses were labeled as skilled at employing policies and tactics, tacking in changing political winds, adjusting the balance of power among the elite groups, isolating dissidents, manipulating the media, maintaining a monopoly of repressive power, and exercising exclusive rights to "revolutionary" ideals that provide legitimacy to the system.[12]

The research goes on to look at the immediate challenges to the system. During the 1970s, Mexico experienced good economic growth and wage gains as a result of its oil reserves and the likelihood of more oil being discovered. The country borrowed heavily to finance infrastructure improvements and government spending on social programs. Due to an economic crash and falling oil prices in the early 1980s, the Mexican economy fell into significant trouble. The economic crisis was one of the big challenges described by the Agency research experts. GDP and living standards were slipping. The Mexican government made major economic adjustments: they slashed government spending, reduced consumer subsidies, and devalued the peso sharply. Mexico had an enormous foreign debt. By 1985, it owed $97 billion to creditors, while U.S commercial bank exposure to Mexico stood at $25.2 billion that year, a factor closely followed by the CIA.[13]

The zero-sum economic growth in Mexico was believed by the Agency to be undercutting the traditional rules of the Mexican political game. The PRI's blue-collar labor sector, primarily represented by the CTM had suffered great deprivation without much clamor, but the Agency researchers did not believe that indefinite sacrifice was likely. Moreover, the chances for wildcat strikes and possibly violent labor unrest would increase.[14]

The CIA report concludes that U.S. political and economic interests would be substantially affected by conditions in Mexico. The security of the border was seen to rely on the continued existence of a stable Mexico. Other U.S. interests, such as illegal immigration and drugs, as well as Mexican oil, trade, investment relationships, and willingness to make payments on its debt, would be affected by Mexico's success in dealing with the economic and political challenges it faced.[15]

The research shows the CIA priorities of the time and how closely the Agency was watching Mexico as conditions changed. Chronologically, the first significant paper to show up is "The Opposition Left in Mexico," dated June 1982. Given DCI Casey's concerns, the timing is no surprise. The twelve-page paper begins by noting in an "Overview" that organizational activity from the left has increased significantly during the past few years. It goes on to discount a threat from the left in the July 1982 presidential election because of the PRI's ability to contest any of the left's efforts to claim constituency groups and that the PRI had developed tactics for containing, co-opting or eliminating opposition elements. The Agency believed that the parties of the opposition left recognized that they could survive only by following government rules. In general, the CIA concluded that leftist leaders appeared committed to nonviolent change.[16]

The "Opposition Left in Mexico" goes on to evaluate every party on the political left. It notes that progress toward leftist unity had arrived with the formation of the communist-dominated Unified Socialist Party of Mexico which reflected a commitment on the part of communists to nonviolent reform. The nine largest parties on the left recognized by the government had a total membership of about 200,000 out of a total population of 70 million. The smallest of these nine, the Revolutionary Workers Party [Partido Revolucionario de los Trabajadores] (PRT), is worth a closer look because it will play an essential part in the events that took place at Ford Cuautitlán later in the decade.[17]

The paper, which carries the DCI's seal and is marked secret, devotes four paragraphs to the PRT, the Trotskyist party founded in 1976. The Agency estimated its membership at 8,000, and according to U.S. Embassy officials, party members are primarily students, professors, public school teachers, and doctors, with some strength within electrical and nuclear energy workers' unions. The Agency speculated that the group could aggravate disunity among the left and this could be the reason the government recognized the party. The party fielded the first female presidential candidate in Mexico, Rosario Ibarra de Piedra. She had gained national prominence for founding the Committee for the Defense of Political Prisoners,

Exiles, Fugitives, and Disappeared Persons, when her son disappeared after being arrested and accused of being a communist.[18]

The Intelligence Estimate of 1984 also mentioned the PRT. It comments that the PRT had avoided manipulation by the PRI and has attracted considerable attention because of its strident anti-government positions. It describes Ibarra de Piedra, its presidential candidate in the 1982 election, as charismatic. The CIA believed the PRT stood a good chance of attracting new support from alienated youth and disenchanted middle-class professionals.[19]

Later, in December 1983, CIA research undertook a study of Mexican labor unions. The document, called "Mexico: Labor–Government Relations," starts out by reporting:

> Mexican labor unions—almost wholly co-opted by the ruling party—are showing few signs of militancy despite soaring prices, declining real wages, rising unemployment, and shortages of food and consumer goods.... The continued loyalty of organized labor—constituting only an estimated 20 to 25 percent of the nation's workforce but politically influential beyond its numbers—is essential for the maintenance of IMF-mandated austerity and for short-term political stability.... US and multinational firms are likely to face increased problems from unions when the economy begins to recover.[20]

The Agency viewed organized labor in Mexico as integrated into the post-Revolutionary corporatist structure by an elaborate system of rewards and control. Union leaders helped organize pro-government demonstrations and supply enough votes for the PRI to justify claims it represents the majority of Mexicans. Strikes and work stoppages were rare.

> Recalcitrant workers are expelled from their locals and, because of strict union shop requirements, lose their jobs. Dissident victories in shop elections are voided. Union thugs exert physical "persuasion" when necessary.[21]

The document devotes an entire page to the key role played by 83-year-old Fidel Velázquez, who has been in command of the CTM since 1941. His unquestioned authority in the organization allowed him to run the labor federation like a microcosm of the PRI. The CIA scholars say that in return for the vast patronage they give to Don Fidel the PRI leaders expect him to head off dissent within labor and to persuade the rank and file to acquiesce to policies that would cause riots in other countries. The paper notes that the process of finding a successor to Velazquez will test the political system.[22]

The union report concludes with the warning that if the economic crisis and consequent labor problems become unmanageable—a scenario they found to be an unlikely but possible outcome—the implications for the U.S. assume significant proportions. The U.S. would then face an unprecedented set of economic, political, and social problems south of its border.[23]

The Mexico City Earthquake

At 7:19 a.m. on September 19, 1985, Mexico suffered an earthquake which measured a magnitude of 8.1 on the Richter scale and was followed two days later by a major aftershock. It resulted in between 5,000 and 20,000 deaths, and the collapse of over 400 buildings, as well as major damage to another 3,000. The collapsed buildings included two public hospitals, many government buildings, several tourist hotels, and the main telephone building.[24] An apartment building in downtown Mexico City, named Nuevo Léon, which was home to 1,200 residents, collapsed. The dead bodies pulled from the ruins were carefully recorded—472 were recovered. At 7:38 p.m., another earthquake, measuring 6.5 on the Richter scale, struck. Hundreds of people still trapped in the rubble from the first quake died when it shifted. At the end of the year, 180,000 homeless refugees were still living in lean-to shelters on the streets of Mexico City.[25]

The devastation to so many buildings laid bare the failure of the government to enforce building codes. Corruption was suspected as the primary cause. The residents of Nuevo Léon had complained for years about how damage done to the building in a quake a few years earlier had not been repaired. At the time the building collapsed on September 19, the residents had hung a banner down the side of the building denouncing the inadequate repairs. The engineer responsible told them Nuevo Léon was "one of the three safest buildings in Mexico City."[26]

The army was sent to protect factories instead of aiding rescue. They were supposed to prevent looting but were seen looting themselves. The Ministry of Foreign Affairs rejected aid from the U.S.[27] The earthquake revealed torture chambers when the Mexican equivalent to the U.S. Justice Department building collapsed. Rescuers came across the bodies of six men who had been arrested by federal police four days before the quake. Medical examiners announced they all showed signs of torture and two had died from it.[28]

The PRI government was paralyzed. Citizens were left to cope with rescue and relief on their own. The people of Mexico City formed organizations and began making decisions themselves. They formulated demands calling on the government to rescue all survivors, to prosecute officials responsible for structural weaknesses, and to rebuild instead of relocating people. Within days, a grassroots movement began to spread across the city. On October 24, the movement named itself the Coordinadora Única de Damnificados (the United Coordinating Committee of Earthquake Refugees). On October 26, they called for a march and 40,000 people showed up.[29]

Alongside the victims' mobilization, a more militant political movement emerged from the National Autonomous University of Mexico, which had 200,000 students at the time. A group of leftist students headed out to the streets to help. They began work digging out at public housing projects and hospitals assisting the search for survivors and recovering the bodies of the deceased. The students also challenged the bulldozers sent in to clear out the rubble, which also killed a few of the remaining survivors and destroyed the remains of the dead, making identification impossible. Within 48 hours, the army command ordered the affected areas off limits, claiming it was a safety issue. Fights broke out between the students and the army, which used tear gas in the confrontation, but the students held their ground. The university groups helped repair telephone lines and the electric grid, directed traffic, and kept an independent census of the dead. The radical students won broad support among the people of Mexico City.[30]

The following April, the CIA disseminated a secret paper assessing the political impact of the quake. The document was entitled "Mexico: Political Implications of the 1985 Earthquakes—A Comparison with Nicaragua and Guatemala." In this case, they incorrectly weighed the political ramifications of the event.

In 1972, Nicaragua experienced an earthquake. The overthrow of the Somoza government by the Sandinistas in 1979 was attributed to poor handling of the relief effort by the regime. The CIA analysts described this as a generally held belief.[31] The CIA examined three aspects of the de la Madrid (PRI president of Mexico) government's handling of the quake: corruption in the relief effort, the portion of the population assisted, and ability to handle the earthquake. The research indicated that because of government performance, it was unlikely that the event would affect the country's long-term political stability. The report mentioned a factor different from the situation as it developed in Nicaragua in the 1970s. That was the formation of popular self-help quake relief groups.[32]

The Agency noted as somewhat of an afterthought that high-ranking Mexican officials had become increasingly worried due to the spontaneous organization of the new groups in the quake's aftermath. These groups filled a vacuum created by the failure of traditional political institutions to respond to the disaster, and officials believed they posed a threat to political stability. The CIA and the U.S. Embassy dismissed these concerns as premature and an overreaction.[33] In actuality, these groups would be the catalyst for a nationwide political upheaval that would challenge the PRI's 60-year history of Mexican rule. The poor handling of the quake called into question the legitimacy of PRI rule. These local organizations developed into an opposition force to the PRI establishment. The newly awakened people would make themselves heard in the 1988 election.[34]

Election Fraud

The July 6, 1988 election developed into the biggest challenge to the Mexican ruling elite since the 1910 revolution. The country would stand on the brink of fundamental change. During the run-up to the 1988 election, the impact of the economic crisis became intense. Inflation reached a high of 160 percent in 1986. Wages rose by only one-third of that amount.[35]

Cuauhtémoc Cárdenas, who was the son of a revered former president of Mexico, Lazaro Cárdenas, defied the PRI dictatorship in 1988. While president of Mexico between 1934 and 1940, the elder Cárdenas had realized many of the objectives of the Mexican revolution, like land reform and the nationalization of the oil industry. Cuauhtémoc moved quickly into the PRI hierarchy, becoming a senator in 1975 and then, in 1980, a governor of the State of Michoacán. In 1985, he argued at an academic forum that since his father left office the PRI had abandoned the revolution's commitment to social justice. In the following years, he spoke out aggressively against President de la Madrid's economic policies, which had impoverished millions. Cárdenas, along with some other PRI dissidents, began advocating publicly for a more democratic nominating process in the PRI. De la Madrid responded by having Carlos Salinas de Gortari chosen as the PRI candidate for president in the 1988 election. A week after Salinas's selection, Cárdenas accepted the nomination for president of a small party, the Party of the Authentic Mexican Revolution (PARM). The PRI expelled Cárdenas immediately.[36]

During the following weeks Cárdenas won the support of hundreds of Mexican leftists, who formed an alliance composed of six parties to support his candidacy. They called it the Frente Democrático National (Democratic National Front). In addition to the PARM, these parties on the left included the Popular Socialist Party (PPS) and the Social Democratic Party. Later, an agreement was reached with the Mexican Socialist Party to support Cárdenas in the 1988 contest, and it was integrated into Democratic National Front. The Mexican Socialist Party was founded in 1987 as a merger of the Unified Socialist Party of Mexico, the Mexican Workers Party, the

Communist Leftist Union, the People's Revolutionary Movement, and the Revolutionary Patriotic Party.[37]

Violence took place in the run-up to the election. Many individuals in the political parties who supported Cárdenas were killed in places like Michoacán, Oaxaca, and Morelos, with some estimates as high as 600 dead.[38] The violence included the 1988 assassinations of Cárdenas' close aide Francisco Xavier Ovando and his assistant. They were killed while they were driving in Mexico City on the eve of the federal election. They had created a nationwide network of polling-place informants and the murders destroyed Cárdenas' ability to compile independent voting results.[39]

The PRI candidate in the 1988 election, Carlos Salinas de Gortari, had been President de la Madrid's Budget secretary, but had never served in an elected position. His lack of skills as a campaigner showed up in the new world of contested elections in Mexico. No PRI candidate for president had ever received less than 76 percent of the vote, but authorities knew this time it would be much closer.[40] Cárdenas was greeted with throngs of enthusiastic supporters everywhere he went.

The Mexican election system had changed little since the revolution. Ballots were counted by hand in each of the 54,000 polling places. Tally sheets and ballots were then trucked to the country's 300 election districts. Four days after the balloting, election officials would add up the results from each polling place in their district and send the results to Mexico City. For the 1988 election, the government had developed a new mainframe computer system to speed up the process. The secretary of government (similar to an interior minister or attorney general in the U.S.) had intended to keep it a secret from the opposition parties, but when they found out about it the government was forced to let representatives from each campaign view results on terminals at the Government Secretariat building on election eve.[41]

The PRI had programmed the computer to allow the opposition campaigns to see only results from districts that Salinas was projected to do well in, and early in the evening the terminal screens were blank. The representative of the conservative opposition party, the National Action Party (PAN), was inadvertently able to access all the election results. He told the representatives of the other campaigns to come look at his terminal. Cárdenas and the PAN candidate were winning in every part of the country. When the government learned that the opposition was seeing this, they shut down the terminals at 7:50 p.m., claiming the system had gone silent or, as was often said, "the system crashed" (also meant as a reference to the political system). The secretary of government was caught lying to the opposition about what building the computer was located in and why the terminals had shut down.[42]

It was a PRI election catastrophe without precedent in Mexican history. There were fraudulent practices all over the country. Roving bands of PRI supporters cast ballots in multiple precincts; opposition poll watchers were expelled from polling places; ballot boxes were filled with ballots marked for Salinas before the polls opened; polling places in Cárdenas areas never opened, or closed with hundreds of people still waiting in line; and thugs stole ballot boxes. Thousands of burned ballots marked for Cárdenas were found. Others were dumped in ravines or found floating in a river. In the 300 separate congressional elections, there were 255 formal accusations of fraud. The number of votes for president far exceeded the number of congressional votes, indicating that votes for Salinas had been added to totals.[43]

At 2:00 a.m., the computer terminals were turned on. They showed Salinas with 45 percent of the vote, Cárdenas with 38 percent, and the PAN candidate with 17 percent. The next day, the government declared Salinas the winner with 50.4 percent of the vote and Cárdenas with 31.1 percent. The opposition parties were not having it and issued a statement denouncing the election results as fraudulent.[44]

On July 16, three days after the official results were announced, 200,000 rallied in support of Cárdenas at Zócalo, the central square in Mexico City and, prior to the colonial era, the central plaza of the Aztec empire. Many of them were advocating open confrontation with the PRI. In Michoacán, Cárdenas backers occupied town halls in several cities. In the streets, people chanted "the people vote, and Cárdenas won."[45] Cárdenas declared himself the election winner and began a nationwide tour, with the crowds shouting for action to defend the true vote. Seeing the swelling anger, the PRI threatened violence.[46]

A 24-hour debate preceded the final vote in Congress to certify the Salinas victory. One PAN deputy, Vincente Fox, proposed opening the ballot boxes and recounting the ballots. He led 30 deputies into the basement where the ballot boxes were kept. They were met by soldiers. Fox later wrote that a soldier threatened the group saying, "take one more step and you die, motherfuckers!" The PAN would later vote with the PRI to burn the ballots and boxes.[47] The PRI outnumbered the opposition deputies by 260 to 240. Every PAN deputy voted against certification and the 136 members of the Cárdenas Front walked out before the vote. Four days later, Cárdenas supporters flooded Zócalo in a demonstration that one Salinas supporter called, "the most powerful and most radical concentration of people in our history."[48] Some estimates of the number reached 1,000,000 people. When Cárdenas addressed the crowd, he advocated pursuing legal, peaceful means to remedy the election fraud.

A month after the election, the CIA issued a paper evaluating the events that had just transpired. "Mexico: Assessing the Potential for Short-Term Instability" is a highly redacted ten-page paper that reviews the conditions that caused the erosion of PRI support, focusing on the economic crisis. In the CIA's view, the election seriously challenged the PRI's credibility. They believed the potential for widespread and potentially violent protests existed and were likely to persist. They speculated the PRI would be able to control the situation eventually. The agency reported that the PRI believed the opposition parties would be satisfied with the unprecedented gains made in the legislature. PRI leaders were negotiating behind the scenes with the left which they could co-opt. The opposition stayed within legal means to challenge the election, and these were firmly in the hands of the PRI. Salinas was inaugurated in December 1988.[49]

One of Reagan's and Casey's stalwarts in the anti-communist offensive in Central America was John D. Negroponte.[50] Negroponte had been a foreign service officer in Asia and an aide to Henry

Kissinger. He had been able to convince Kissinger that he was conceding too much to the North Vietnamese in secret negotiations in 1972 and those fell apart. The American war effort continued in Vietnam for two more years, but finally, the parties reached a peace agreement with the same terms in late 1973. Kissinger blamed Negroponte for many of his problems in the negotiations and when he became Secretary of State banished his former aide to a foreign service post in Ecuador.[51]

Negroponte persevered, and Ronald Reagan appointed him as ambassador to Honduras from 1981 to 1985. Honduras was a base of operations for the Contra rebels who waged war against the Sandinista government of neighboring Nicaragua throughout the 1980s. After Congress prohibited aid to the Contras in 1982, Oliver North labored to raise extra-legal money for them, and Ambassador Negroponte worked with the Honduran government to retain their support for the Contra army which would eventually total between 20,000 and 30,000 men. U.S. military aid to Honduras rose from $3.9 million in 1980 to $77 million in 1984, and 1985 economic assistance totaled $229 million.[52] According to the *Washington Post*, Negroponte developed skills in back-channel communications with the CIA during this time to avoid Congress detecting his prohibited efforts in support of the Contras.

> The cables show that Negroponte enjoyed a close relationship with senior Washington policymakers, such as then-CIA Director William J. Casey, that was unusual for career diplomats. He used a back-channel system of communication through the CIA to send messages to Casey and others that he did not want widely distributed.[53]

Between 1981 and 1984, as many as 200 suspected leftists may have been killed for political reasons in Honduras. The CIA aided Honduran security forces that it knew were responsible for this.[54] Negroponte downplayed the human rights abuses in Honduras. The previous U.S. ambassador to Honduras, Jack Binns, had sent several cables to Washington before being recalled in 1981 warning of

"Death Squad" activity linked to General Gustavo Alvarez. Negroponte dismissed talk of death squads and in a cable of October 1983
emphasized Alvarez's "dedication to democracy."

Negroponte's history is important to our story because President George H. W. Bush later appointed him as U.S. ambassador to
Mexico and he assumed the office in February 1989. The CIA station
chief he worked with in Honduras between 1981 and 1985 was
Vincent Shields, whom Negroponte described as a "good friend."[55]
Shields would be assigned as the CIA station chief in Mexico
during Negroponte's tenure there. Shields ended his career in 1997
as a 34-year veteran of the CIA's Directorate of Operations, which
supervises spying and covert operations abroad. He handled controversial operations in Honduras in the 1980s during the Reagan
years, and when he retired in 1997 he was praised by John Negroponte from the DoS and the defense intelligence agency director, Lt.
Gen. Patrick M. Hughes, who recognized him for his role in inte-
grating CIA and military intelligence operations abroad.[56]

Negroponte and Shields were joined in the Mexico assignment by another experienced foreign service and national security
expert, Robert Pastorino. Pastorino had served in Mexico City as an
economic and political counselor from 1984 to 1985. He was then
sent to Honduras as deputy chief of mission from 1986 to 1987.
President Reagan appointed him as special assistant to the president for national security affairs and director of Latin American
affairs on the National Security Council staff in 1988. Pastorino was
appointed as the deputy chief of mission at the U.S. Embassy in
Mexico City in 1989. In that capacity he helped draft the first con-
ceptual paper on NAFTA.[57]

Presidents-elect George H. Bush and Salinas met in November
1988 in Houston where they resolved to seek "dialogue, constant
negotiation and the use of new and imaginative forms of understanding." Bush's resume included a stint as DCI between 1976 and
1977. Negroponte's appointment followed quickly. President Salinas
accepted Negroponte as ambassador before the nomination had
been officially announced or even confirmed by Washington thus
circumventing political opposition in the legislature. Negroponte's

nomination met fierce criticism in the Mexican congress because of his previous posts in Vietnam and Central America and his close ties to American intelligence agencies.[58] Negroponte's most enduring legacy from his time in Mexico would be his role in facilitating the successful negotiations in 1990 and 1991 between Presidents Salinas and Bush for a North American Free Trade Agreement (NAFTA).[59]

William Webster, the new DCI who had replaced Casey, told the *LA Times* in February 1989 that unrest in Mexico "will receive far more attention...than in the past."[60] The Reagan administration responded to the 1988 election crisis in Mexico by sending in a diplomatic and intelligence team with strong links to national security and with extensive covert operations experience.

In 1987, amid the turbulence of the decade, Ford Motor Company would begin negotiations with the CTM over a new contract at its Cuautitlán Assembly Plant (CAP) located just outside of Mexico City.

6

U.S. Auto Companies Move South

A key episode in CAP's [Cuautitlán Assembly Plant] union-management relationship was the 1987 100-day work stoppage that coincided with the government's shift to a policy of economic liberalization.... The contract buy-out resulted in an immediate payroll cost reduction of 40 percent. The CTM's national leaders acquiesced to these events and pressed the local union to sign a new contract that dismantled some of the previous restrictions on management action.

P. Roberto Garcia and Stephen Hills, "Meeting 'Lean' Competitors: Ford De Mexico's Industrial Relations Strategy"

In the 1980s, the Big Three automakers (General Motors, Ford, Chrysler) began a fundamental restructuring of their operations. This transformation was forced by two oil crises and a resulting increase in demand for small fuel-efficient vehicles, by more stringent regulations on safety, energy, and the environment in the U.S., and a drastic fall in vehicle demand overall. Japanese automakers were able to take advantage of the changing competitive dynamics using new technologies and production methods, like lean production and just-in-time delivery. They also held a competitive cost advantage over American operations.[1]

During the U.S. military occupation of Japan following World War II, occupation forces initially encouraged unions as a democratic force that could oppose re-militarization. In the poverty and hardship in early post-war Japan, unions proliferated. The unions battled with employers as they both struggled to adjust to the newfound rules and power being given to workers. As the Cold War heated up, the U.S. supported purges of the communists who had gained control in the new Japanese unions, and began to restrain support for unionization. In the spring of 1953, a battle began between Japan's strongest auto union and Nissan (backed by the Bank of Japan and the government), eventually leading to the reshaping of the auto industry worldwide.[2]

On May 25, 1953, a 100-day strike and lockout began at the Nissan plant involving 7,000 union members. In Japan, unlike the U.S., middle management employees were allowed to join the union. A new union, supported and funded by Nissan management, was created to challenge the striking union. The new union organization, led by members of management, contested with the old union for membership. Fistfights between the factions took place regularly. The noncommunist leftist leader of the striking union was arrested and jailed after charging a company barricade. By early September, Nissan broke the strike and defeated the old union, and it was replaced by a new company union, which became the workers' representative. Out of this new union–management relationship was born the production methods that would soon dominate manufacturing worldwide: lean manufacturing.[3]

The new production system was initially called just-in-time production. It was further refined as the Toyota Production System, then came to be called lean manufacturing. Lean manufacturing is a method that focuses on minimizing waste while maximizing productivity. The system requires a high degree of cooperation from the workforce, and if a union represents those workers, it requires a collective bargaining agreement that allows employers the necessary degree of flexibility. The transition to lean production would become a point of contention at Ford Cuautitlán in the late 1980s.

The U.S. auto industry's competitive challenges were closely observed by Professor Harley Shaiken of MIT. Shaiken, who spent several years working on a GM assembly line, believed that while job losses to Japanese industry were the most apparent danger to American workers, they were not the most severe threat. Shaiken believed the new competitive landscape would provide the American companies an excuse to locate their factories in developing countries with weak or non-existent unions. Shaiken's concerns were a forewarning.[4]

The Move South

The U.S. Big Three reacted to Japanese industrial competition by outsourcing the production of parts and small vehicles to low-cost countries overseas. First among these was Mexico. Mexico was an attractive low-wage country to locate in for a number of reasons: its geographical proximity to the U.S., the government's unilateral adoption of free trade and pro-investment policies, the quality of the labor force, the lack of unions in northern Mexico, and the overall weak state of unions across the country.[5] By 2010, one out of every four automobiles imported into the U.S. had been assembled in Mexico.[6]

In 1980, General Motors (GM) began constructing a new assembly plant at Ramos Arizpe. This initiated the corporate auto-maker's campaign to reorganize the Mexican auto industry by moving it northward. GM's Mexico City-area plant had a militant local union that had conducted six strikes between 1965 and 1979.[7] In 1980, GM refused to agree to contract terms with the local, and a 106-day strike followed, which ended in defeat for the Mexico City union. This GM victory allowed them to open the Ramos Arizpe plant with a different union federation that had a weaker union tra-dition. The lower wages and more ineffective unions in northern Mexico attracted other new investments as well, following the GM move. These included Chrysler Saltillo (engines and trucks), Nissan Aguascalientes (engines and cars), and GM Silao (trucks). Ford Motor also began investing in new plants in northern Mexico in the early 1980s.[8]

Ford seemed to be the best prepared of the auto companies for a global strategy, given the size of its international operations. By 1990, Ford was the second largest auto manufacturer in the world, with operations in 200 countries and territories employing 350,000 workers. It followed a less aggressive strategy than GM or Chrysler of outsourcing parts and small vehicles. The Ford determination was partly due to its decision to adopt the lean production model that the Japanese had developed. It would therefore require a much more cooperative labor relations model than Ford had previously been using. In the U.S., the union contractual changes necessary would compel Ford to enter into job security provisions with the UAW that would impede the transfer of production operations to Mexico.[9]

In the 1970s, Ford had increased its Latin American investments to produce parts for export markets. The value of this production was insignificant. GM became the leader in Mexico. By 1989, GM had 25 maquiladoras in Mexico, employing more than 25,000 workers compared to Ford's 7,000 and Chrysler's 5,000.[10] In Mexico, a maquiladora is a sub-contractor factory operation that imports materials and equipment on a duty-free and tariff-free basis for assembly, processing, or manufacturing and then exports the assembled, processed, or manufactured products, sometimes back to the raw materials' country of origin. Ford also established joint ventures with a Mexican company to produce 750,000 radios annually and joined in a collective glass manufacturing operation there.[11]

Following the passage of NAFTA in late 1993, total employment in the maquiladoras would jump from 450,000 to 867,000.[12] By 2000, an industrial trade magazine counted a total of 3,384 maquila plants employing 1.2 million workers. Of those, 214,000 were employed making auto parts. In 1999, those workers earned an estimated $1.75 an hour.[13] NAFTA permanently tied the Mexican economy to a low-wage export strategy.[14]

Ford made investments in Mexico in the 1980s principally to strengthen its small car strategy. The establishment by the automaker of an engine manufacturing plant in Chihuahua in 1984 was primarily a response to GM's and Chrysler's competitive moves in the late 1970s and early 1980s. In 1987, it finished its Hermosillo, Sonora, assembly plant, which built small cars for the U.S. market. The plant was a significant change from previous operations in Mexico. Ford had used obsolete technology in Mexican facilities before opening Hermosillo. By the late 1980s, the Hermosillo plant was the only North American complex that combined stamping, manufacturing, and assembly, making it one of the most modern production operations in the world. It also allowed Ford to experiment with lean production in its new labor contract with the CTM.[15]

Ford Hermosillo and Chihuahua were producing almost exclusively for export, while the older Cuautitlán plant produced for the contracting domestic Mexican market.[16] When the Hermosillo and Chihuahua plants were completed and began production, all three Ford facilities would have unique local contracts. Ford paid workers at each plant a different salary. While the labor contracts had a differing expiration date, they would form a National Ford Workers Union in the CTM.[17] In the U.S., each unionized Ford location operates under a national contract with the same expiration date.

Ford Cuautitlán

Ford's operations in Mexico had begun in 1925 with the construction of an assembly plant in Mexico City. In 1962, construction for a new facility began 25 miles outside of Mexico City in Cuautitlán, which is in the State of Mexico. (Mexico City, like Washington, DC, is in a Federal District.) The CTM union affiliation traveled from the old plant on the north side of Mexico City to the new facility at Cuautitlán.[18]

In the 1960s and 1970s, several PRI governmental administrations rewarded the CTM's political support by enacting strong labor laws. During this period, the Cuautitlán union leadership was able to wrest a robust degree of shop floor control from Ford management. Their contract contained 17 broad job categories, with each classification linked to the one before it. Management was required to hire only entry-level employees. Layoffs had to be in the order of reverse seniority. The system protected employment security by its narrow definition of the jobs and who was allowed to do them. Ford found these and other contract provisions burdensome and prohibitive to productivity improvements, and they also made implementing the lean production system they envisioned impossible. Managers determined to get rid of them.[19]

When the economic crisis first erupted in 1981, Ford decided to terminate some workers at Cuautitlán. When these workers learned that the company would fire them, a few started to scratch the automobiles at the plant and cause damage to the units, as a protest against their dismissal. The CTM informed the Cuautitlán workers that to compensate for the losses caused by this, Ford would cut by 30 percent the salaries of those hired after that incident. It is likely that this story was a cover for the CTM, who may have agreed to a two-tier wage system in which newly hired workers are paid less than senior ones. The two-tier wage system was also being introduced in the U.S. at Big Three auto companies at about the same time. In both cases, the new lower wage rate would become a source of discord in the future.[20]

In 1987, contract negotiations between Ford and the CTM began in the wake of another peso devaluation and an economic crisis in Mexico. The head of the National Ford CTM was Lorenzo Vera Ozorno, who had sole authority under Mexican law to negotiate for the Cuautitlán workers. Inflation was rampant, and vehicle sales had declined to leave an excess of workers at the plant. A layoff would eventually have to take place. The government, which held a form of wage-freeze authority, authorized a 23 percent wage increase that year in response to the 133 percent inflation rate. Vero Ozorno and Ford agreed on a solution to their problems. Ford would refuse to match the 23 percent wage increase approved by the government and offer only 16 percent. Vera Ozorno would call a strike at the plant over the wage issue but, while on strike, Ford would pay the workers 50 percent of their salaries. In reality, this would be a subsidized layoff but with a hook.[21]

Mexican labor law allowed employers to terminate a labor contract after 60 days if the workers were on strike. For two and a half months, this strike went on before Ford terminated the contractual agreement and fired all 3,400 workers, offering to negotiate a new contract. Mexican law required that employers pay three months' salary in severance in this circumstance, and Ford offered the workers four months' salary. According to Ford de Mexico industrial relations managers, the firm exercised a legal separation clause at this time. The government Ministry of Labor ruled that the new agreement would have to be ratified by a majority of the workers. The workers, believing that Ford would call back most people, were offered a four-month bonus (the severance pay) if they approved the agreement. After two and a half months on strike at half pay, they accepted the deal and returned to work under the new contract terms.[22]

Ford rehired 80 percent of the workers under the new contract. Ford did not call back approximately 600. Many of the Ford workers believed the company used the opportunity to eliminate trouble-makers, unreliable workers, the injured, and individuals with absenteeism problems. Those that they rehired would receive the new wage at the lower rate established in 1981. The contract termination resulted in an immediate payroll cost reduction to Ford of 40 percent.[23]

Under the new contract, Ford also achieved more shop-floor flexibility, which they needed to pursue lean production. For example, they reduced job classifications from 17 to seven. What would take ten or 15 years to accomplish at a UAW-represented auto plant in the U.S., in terms of cost reductions and contract changes, was accomplished by Ford in a few months in Mexico. The new contract and the method Ford and the CTM used to achieve it became a source of bitter conflict in the coming years.

Emergence of Democratic Unionism

In 1987, in the middle of the conflict, Fidel Velázquez, the general secretary of the CTM, asked Ford to deposit in the Laborers' Bank all the severance payments required for the termination of the contract. Lorenzo Vera Ozorno, who had been negotiating with Ford for the CTM, rejected the proposal. As a result of that dispute, the CTM removed Lorenzo Vera Ozorno as the general secretary of the National Ford Union. The Ford Cuautitlán dissidents believed that this was a violation of Mexican law. With the approval of only the local union committees at Hermosillo and Chihuahua, the CTM appointed a new general secretary, Hector Uriarte Martinez. Since they were on strike and without a contract, the Cuautitlán workers had no say in this new National Ford CTM leader. The Mexican Federation needed to designate a new general secretary and national Executive Committee to conclude the strike and return the workers to their jobs. Uriarte and the new national committee took office in late summer.[24]

When the Ford Cuautitlán workers did return to work in the fall of 1987, they were without a local union committee. The Ford CTM plant committees were composed of a General Secretary, Work Secretary, Minutes Secretary, Statistics Secretary, Treasury Secretary, and a Sports Secretary. The local plant committee's power rested in authority granted to them by the workers, but Mexican labor law did not recognize it. In the early months of 1988, the CAP workers elected a new local committee by a popular vote. These new members of the Cuautitlán committee had opposed the ratification of the contract of 1987.

Both the 1987 contract with Ford and Vera Ozorno faced opposition from within the plant. The PRT and some other leftists had successfully been organizing at Cuautitlán since the early 1980s. Political activists had founded the PRT in the wake of the PRI's crushing of the student movement of 1968.

The 1968 student movement began in July of that year with a brawl between teenagers from rival high schools at a football game in Mexico City. Riot police attacked the kids and followed them into a vocational school where they beat students and teachers alike. That led to days of skirmishing between the young people and the police. The repression that followed drew more people into the fighting, including some from the neighborhoods. Diaz Ordaz, then president of Mexico, ordered the army to assault one of the high schools using a bazooka to blow apart a door. The following day, 50,000 students and professors marched in protest of the government's actions. By mid-August, every college, university, and preparatory school in Mexico City, and many as 31 universities in other Mexican states, had joined in a student strike. They called for freeing the jailed students and railway union leaders imprisoned from a 1959 strike, compensation for injured protesters, the disbanding of the riot police, and the repeal of vague laws used to jail dissenters. On August 27, 400,000 joined a march to Zócalo, the central square.[25]

The movement gained momentum and attracted broad public support. It became a threat to the public image the government wanted to project at the 1968 Olympic Games, scheduled to start on October 12 in Mexico, the first developing country to be selected to host the games. On September 18, the army occupied the National Autonomous University of Mexico, the largest university in Latin America, with 100,000 students, and arrested 500. By late September, Mexico City was under a near state of siege.[26]

National strike leaders called for another protest rally on October 2. It would be held in the commons area of a downtown housing project called Tlatelolco. The commons area was called the Plaza de las Tres Culturas (Plaza of the Three Cultures). The student rally would prove to be the violent birth of a new political generation of Mexicans.[27]

About 8,000 people attended the rally. More than 10,000 soldiers and police were present. Helicopters hovered close overhead and dropped two flares on the protesters. The crowd panicked and tried to flee, but authorities blocked escape routes. Soldiers began firing into the crowd with automatic weapons. Hundreds of plain-clothes police assaulted the student leaders who were inside a nearby apartment building. Unidentified snipers on the roof fired on both demonstrators and the military. The shooting continued throughout the night. Estimates were that 300–500 students were killed and 2,000 arrested. The CIA reported in 1985 that according to Embassy cables, over 300 were killed and 1,000 wounded.[28] The incident is called the Tlatelolco massacre.[29] The CIA produced daily reports on the student movement, and the U.S. military sent assistance to Mexico during the crisis. Philip Agee, who had been assigned to monitor the Olympics in Mexico City, resigned from the CIA in disgust.[30]

Mexicans saw the army and a vast array of security forces used against peaceful protesters. The judiciary proved to be no more than a kangaroo court. Authorities charged hundreds of student leaders with murder, and the courts imprisoned them for years. The Congress completely supported President Diaz's action. The media reported nothing more than government propaganda and the Catholic church remained silent.[31]

A young medical student, Jesús Piedra Ibarra, outraged at the injustice of Mexican society, became active with an urban guerilla group, the Liga Comunista 23 de Septiembre (the 23 of Septem-

ber Communist League). His mother, Rosario Ibarra de Piedra, sent
him out one evening in 1973 to get cheese. She never saw him again
and later learned that the police had detained him. He became one
of the *Desaparecidos* (disappeared). Rosario Ibarra's efforts to find
out what happened to her son and other Desaparecidos would lead
her to collaborative efforts with the PRT. She became one of the
most determined opponents the PRI elite ever faced.[32]

The PRT had grown very quickly since its founding in 1976 as
it absorbed smaller Trotskyist bands. Militants from different social
movements and guerrilla organizations joined. Non-Trotskyist political groups also merged. It grew into a genuine political party, not
just a Trotskyist sect, with 8,000 members in 1982 according to the
CIA.[33] In 1978, the PRT became a legal political party, and in the
1982 election, Rosario Ibarra de Piedra, now a nationally known
human rights activist, ran for president. The PRT openly advocated
gay rights and openly supported gay candidates in the 1982 election.
In that election, a handful of PRT members won seats in Parliament.
After the election, the PRT received leaked information that came
from Mexican military intelligence. Ibarra de Piedra had in reality
received more votes than had been officially recognized. Official
results showed she had 416,448 votes, but the PRT believed that the
actual tally was approximately one million votes in her favor.[34] This
period of PRT expansion coincided with the emergence of neoliberalism in Mexico.

Hector de la Cueva, a founding member of the PRT, began
working at CAP in the early 1980s. In the atmosphere of violent
repression, activists had to do work clandestinely. Unlike most in
the CTM, the CAP local union had an inner life and "simulated"
meetings and elections. These legal union activities provided opportunities for organizing, and within that environment, some PRT
members were able to win elections, not only at Ford but other factories as well. The CAP union adopted a democratic secret ballot
election, resulting in a PRT member Francisco Ferruzka being
elected general secretary in 1984. Hector de la Cueva and other PRT
members began putting out an underground shop newspaper called
El Pistón (the Piston or Percussion Cap). The paper had a very loyal

following among the workers. Ford never found out who was publishing the paper, though they fired many suspected of doing it.
When workers ratified the 1987 contract, Ford fired 600 workers,
including those they believed to be "troublemakers." Hector de la
Cueva was one of them. He remained active at the Ford factory as
an advisor to the workers.[35]

The PRT had opposed the strike called by Vero Ozorno in 1987,
fearing Ford would use it as an opportunity to terminate the existing
contract. They had advocated for voting against the contract in
the 1987 ratification vote. Events were soon to prove them right.
PRT-supported candidates won the 1988 local CAP union elections.
After that point, the local Executive Committee was composed
entirely of PRT members and their supporters throughout the
decade.[36]

The CIA closely monitored leftist attempts to organize Mexican
workers during the 1980s. In December 1983, the Agency noted:

> Opposition political parties have made little headway in building
> a following among workers. Although Marxists have managed
> to attract enough support to establish footholds in many PRI-
> affiliated unions, we believe the PRI's success in co-opting leftist
> leaders has undermined even this limited foundation.[37]

There is no evidence that the PRI had any success in co-opting the
PRT. Cueva and his comrades at Ford Cuautitlán were having great
success in organizing.

AIFLD Arrives

Meanwhile, AIFLD had established an office in Mexico City in
the mid-1960s. It was a successor to the PTTI in Mexico, where
William Doherty had set up shop as the regional director in 1955.
The transition between PTTI and AIFLD is murky.[38] Both Doherty
and Jesse Friedman claimed Doherty had been working for AIFLD
a year before the founding date.[39] Jesse Friedman was an AIFLD
agent in Mexico between 1963 and 1966, and worked in Washington, DC, at the AIFLD headquarters between 1967 and 1995, rising

to be AIFLD deputy director. He said his work required him to travel to Mexico six or seven times per year.

Friedman's career followed a track similar to that of William Doherty Jr. He was stepson to a person with strong links to the CIA, Serafino Romualdi, the first executive director of AIFLD. After graduating from college in 1958, he began working for the Department of Labor. Then, from 1958 to 1959, Friedman developed some nebulous ties to unions (he claimed to have been a member of the Hotel and Restaurant Workers Union in 1958) and learned Spanish. In 1959, he began working at the AFL-CIO headquarters in Washington, DC. In an Association for Diplomatic Studies and Training (ADST) interview in 1995, he cited working for AIFLD in Peru during 1960, a full two years before the Institute was officially established. He spent the rest of his career working for government-funded labor organizations.

In 1983, a new funding source had been proposed by the Reagan administration for AIFLD and some other CIA operations. Congress passed the National Endowment for Democracy (NED) Act. The NED would receive money from Congress or the U.S. Agency for International Development (AID) for "democracy building" overseas.[40] A few months later, the Free Trade Union Institute (FTUI) was set up to receive funds from the NED and distribute them to AIFLD, AALC, AAFLI, FTUC, and International Trade Secretariats like the PTTI.[41] The FTUI was another quasi-official organization of the AFL-CIO.[42] One of its first board members was Irving Brown, and William Doherty Jr. was a principal staff member.[43] Both were linked to the CIA. Perhaps Paul Somogyi best explains the FTUI–NED relationship. Somogyi was an AIFLD country director in Mexico during the 1980s. In 1986, he became the assistant director of the International Affairs Department for the AFL-CIO and in the 1990s was the executive director of the FTUI:

FTUI was one of the four civil pillars of the National Endowment of Democracy (NED, a private, non-profit funded directly by the U.S. Congress), the other three pertaining to the Center for International Private Enterprise (CIPE), which was the international

arm of the American Chamber of Commerce; and the two political party institutes (NDI/National Democratic Institute) and
IRI/International Republic Institute), all creations to do for their
respective sectors what FTUI was doing for labor.[44]

The NED necessitated more vigorous financial reporting
and accounting than the previous AIFLD funding streams had
required.[45] AIFLD would have to prepare budgets and substanti-
ate expenses. The new accounting procedures were a problem for
AIFLD. NED was unable to close out several of the grants given to
the FTUI during the 1980s because it never submitted the proper
paperwork. AIFLD never properly closed one of these grants before
dissolving in 1996.[46]

The budget proposed by AIFLD from the NED in 1985 for
Mexico requested money for something called "The Civic Education Mexico Awareness Project":

BACKGROUND
The Mexican Confederation of Workers (CTM) has historically
been active in civic education. Recent economic problems in
Mexico indicate a clear opportunity between FTUI and the CTM
in this most important area.

OBJECTIVE
To strengthen the political action structure of the CTM through
the training of grass-roots, trade union political activists to foster
democracy in Mexico.

The CTM was virtually a component of the PRI and always supported its candidates. The proposed NED/AIFLD grant was, in fact,
a subsidy for the repressive PRI and its six decades of one party political domination of Mexico. In the third quarter of 1985, this is how
the FTUI/AIFLD summarized the work:

PROGRAM OBJECTIVE
To strengthen ties between the Confederation of Mexican Workers
(CTM) and the AFL-CIO.

RESULTS/ACCOMPLISHMENTS

Owing to unanticipated local problems, the program by mutual agreement has not gone forward.[47]

What these unanticipated local problems were is not known. Perhaps the earthquake of 1985 and the resulting political turmoil was responsible for the program being scrapped.

By 1986, AIFLD had located its office in the new CTM building in downtown Mexico City.[48] The alarming results from the 1988 election were causing grave concern there, as well as in Washington. Political forces opposed to the PRI and its programs were gaining strength. The U.S. auto companies had become major employers in Mexico, and they too were becoming concerned about the unstable political situation and worker demands for wage and benefit increases. These currents would coalesce at the Ford Motor Company's Cuautitlán Assembly Plant in 1989, where there would soon be a deadly clash between these contending forces.

7

The Coup

SUBJECT: LABOR STRIFE AT FORD PLANT

1. ON JAN. 8 VIOLENCE AT CUAUTITLAN-IZCALLI FORD MOTOR PLANT, WHICH INJURED AT LEAST TEN WORKERS (EIGHT WITH GUJQQT QQQQMQ, FORCED THE COMPANY TO TEMPORARILY SUSPEND OPERATIONS. UNION MEMBERS HAVE CHARGED THAT SEVERAL HUNDRED LABOR AGITATORS HIRED BY THE HEAD OF THE CTM AFFILIATED UNION IN THE FORD PLANT, HECTOR URIARTE, INFILTRATED THE PLANT DURING THE MORNING SHIFT WITH THE AIM OF INTIMIDATING DISSIDENT WORKERS. PASTORINO

U.S. Embassy in Mexico City cable to U.S. Secretary of State,
January 11, 1990

On April 19 and 20, 1988, a joint meeting of the AFL-CIO and the CTM was held in the twin sites of Brownsville, Texas, and Matamoros, Tamaulipas, Mexico. A few documents concerning these meetings are found in the Reuther Library at Wayne State University.[1] The records of the International Affairs Departments of the AFL-CIO and the UAW for this period are not open to researchers.

The labor federations held the first meeting at the Sheraton Plaza Royale Hotel in Brownsville. Of the 18 American labor union officials in attendance, seven were AIFLD officers, staff, or former staff. These included: AFL-CIO Secretary-Treasurer Tom Donahue (he held the same position in AIFLD); AFL-CIO Vice-Presidents Owen Bieber (UAW President) and William Bywater (International Union of Electrical Workers President), both AIFLD trustees on its board of directors; AFL-CIO Assistant Director Paul Somogyi, International Affairs Department (Somogyi had been the AIFLD country director in Mexico in the mid-1980s); William Doherty, Executive Director/AIFLD; Jesse Friedman, Deputy Director/AIFLD; and Roberto Torres who was listed as secretary-treasurer of the Inter-American

Regional Organization of Workers (ORIT-Mexico) but was also the current AIFLD country director in Mexico.[2] The meeting began with a welcome by Tom Donahue and a response by CTM General Secretary Fidel Velázquez. The meeting then moved into a discussion of the "twin plant program" and its impact on the national and local scenes. The "twin plant" was what the labor federations called the Maquiladora system, where parts were exported duty-free from the U.S. then assembled in a Mexican border plant and sent back. The second meeting duplicated the first agenda but was held at the Hotel Presidente in Matamoros with Velázquez giving the welcome and Donahue the response. The group discussed a joint communique by the AFL-CIO and the CTM.

One of the participants at the Brownsville/Matamoros meeting was Owen Bieber, President of the UAW. In 1981, he had brought the UAW back into the AFL-CIO. Strikingly, he was also a member of the AIFLD board of directors from at least 1986 to 1992. His name appears on the bottom of AIFLD/Mexico stationery during those years.[3] The Reuthers' previous problems with AIFLD had not deterred Bieber from joining the board and giving the UAW's endorsement to its efforts.

On May 20, 1988, Bieber received a letter from Paul J. Somogyi, the assistant director of the AFL-CIO International Affairs Department. At the April meeting, the unions agreed to form joint industrial groups, and Somogyi was in charge of coordinating that effort. He was very familiar with Mexico and AIFLD. A 1986 voucher found in the AIFLD files at the University of Maryland lists his name and an address on a voucher for the ORIT office, which was on the third floor in the CTM building in Mexico City. (Edificio CTM, Vallarta No. 8, TERCER PISO, Mexico D.F., Mexico 06030.) In 2019, this was still the CTM address in Mexico City. ORIT is the Spanish acronym for the Organización Regional Interamericana de Trabajadores, translated as Inter-American Regional Organization of Workers. It was the regional organization of the ICFTU based in Brussels, Belgium. The AFL-CIO maintained control when it left that organization in 1969 and again when it rejoined in 1983.[4] ORIT also had an interesting history with the CIA. Philip Agee called ORIT "a principal mechanism for CIA labor operations in Latin America."[5] Additionally, Somogyi is listed on AIFLD letterhead as the AIFLD country director in Mexico in 1986 using the same address as the ORIT one except that the CTM building identification doesn't show.[6] From these addresses, it is certain that the Somogyi, ORIT, and AIFLD occupied an office in the CTM headquarters building during the 1980s and would have had constant exposure to the CTM and information about events at Cuautitlán

After learning of this history, I contacted the retired Somogyi, who wrote to me about his past. He described his roles in AIFLD, the AFL-CIO, and the FTUI as being primarily financial/administrative. He was officially AIFLD's country program director for Mexico from 1981 to 1986, but that was primarily a mechanism to cover his salary and benefits while he served as treasurer of ORIT. He was nominated as the candidate of the AFL-CIO for the position, and while there was some opposition to his candidacy in ORIT's convention in 1981, it was a foregone conclusion that Somogyi would be elected. The CTM built a new headquarters, located on the Plaza de la Revolución, prime real estate in downtown Mexico City. It insisted that the ICFTU base its regional offices in the new building, and it became the ORIT base of operations and subsequently Somogyi's and AIFLD's.[7]

By January 1988, Somogyi was no longer the AIFLD/ORIT-Mexico country director. His name has been whited out on the AIFLD stationery for that year and replaced by Robert Torres. In 1986, Irving Brown had left the AFL-CIO for health reasons and was replaced as the director of the International Affairs Department by Tom Kahn. By 1988, Somogyi had become the assistant director of the International Affairs Department of AFL-CIO. He would go on to become the executive director of the FTUI and would remain at the head of that organization in 1996 when it transformed into a new organization.[8]

In his message to Bieber, Somogyi references a letter from AFL-CIO President Kirkland designating Bieber as the chairman of his industrial group, the Automotive/Transportation Equipment Committee, that will meet with its counterpart group affiliated with

the CTM. While the message does not identify the chairman of
the Mexican auto group by name, it is clear from other documents
that Hector Uriarte, the general secretary of the Ford CTM, was on
this committee and would have been the logical choice as the CTM
chair.[9]

Steve Beckman worked in the International Affairs Department
of the UAW between 1985 and 2007. Unaware of Bieber's position
as AIFLD trustee, he was in attendance at two cross-border union
meetings in 1988.[10] Beckman remembers the AFL-CIO meetings as
being a "farce" because nothing really happened. He recalls Uriarte as
being uninterested in the UAW and not engaged in the cross-border
process. Paul Somogyi was someone Beckman didn't have anything
in common with politically:

Regarding Somogyi and the AFL-CIO international affairs crew
in general, it's true that I was relatively new at being a part of these
activities and not aware of all the relationships and affiliations, but
I knew enough to know that these were not people I wanted to get
to know any more than was required to get through the process
that was set without our input.[11]

Concerning the CTM/AFL-CIO meetings that year, Beckman
said that the CIA was "in the air," but he couldn't discern the
relationships.

Don Stillman and Steve Beckman discussed a letter by Somogyi
dated May 20 in an inter-office communication addressed to Bieber
dated June 1, 1988. They tell Bieber that CTM does not represent
all unionized auto workers in Mexico. They explain that a national
CTM-affiliated union represents Ford and Chrysler workers at the
non-border plants and 60 percent of such GM workers. The Stillman/
Beckman analysis would make the Ford CTM the largest and best
organized CTM union in auto and the most likely to be assigned to
lead the CTM industry group. Uriarte had been appointed general
secretary of the Ford CTM following the 1987 strike. A memo from
Stillman and Beckman to Bieber on September 28, 1988, suggests
October 20, 1988, as a suitable date for the Automotive Commit-

tee to meet in Washington, DC, as Bieber would be in town that day. Beckman and Stillman had proposed Juarez, Mexico/El Paso, Texas, as a site for the Automotive Committee meeting because many auto-related industries were located in the area.[12] Beckman does not know why the participants changed the meeting to Washington, DC, or who changed it. Beckman and Stillman also suggest that the Mexicans might not be interested in a meeting because of the serious defeats they (the CTM/PRI) had suffered during the July elections. The Beckman/Stillman proposed agenda for the Automotive Committee meeting was ambitious, focusing on Maquiladora plants and union organizing.[13]

Bieber, Beckman, and at least three other Mexican CTM auto union officials were in Washington, DC, on November 11, 1988. Beckman does not know how long the Mexicans were in Washington or who else they met. Both Beckman and Mark Anderson are skeptical that an Automotive Committee sub-group meeting took place, as neither were in attendance. Mark Anderson, from the AFL-CIO International Affairs Department was also in Washington on November 11. He agreed with my speculation that the Mexicans were meeting with CIA representatives or go-betweens.[14]

This group was on the passenger list of a private jet plane that flew from Washington to San Diego on November 11. A memo from Paul Somogyi to Tom Donahue dated November 9, 1988, lists the confirmed passengers on the flight as Tom Donahue, Owen Bieber, Steve Beckman, William Doherty, Tom Kahn, who may have had to cancel at the last minute (Kahn was the international affairs director of the AFL-CIO, replacing Irving Brown), Mark Anderson, plus three or four Mexican auto workers, Victor Betancourt (GM), Jorge Rodriguez Leon (Nissan), and Hector Uriarte (Ford), plus possibly Ricardo Chavez Narvaez (Ford). The plane's amenities included an onboard continental breakfast, lunch, and a complete bar.[15] These were quite luxurious accommodations for a Mexican autoworker in his twenties like Uriarte. Beckman noted that this was the only time in his career that he was on a private jet flight, and he was not comfortable. He stared out the window much of the trip. The AFL-CIO made a special effort to fete the Mexicans and their hosts.

The five-and-a-half-hour jet flight to San Diego brought its passengers to another AFL-CIO/CTM cross-border organizing committee meeting in San Diego and Tijuana held on November 11 and 12. Tom Donahue had urged the industrial committees and the border committees organized with state AFL-CIO officers from Arizona, New Mexico, and Texas to meet before November 11.[16]

Bieber attended at least five meetings with Uriarte in 1988; two in Brownsville/Matamoros, one in Washington and two in San Diego/Tijuana. He also spent five-and-a-half hours with him on a charter jet flight. There is other evidence that Bieber knew Uriarte. Beckman would mention him in an inter-office communication to Bieber dated February 15, 1990. "It appears that the problems at the Cuautitlán and Chihuahua Ford plants have been, for the most part, resolved by a 27 percent wage increase, but Hector Uriarte has not been apprehended."[17] No explanation was necessary of who Uriarte was or why he would need to be apprehended.

The record suggests that the UAW was involved in the cross-border meetings due to their concern with auto job losses to Mexico. In the June 1 communication, Stillman and Beckman propose two arguments that the UAW can make to the CTM regarding U.S. job losses:

...first, American workers are losing jobs to Maquiladora production and shifting to alternative available jobs would mean living standard reductions comparable to those suffered by Mexican workers in recent years, and; second, preventing the loss of these jobs through cutbacks in Maquiladora operations should be offset by new American policies to address the impact of the debt crisis on Mexico. We can develop a list of specific items to be included over the next few weeks.[18]

Given these goals and their interest in unionizing the Maquiladoras, it is difficult to understand how Bieber could have believed that working with AIFLD would have advanced a trade union agenda in Mexico. In 2020, Beckman wrote to me about Doherty, "With respect to Bill Doherty, it's true that I don't remember anything outrageous he said in the brief time I listened to him talking, but it certainly didn't change what I thought of AIFLD or his adverse impact on independent trade unions in Latin America."[19] The UAW and the Reuthers had a history with AIFLD that the UAW president would have been aware of. Perhaps this was part of the problem. Bieber and Victor Reuther were in 1988 locked in a fierce internal union dispute.

Bieber and Uriarte may well have commiserated about the difficulties of being national automobile workers' union leaders during their meetings in Brownsville/Matamoros, Washington, and San Diego/Tijuana. Bieber was facing a challenge by the New Directions movement led by Jerry Tucker, a dissident assistant region director. Tucker lost his election for the position of region director by a margin of 0.16 votes out of a total of 650 cast at the 1986 UAW convention (delegates have voting power proportional to the size of their constituency). The Department of Labor found that some of the delegates were elected improperly and ordered a new election. In the new election, Tucker won with 52 percent of the vote. Aided by Victor Reuther, Tucker was challenging Bieber and his caucus on the issues of the cooperative programs that the Big Three auto companies wanted. He also advocated more rank-and-file participation in the union. Reuther and Tucker were very critical of Bieber and his caucus's tactics, which they believed to be undemocratic. The 1989 UAW convention was going to be a battlefield on these and other issues.[20]

The Battle at Ford Cuautitlán

Hector Uriarte Martinez faced his own problems with the local union at the CAP. Uriarte was from Hermosillo and had likely been a Ford employee at the new plant before taking charge of the Ford CTM union. A cable from the U.S. Embassy in Mexico City to the Secretary of State sent on January 11, 1990, describes him as follows:

URIARTE, WHO IS A PROTÉGÉ OF CTM SECRETARY GENERAL FIDEL VELASQUEZ, TOOK OVER THE LEADERSHIP OF THE UNION AFTER A 1988 STRIKE AT THE FORD PLANT. YOUNG (LATE 20'S) AND POLITI-

CALLY AMBITIOUS, URIARTE, ACCORDING TO OUR LABOR CONTACTS,
IS BEING GROOMED FOR A MORE IMPORTANT LEADERSHIP ROLE IN
THE CTM BY VELASQUEZ.[21]

(Robert Pastorino, Deputy Chief of Mission)

At the CAP, Uriarte faced a capable and united opposition to both himself and the CTM. Following their election in early 1988, the new local Executive Committee began making changes. The reform leadership made efforts to regain the losses suffered under the 1987 contract. They followed a new strategy of actively engaging the union membership in the process. The local began doing previously unheard-of things, like holding union meetings where the local Executive Committee listened to the workers.[22] Due to their efforts to institute contract changes, "the local committee of Cuautitlán had grown in fame and recognition" throughout Mexico.[23]

After being appointed as general secretary to replace Vera Ozorno in 1987, Uriarte would face re-election in July 1989 after finishing Ozorno's term of office. The local committee at CAP was planning to challenge him in this election. As the largest local union in the Mexican national Ford union, they would be able to mount a serious threat. The membership at Ford Cuautitlán was larger than those of Hermosillo and Chihuahua combined. The Cuautitlán candidates were almost certain to win.[24]

In the run-up to the July 1989 Ford CTM national election, the CAP candidates seemed to be gaining strength. Ford Motor management in Mexico acted as if they supported the candidacy of Uriarte and the CTM status quo and so made a sizable profit-sharing distribution to the workers. The payment amounted to even more because Ford did not withhold taxes from it. According to the secretary-treasurer, Escobar Briones, the payment "represented a millionaire's sum."[25] The windfall did not appear to be enough to shift the election to Uriarte.

On June 22, 1989, Ford Motor, with the tacit support of the CTM, fired four of the six members of the CAP Executive Committee. The following were discharged: Juan Ramón Ramirez, Secretary of Labor; Marco Antonio Jiménez, Secretary of Statistics; an individual whose first name was Jesús who was Secretary of Minutes; and Raul Escobar Briones, Secretary of Finances. The growing strength of the union had led to work stoppages and slowdowns. The union and the workers began to challenge Ford's hegemony in the workplace. Such workplace actions were similar to the formative days of the UAW at the plants in Flint, Michigan, where there were 170 wildcats and slowdowns in early 1937.[26]

Ford fired the local executive members at CAP (according to those workers interviewed) for supporting these work stoppages during early 1989. The firings left only General Secretary Isaac Murano and Hugo Ontiveros, Secretary of Sports, as active Ford employees. One month later, in July 1989, without significant opposition, Hector Uriarte was elected to a six-year term as the head of the Ford CTM national union.[27] Just a few months before, Uriarte had joined two other Mexican union officials in the trip to Washington, DC, where they met with AFL-CIO and AIFLD officials and perhaps others. With the firings and Uriarte's election, the conflict at Ford Cuautitlán began in earnest.

The June discharges sparked the formation of the Ford Workers Democratic Movement (FWDM). Mexican labor law prohibits arbitrary firings of union leaders. Still, with the legal system firmly under control of the PRI, the fired Executive Committee members did not count on the government approving their legal demands for reinstatement. The dismissals had created a climate of fear in the plant. Many workers believed that if Ford could fire the union leaders, they too could be next to go. The discharged Executive Committee members set up a camp in front of the assembly plant. The FWDM started a rank-and-file newspaper called *En La Línea* (*On the Line*, a reference to the assembly line). The paper contained information about working conditions at CAP and general information about the labor movement.[28]

The activists initiated a new tactic to build the fledgling FWDM and create support for the fired leaders. The wives of the fired Executive Committee members came to the plant with cookie jars and asked for donations for the movement. The courage displayed by the women in publicly standing up to Ford and the CTM emboldened many workers. They knew that as long as the sacked leaders kept fighting for reinstatement, Ford would be reluctant to fire more workers. With this act, the majority of workers inside the plant began to support the fired leaders. The women's actions marked a turning point in the battle with Ford and the CTM. Firings, a tactic the CTM had used for decades to control dissent, was failing.[29]

The end of July saw another new method taken up for building the movement. Two of the fired Executive Committee members, Marco Antonio Jiménez Cervantes and Juan Ramón, started a hunger strike. It began in August and would continue until September 13. The hunger strikers initially stationed themselves in front of what were the general offices of the Ford Motor Company in Mexico City and later transferred the location to the monument of the Ángel de la Independencia. El Ángel was built in 1910 to commemorate the centennial anniversary of the Mexican War of Independence from Spain. The hunger strike made it into the newspapers and on to some of the broadcast media outlets, and then it steered the press to the factory where they interviewed the fired leaders.

The hunger strike was not enough to make Ford relent on the discharges, however. Law enforcement removed the workers from El Ángel. According to a study in the *British Medical Journal*, hunger strikers begin to feel severe starvation symptoms after around 35 to 40 days. That's when many develop confusion, hallucinations, and convulsions. Shortly after, they begin to experience organ failure, leading to death directly or to fatal heart attacks.[30] After 38 days, the FWDM called off the hunger strike. The hunger strike action brought the Ford conflict to the public's attention. The movement gained a voice. The demands of the workers at Cuautitlán were kept alive.

The fired Executive Committee continued to act as the leadership of the local union throughout 1989. The workers in the plant rejected the national Executive Committee's attempts to direct the local, as it was clear that they had gained office through the firings of their potential opponents. In December, a major problem developed in the plant. In the spring, Ford had made profit-sharing payments to the workers but did not withhold the taxes, in an effort to benefit the election of Uriarte. In December, Ford de Mexico withheld those taxes from paychecks and also from a year-end bonus. It resulted in tiny paychecks and reduced annual bonus payments. Some workers received nothing, and others were told that they actually owed money to Ford. A U.S. Embassy cable from January 13, 1990, explains:

A SENIOR FORD COMPANY REPRESENTATIVE BRIEFED US ON THE DISPUTE FROM THE COMPANY'S PERSPECTIVE, ... URIARTE HAS BEEN ACCUSED OF DIVERTING DIVIDEND PAYMENTS AND CHRISTMAS BONUS FUNDS TO A UNION ACCOUNT. COMPLICATING THE PROBLEM, ACCORDING TO FORD, WAS THE COMPANY'S OWN POOR JUDGEMENT ON THE ISSUE OF BONUS AND DIVIDEND PAYMENTS. ACCORDING TO FORD, PROFIT SHARING PAYMENTS ARE DOWN, AND THE CTM HAD REQUESTED THAT TAXES ON THESE FUNDS AND CHRISTMAS BONUSES BE DEDUCTED AT YEARS-END, A DECISION THAT WAS APPARENTLY NEVER COMMUNICATED TO THE WORKERS. AS A RESULT, FORD IS BEING ACCUSED BY WORKERS OF BEING IN LEAGUE WITH URIARTE'S PLANS TO DEFRAUD WORKERS. REDUCED PAYCHECKS PROMPTED UNION UNREST, WHICH BEGAN DECEMBER 22.

(Robert Pastorino, Deputy Chief of Mission)[31]

Ford had reached the agreement about withholding taxes at the end of the year with the national CTM, to whom none of the workers were listening. They had since fired four of the six Executive Committee members, and communication with the workers at CAP was at a minimum. Assembly plants are fertile soil for rumors, and many workers believed Uriarte had diverted their money to CTM accounts. On December 21, 1989, the workers walked off their jobs and went outside. They blocked the federal highway near the plant and called the media to air their grievances. They demanded the restoration of their salaries and bonuses. The workers picked a commission of 22 representatives to assist the local Executive Committee in negotiations on the issue.[32]

Ford refused to negotiate with the commission, saying they only recognized the authority of the national CTM Executive Committee. As a result of Ford's refusal to negotiate, the local committee then decided to call for the CTM to meet with them. On December

22, the expanded leadership group went to Edificio CTM, Vallarta No. 8, the CTM building in Mexico City, and requested a meeting with Secretary General Fidel Velázquez Sánchez. Perhaps they walked past the AIFLD office on the third floor. A spokesman for the confederation initially told them that they would not meet with the local Executive Committee, but when they found they could not get the workers to forsake the local committee, Velázquez agreed to meet the group.

In that meeting, the CAP workers put forward the demands for a partial payment of the salaries, a year-end bonus, reinstatement of the fired Executive Committee members, and a new democratic congress of the CTM. Secretary General Fidel Velázquez agreed to meet with the local committee again on January 8. The Cuautitlán workers continued to refuse to recognize the authority of Hector Uriarte and the National Ford CTM.[33]

Like U.S. assembly plants, Mexican operations have a holiday shutdown from Christmas through New Year's Day. The workers agreed to return to work on January 3, 1990.

Threats of violence had been a standard CTM tactic. Those forces in the plant opposed to the democratic movement at Cuautitlán continued to follow that path. Jaime Flores Durán, a leader, was targeted in December before the break. At the end of a work shift, two "vigilantes" led Flores Durán to a scrap heap on the periphery of the Ford complex and told him to start digging a ditch. These men were employees of a private company contracted by Ford to provide plant security. They began an interrogation, asking, "Are you a Marxist? Communist? Who is with you?" They asked him repeatedly if he knew what the ditch was for, implying it was a grave for him, threatening his life. These company-affiliated thugs demanded he work overtime, but he refused, left the plant, and told some fellow workers about it. They resolved to be ready for more of this kind of thing in the coming days.

The next day, the plant security men returned to Flores Durán's worksite and took him back to the ditch near the scrap heap. When his fellow worker and activist Gabriel Abogado found him missing from his usual workstation, Abogado organized a work stoppage of the assembly lines. Flores Durán took advantage of the disruption caused by the work stoppage to escape back into the assembly area and tell the others what had happened.[34]

On January 3, work resumed at the CAP. On Friday, January 5, local leaders came to the plant to hand out a leaflet calling on workers to go to a scheduled meeting with the CTM's general secretary, Velázquez.[35] Soon, about 30 thugs, protected by municipal and federal highway police, attacked six workers handing out the leaflets in the vicinity of the plant; Marco Antonio Jiménez, Jaime Peña Silva, Antonio Galinda, Alfredo Arista, Francisco Ferrusca, and José Sánchez. All were members of the commission or the local Executive Committee. These leaders were then taken away. When the workers in the plant learned of the disappearances, they stopped work and halted production but remained in the plant. They conducted a sit-down strike and barricaded themselves in the Ford complex. The organizers in the plant contacted the Mexican Secretary of the Interior, the National Front Against Repression, a human rights group, and the Mexico City newspapers to report the disappearances.[36] In the afternoon, the Ford workers located the leaders. The kidnappers had released them at the Tlalnepantla police station. By 6:00 p.m., the six were free, and the workers left the plant for the weekend.

The forces that had planned the January 5 attack did not identify themselves. Their group may have included individuals from Ford, the CTM, Mexican gangsters, and some in law enforcement who may have blocked traffic. A question remains as to who could pull such a group together.[37] The work stoppage came as a surprise, and pulled Ford publicly into the dispute. Over the weekend, the shadowy grouping would formulate plans for a new attack.

On the evening of January 5, the Executive Committee and shop floor leaders met at Antonio Galindo's house (Galindo had been one of the six shanghaied that day) to discuss the January 8 meeting that Velázquez had agreed before Christmas to hold. The meeting with Velázquez would never take place because the workers would instead meet with violence on a still larger scale.

The local Executive Committee reconvened on Sunday evening, January 7, when they learned that strange things were going on in the CAP. Unknown people were entering the plant. Ford personnel were providing them with uniforms and Ford ID badges.[38] The workers in the plant told the committee it looked like these individuals were going to be present at the start of work on Monday morning. The Executive Committee prepared tactics to use the following morning for what was shaping up to be a confrontation.[39]

Outside the Cuautitlán plant, a group of 300 *golpeadores* gathered, to borrow the term used by the Mexican press. The word translates into English as hitters or batterers, but it implies a substantive purpose. They began arriving around midnight on buses identified as "Gregorio Velázquez's"—Fidel's brother's company.[40] They were wearing Ford uniforms and ID badges and were armed with clubs, pistols, and machine guns.[41] They were under the tactical command of Wallace de la Mancha.[42]

Mancha's national origins are unknown. It was speculated at different times that he could have been Cuban, Guatemalan, Puerto Rican, or Mexican.[43] Mancha was a participant in the violence of Mexican unions on behalf of the CTM for many years. But none of his previous actions had reached the level of what he was about to initiate at CAP. Before November 1988, he had not attracted much attention. In the wake of the PRI election fraud of that summer, he would soon become notorious for an attack on striking workers at the Babcock and Wilcox company where he allegedly shouted, "Wallace de la Mancha has arrived, you bastards."[44] Mancha's thugs shot a journalist from *La Jornada* during the violence there, and two other people were killed.[45]

Mancha described himself as "short and ugly." He wore jewels, a bracelet, a gold watch, a nicely pressed sports suit, and cologne.[46] His relationship with the CTM was unclear. At times Fidel Velazquez had denied knowing him. Mancha recruited his soldiers from gang members or young people who wanted an industrial job and thought serving with Mancha could provide one.[47] Uriarte's involvement may have been critical in recruiting these *golpeadores* for the Ford Cuautitlán operation. They would have needed to be assured that there would be no retaliation on the part of Ford or the Mexican government. Uriarte would seemingly have been essential to coordinating the assault with the Ford plant. He knew where to get Ford uniforms and ID badges from his previous employment and contacts.[48]

The expense and logistics of pulling together 300 men in the middle of the night, arming them with clubs, firearms, and even some machine guns, providing communication equipment, getting them in Ford uniforms, and then securing each a company ID badge were daunting. These tasks far outstripped the financial and organizational capacity of the CTM. The Ford Cuautitlán factory complex consisted of five buildings: an engine plant, a foundry, a paint building, a body build shop, and a final assembly plant. The large group of *golpeadores* was divided up, with a trusted lieutenant assigned to each area to ensure that all instructions were carried out.[49]

Wallace would not go into the complex himself but placed a trusted lieutenant in charge, Guadalupe Uribe Guevara. Uribe had been working for Mancha as a shock trooper since 1974.[50] In addition to being an associate of Wallace de la Mancha, he was also a minor CTM official in Mexico City. Uribe brought along his two sons to assist in the venture.[51]

After several witnesses claimed to have seen him outside the CAP on January 8, Mancha wrote a letter to the editor of the newspaper *La Jornada* which was printed on January 10, denying he was involved in the attack.[52] The amount of attention Mancha was attracting, and the publicity the Ford battle drew, would not sit well with his employers. Wallace de la Mancha was 58 years old on the morning of January 8. He would be dead at 59.[53]

Some witnesses said they observed Hector Uriarte with the *golpeadores* on January 8. The CTM's attorney, Juan Moisés Calleja, a former minister of the Supreme Court of Justice, stated that he didn't believe that authorities would find or arrest Uriarte. Calleja told the press that he was prepared to testify he had been with Uriarte on the morning of the shooting.[54] Another account has Uriarte give Mancha the signal to enter the plant complex over the phone, which seems more likely.[55] Velazquez was 89 years old on January 8, and many suspect Calleja and other staffers were running the CTM.[56]

The activists reported for work on January 8, expecting trouble. When reporting for work at the beginning of a shift, workers in a Ford assembly plant first go to a small coverall locker to retrieve a clean pair of coveralls. That morning ten leaders of the January 5 work stoppage found that the locks on these lockers had been changed, preventing them from getting coveralls. A notice was posted on each of their lockers telling them to report to the locksmith to be assigned new ones. When they approached the locksmith, they could see unusual characters loitering in the area. All but one of them decided to go directly to their workstations. That unfortunate worker was beaten.[57]

When the rest of the workforce arrived for the morning shift on January 8, they found 300 strangers on the assembly lines. These were easily identifiable as not being genuine Ford employees because they wore tennis shoes instead of the required leather shoes, and they were wearing the Ford ID badges around their necks. Ford employees would keep them in their pockets so they wouldn't get caught on things, come loose, and be lost. Many of the *golpeadores* were drunk or on drugs. The intruders immediately started to harass and intimidate the workers. The leaders had prepared for this event, and the workers picked up tools and organized themselves to fight back. The workers knew the plant and outmaneuvered the *golpeadores*, who felt cornered, took out their guns, and opened fire. A voice came over the company loudspeaker, telling the workers to do as they were told.[58] Escobar Briones remembers the voice on the loudspeaker saying, "Do not run; those are only blanks."[59] Nine workers would go down wounded, one of them fatally.

In an interview nine years later, a reporter asked Uribe if he had trouble obeying an order to shoot the Ford workers. He said, "No, there were no orders. The conditions were met—I had to defend myself. I didn't want to fight, but that's how things happened."[60]

The local leaders notified the press about the incident, and a radio station began broadcasting reports on it almost immediately. When the wives of the workers heard about the injuries, they went to the factory, joining a throng of reporters and onlookers who had gathered outside the plant. Ford security guards had closed the gates and pre-

vented ambulances from coming in. The women began pushing on
the fence gate surrounding the complex, and they managed to push
the fence down and open the gate allowing the ambulances and press
to enter the factory along with them. With the fence down, most
of the Ford management fled, leaving a small contingent behind.[61]

In the ensuing turmoil, and with the rapid retreat of the main
body of *golpeadores*, three of their number (Armando Salgado Jara-
millo, Constancio Escobar Hernández, and Juan Enrique Hernández
Avalos) were separated and detained by the workers.[62] These had
their hands tied tightly behind their backs with wire, and the workers
decided to lynch them as an example to others. When Ortiz Mon-
asterio from the Human Rights Department of the Secretary of the
Interior arrived at the scene, they changed their minds and turned
the *golpeadores* over to the police, who detained them. The police
would only prosecute the three captured thugs if someone would
file charges, so several of the CAP workers went to the police station
and did so.[63]

According to Ford Motor's account, given to the U.S. Embassy in
the immediate aftermath, the *golpeadores* had entered the CAP with
police, whom Ford had requested come to the plant that Monday
morning:

5. SEVERAL DAYS AGO, FORD BROUGHT LEGAL ACTION TO EJECT
SOME DISSIDENTS FROM PLANT GROUNDS WHO WERE NOT FORD
EMPLOYEES. ON JAN. 8, STATE POLICE ARRIVED TO EVICT THESE
INDIVIDUALS, AND DURING THE SECOND SHIFT, A NUMBER OF
ALLEGED NON-UNION/NON-FORD EMPLOYEES INFILTRATED THE
SHIFT CHANGE AND USED VIOLENCE TO INTIMIDATE WORKERS
AND SHUT DOWN THE PLANT, UNHINDERED BY THE POLICE
PRESENCE. NON-COMPANY WORKERS ARE ALLEGED TO BE MEMBERS
OR SUPPORTERS OF THE REVOLUTIONARY WORKERS PARTY (PRT) A
TROTSKYITE POLITICAL PARTY WHICH LOST ITS LEGAL REGISTRA-
TION IN JULY, 1988.[64]

(Robert Pastorino, Deputy Chief of Mission)

Ford de Mexico's upper management demonstrated a great deal
of confusion in this meeting with the Embassy officials and seemed

to believe that the *golpeadores* had been PRT members. It is unlikely that Ford lied to the Embassy, as the newspapers would dispel this interpretation within a few days. This cable seems to exclude the possibility that Ford's upper management played a significant role in planning the violent attack. Ford Motor had not used violence against their workers in their plants since the infamous "Battle of the Overpass" in 1937. In the widely photographed encounter, Henry Ford's security goons pummeled Walter Reuther and UAW staffers attempting to hand out leaflets to workers at the Dearborn, Michigan, complex. The press photographed the bloodied UAW men, and the pictures were published around the country, resulting in what must be a contender for the worst public-relations disaster of the twentieth century. The idea that Ford management would have agreed to gangsters and the CTM coming into the plant to commit violence against its workers is therefore not credible.

The question remains: why did Ford call police into the plant on January 8, as they reported to the Embassy a few days later, and why were signs placed on the uniform lockers instructing the local leaders to go to the locksmith? The notices on the lockers indicate Ford's participation, as only Ford management would know which worker was assigned to which locker. A likely explanation would be that after enduring two unauthorized strikes in the last few weeks, Ford had decided to fire the strike leaders after the work stoppage on the previous Friday, and had called the police to remove them from the plant. Ford put the notices on the uniform lockers to get the leaders to go to a location where their removal could quickly take place. The ten workers who had notices placed on their lockers had been organizers of the January 5 work stoppage. By preventing the leaders from reporting to their workstations, management hoped to avoid another strike over their discharges. Ford would have had to notify the CTM of the firings, and Uriarte would have been privy to that information. The CIA had informants in Latin American police stations in major cities. They could have coordinated the *golpeadores'* entry into the plant alongside the police.

In 1991, Ford Motor told the UAW bargaining chairman at the Ford assembly plant in St. Paul, Minnesota, Ted LaValley, that they had agreed to allow a group to come into the plant on January 8 to "talk" with the workers.[65] Ford may have hoped that this group could have dissuaded the workers from a new work stoppage in response to further firings. Ford may have assigned people to the plant loudspeaker system in anticipation of a work stoppage when the workers learned of the leader's dismissal. This seems to be the best explanation for Ford management's role in the January 8 events, though there were likely CTM supporters and individuals in the complex who could have been bribed to play a different role. If U.S. ambassador John Negroponte or CIA station chief Vincent Shields had advocated for some retaliatory action against the FWDM/PRT, Ford would have agreed to a group coming into the plant. Ford Motor Company has not responded to several requests for comment for this book.

Concurrently, the CTM, a labor federation known for its servility and obeisance to foreign employers, would not have entered an employer's factory, shot its employees, damaged property, caused a long strike, and loss of production unless it was quite sure it would be protected from retaliation. Freedom from retaliation was something that the CIA was in a position to guarantee.

The workers had survived a well-financed, violent attack on their movement. To remain safe, they decided to secure the entrances and stay in the plant. As night fell they notified the press of their demands: 1) No more attacks on the factory; 2) Those responsible for the crimes committed on January 8 must be punished; 3) Full pay for the lost salaries due to the pay withholdings of December; 4) Reinstatement of the fired Executive Committee members; and 5) A national democratic congress to be held on union rights. In support of these demands, the workers began a strike, and after determining the only bargaining power they had was control of the factory complex, the workers decided they would occupy the plant.[66]

8

The Strike

IN OF ITSELF, THE FORD DISPUTE IS A POTENTIALLY SERIOUS PROBLEM FOR PRESIDENT SALINAS'S EFFORTS TO ATTRACT INVESTMENT AND BUSINESS TO MEXICO. FOR VELAZQUEZ AND THE CTM IT MAY BE A REFLECTION OF THE INABILITY OF THE CTM GERONTOCRACY TO EFFECTIVELY DEAL AND ADAPT TO AN INEXORABLY CHANGING LABOR SECTOR IN MEXICO. ON THE OTHER HAND, FIDEL HAS FACED AND SUCCESSFULLY RESOLVED SITUATIONS OF THIS TPE [sic] SCORES OF TIMES IN THE PAST. END COMMENT NEGROPONTE.

Department of State Embassy Cable from Ambassador John Negroponte, January 19, 1990, DoS F-2016-16693 C06337074

In 1990, the Cold War was nearing its end, and American workers were about to reap the harvest of the AFL-CIO alliance with U.S. foreign policy and the CIA.

Lane Kirkland had decided to make another attempt to bring the CTM into some agreement that would address U.S. job losses resulting from low wages in Mexico. With the ambassador to Mexico, John Negroponte, Presidents Salinas and Bush had settled on a free trade agreement, and it would take legislative form in 1992. A free trade agreement with Mexico would provide ammunition for Kirkland's critics and might even lead to a challenge to his leadership at the 1995 AFL-CIO convention. The AFL-CIO had developed a close bond with the CTM over three decades of battling communists, socialists, and their allies, and it was worth another effort to try to preserve that. The AFL-CIO/CTM built a close relationship mainly through AIFLD, who had assigned William Doherty Jr., Jesse Friedman, Paul Somogyi, and Robert Torres to Mexico City. In 1990, the AFL-CIO held another joint meeting with the CTM in Tijuana, with Kirkland attending instead of Secretary-Treasurer Tom Donahue. CTM General Secretary Fidel Velázquez would also be in attendance. One member of Kirkland's staff, Mark Anderson, would later recount:

> And it was at the Tijuana meeting where we were talking about the maquilas and the need to improve labor rights and what not where the CTM were telling us that they don't want to be party to anything that would increase wages in the maquilas because it would detract, they thought, from investment. Whereupon Kirkland told me, he said to me, "that's it, I don't want to have anything to do with them you deal with them, but not me," and walked out of the room and flew home.[1]

Early in the day on January 8, Fidel Velázquez held a press conference to blame the dissidents at the Ford plant for the violence that had just taken place, and announced he would not meet with local leaders that day as he had agreed to do before Christmas. Uriarte denied any responsibility for the violence, assigning blame to the Party of the Democratic Revolution (PRD) or the PRT.[2]

The CAP was initially occupied by 2,000 workers (and many of their wives) out of about 2,500 who reported for work on the day shift. That number would ebb and flow as the occupation went on. The workers created a maintenance commission to take care of the factory, so that it would be in condition to start production again when needed. The press was allowed to check that the strikers had done no damage or sabotage to Ford equipment. Messages of solidarity began to pour into the plant from other unions and workers in different factories. Teachers with preschool children came to the factory and gave their lunches to the workers.[3] They received messages of support from the Ford local unions at Hermosillo and Chihuahua.[4] Contributions of food and supplies from supporters allowed the occupation to continue.[5]

The most gravely wounded of the nine shot was Cleto Nigmo Urbina. One worker, Manuel Romero, told the journal *Proceso* that he saw a gunman shoot Nigmo in the stomach at close range, causing him to fall to the ground. When he tried to get up, the gunman held his gun with both hands and shot him again. Romero said a supervisor helped him lift Nigmo and take him to the infirmary.[6] Some of the activists went to the hospital with Nigmo when the ambulances finally got to him. They stayed there on January 8, 9, and 10. Nigmo never recovered consciousness and died on January 10. The Cuautitlán workers reached an agreement with Nigmo's family to hold his memorial service at the occupied Cuautitlán factory complex on January 11. His body was taken to the plant where after midnight, co-workers formed a human chain on both sides of a roadway leading to the factory. As his body passed by, some workers hoisted banners proclaiming "Uriarte assesino"—Uriarte is a murderer.[7] A Jesuit priest from the Centro de Reflexión Laboral (Workplace Reflection Center) delivered the funeral mass. Gabriel Abogado, one of the Ford activists, told the gathering that they would continue the struggle with the memory of the martyr Cleto ever present. The workers demanded that the government prosecute Uriarte, Mancha, and Uribe for Nigmo's murder.[8]

An Embassy cable sent on April 13, 1991, noting a protest by UAW 879 officials at the Cuautitlán plant, gives some background on what happened in January 1990. About Cleto Nigmo, the cable says:

4. COMMENT: AN INTERESTING FOOTNOTE, IF ACCURATE, IS THE COMMENT BY A FORD OFFICIAL THAT THE FORD WORKER, CLETO NIGMO, WHO DIED JAN. 10, 1990 AS A RESULT OF WOUNDS DURING THE JAN. 8, 1990 INCIDENT WAS NEITHER A CTM OR UNION DISSIDENT ACTIVIST BUT A WORKER BYSTANDER WHOSE BAD LUCK IT WAS TO CATCH A STRAY BULLET. SINCE THEN THE COR [Confederation of Revolutionary Workers] ACTIVISTS HAVE MADE HIM THEIR MARTYR. END COMMENT.[9]

(Robert Pastorino, Deputy Chief of Mission)

Nigmo was not one of the union activists, but his murder was not "bad luck." Ford's upper management was not witness to the events, and their comments to the Embassy were undoubtedly intended to deflect their culpability in the death. Ford officials went to the hospital themselves, and the Cuautitlán workers present observed them making offers to Nigmo's family to pay for the funeral, make sure medical bills would be paid, and take care of the family's needs in the future. All of this was likely an attempt to avoid further scandal.[10]

Ford representatives met with Velázquez, the general secretary of the CTM, Labor Secretary Arsenio Farell Cubillas, and Commerce Secretary Jaime Serra Puche on January 10. Velázquez subsequently met with Salinas. The Ford representatives told the Embassy that Velázquez and Serra advised them to petition the Federal Conciliation and Arbitration Board for permission to terminate the contract with the union, and Serra and Velázquez hinted strongly that a favorable labor court ruling would be forthcoming. With a favorable ruling, the company could legally dismiss all or part of Ford's 4,000 workers at CAP. While Ford believed this would be a good strategy for getting rid of dissidents in the workforce (they estimated that there were between 200–400), it didn't address removing the workers occupying the plant. The Mexican government informed Ford that they passed the problem of evicting dissidents occupying the plant to Interior Minister Gutierrez Barrios.[11]

The company was looking for additional help from the Embassy:

FORD REPRESENTATIVES WERE ALSO ADVISED BY SECGEN VELASQUEZ TO SEEK A MEETING WITH PRESIDENT SALINAS ON THE LABOR DISPUTE; ... INSTEAD, FORD HAS NOW SUGGESTED THAT THE AMBASSADOR [Negroponte] TAKE THE OPPORTUNITY TO RAISE THE ISSUE WITH SALINAS IN AN INFORMAL MANNER AT THE EARLIEST OPPORTUNITY. THEY ARE AWARE THAT A PROMINENT EMBASSY ROLE IN THIS DISPUTE COULD TRANSFORM THIS FROM A LABOR ISSUE TO A POLITICAL ONE INVOLVING OUR BILATERAL RELATIONSHIP. THROUGH ALL THIS, VELASQUEZ WARNED FORD THAT THE UNION WOULD OF COURSE HAVE TO TAKE AN ANTI FORD PUBLIC POSITION, WHILE IT IS SEEKING TO CONTROL THE UNION AND WORK BEHIND THE SCENES WITH THE GOVERNMENT FOR A SOLUTION.[12]

The events that unfolded at CAP set off a contentious debate in the Mexican Congress. The PPS, the PRD, the PARM, and the PAN accused the CTM and the Ford Motor Company of having been responsible for the violence.[13] Blas Chumacero, the second highest official in the CTM, blamed Ford saying, "The events were provoked by people from outside the union. Let us speak with clarity: the company is responsible and can always find people at its service for these kinds of illegal acts."[14]

On January 17, Silvestre González Portillo, the head of the National Union of Automobile Workers, CTM (the Ford union was an affiliate of this organization), held a press conference. He called on the Secretary of the Interior to prosecute Wallace de la Mancha for criminal attacks on workers on several occasions, the Cuautitlán attack being the latest.[15] It is difficult to imagine a scenario where the CTM had been the architect of the plan to kidnap the local leaders on January 5 and then assault the plant complex on January 8, and that then this press conference was allowed to take place. Wallace de la Mancha was doing his best to deny any connection to the January 8 attack.[16]

Ford filed with the Federal Conciliation and Arbitration Board the papers necessary to terminate the labor contract, but learned that it would take ten days for the judgment to be delivered, meaning there could be no court decision until January 26. The Mexican government told Ford that they were determined to seek a solution before January 20. Ford later informed the Salinas government that the plant occupation had jeopardized a planned 800-million-peso investment at the Chihuahua engine facility.[17]

The Embassy cable of January 13 ended with this:

10. COMMENT: MANY OF THE ELEMENTS OF THIS DISPUTE REMAIN UNCLEAR AND UNSUBSTANTIATED, PARTICULARLY URIARTE'S ROLE. FROM OUR VANTAGE POINT, VELASQUEZ APPEARS TO BE USING THE THREAT OF A CONTRACT TERMINATION AS LEVERAGE TO BRING UNION MEMBERS UNDER CONTROL, WHILE AT THE SAME TIME ACTING AS DEFENDER OF THEIR JOBS. IF THIS STRATEGY WORKS, WILEY [sic] VELASQUEZ WILL HAVE SAVED THE HIDE OF A FAVORED UNION LIEUTENANT [Uriarte] AT LEAST FOR THE MOMENT. (CTM HAS ADMITTED TO FORD THEY HAVE TO BACK THEIR MAN IN THE PRESENT CIRCUMSTANCES, BUT THAT HE WILL LIKELY BE QUIETLY SHELVED OR TRANSFERRED IN THE NEAR FUTURE.) THE DISPUTE REMAINS A POLITICAL HOT POTATO. (DRAFTED:POL:VMAYER) PASTORINO.[18]

Ford executives flew in from Dearborn, Michigan, and together with the President of Ford de Mexico, Nicholas Scheele, met with Salinas, Labor Secretary Farell, Interior Secretary Barrios, and Commerce Secretary Serra on Friday, January 19.[19] (British-born Scheele would go on to become COO of Ford Motor.) The meetings continued over the weekend. The government officials told the Ford executives they would end the plant occupation on Monday the January 22. They encouraged Ford to move ahead with the petition to terminate the collective bargaining agreement with the Federal Conciliation and Arbitration Board, but warned them not to dismiss large numbers of workers, as authorities would arrest people with links to the CTM for the attack. Salinas and his cabinet secretaries told Ford that the public might see the workers occupying the plant as having been justified in their actions.[20]

On January 21, the workers inside the Cuatitlán complex heard that 200 prosecutors from the State of Mexico were gathering with plans to take over the factory the next day. The Ford workers occupying the plant discussed whether they should surrender the plant and leave or make the authorities evict them. Many felt that surrender would send a bad signal and that they should fight to the end. The majority supported turning the plant back to the authorities and leaving with their dignity intact. They decided that they would wait in the plant until the police arrived but then peacefully end the occupation. Between 200 and 300 workers remained in the CAP that night.[21]

At about 6:00 a.m. on the foggy morning of January 22, 1990, riot police surrounded the plant, then broke through the fence and entered the factory.[22] The workers had agreed that when the police entered the complex, they would concentrate at the main entrance. According to plan, they assembled at the entrance and then received the prosecutors with an ovation. A representative of the workers asked the authorities to do a full inspection to verify that they had done no damage to Ford property. When the inspection was completed, the workers all walked outside. The 15-day occupation of CAP had come to an end.[23]

When they left the factory, the activists set up a camp outside the Ford complex to serve as an organizing center to keep their demands alive. As many as 1,800 workers visited the site daily. When some workers returned to work, they gave money to support the camp operations. Every Friday, volunteers would get on the buses leaving the factory and solicit contributions. These funds were used to buy food for the camp, draft flyers, and give assistance to those who hadn't returned to work.[24]

On January 22, while police were entering the CAP to remove the workers occupying it, Guadalupe Uribe Guevara, two of his sons, and seven others were arrested for manslaughter in the killing of Cleto Nigmo and on weapons charges. The three *golpeadores* caught and turned over to the police on January 8 were released on bail on January 12. Some press sources reported that the CTM had paid their bail.[25] An Embassy cable, dated April 12, 1991, says the three were released for lack of evidence.[26] The three told police that Hector Uriarte and Guadalupe Uribe hired them.[27] The Embassy believed that the government issued an arrest warrant for Hector Uriarte Martinez. The Embassy had unconfirmed reports that Uriarte was already in police custody.[28] If a warrant for Uriarte had been issued, he was never detained. The Embassy cable of April 12, 1991, states, "HECTOR URIATE, THE THEN FORD CTM NATIONAL CHAIRMAN, WAS SUBPOENAED FOR QUESTIONING BUT NEVER APPEARED. HE REMAINS ON THE CTM PAYROLL, BUT IS NOT ACTIVE IN FORD AFFAIRS."[29]

The violence against the Ford workers continued on January 27. Ricardo Cervantes and Héctor Hernández were handing out leaflets and collecting donations for the movement when they were kidnapped and beaten by six men and a woman. After several hours they were released in the same neighborhood where they had been taken. Cervantes and Hernández were told to "quit making a fuss."[30]

Ford announced in the press that they would fire the striking workers if they did not report to work in 24 hours. On January 31, the Ford CTM placed an advertisement in the newspaper urging workers to return to work, warning those who didn't that they would be subject to discipline.[31] The Embassy cabled Washington on February 1 that:

(U) IN THE WAKE OF THE PLANT REOPENING AND THE WARRANTS
ISSUED FOR THE ARREST OF INDIVIDUALS CHARGED WITH THE JAN.
8 VIOLENCE AT THE PLANT, THE CTM IS STILL WRESTLING WITH THE
PROBLEM OF IMPOSING DISCIPLINE OVER ITS FORD UNION MEMBERS.
CTM FORD UNION LEADER, HECTOR URIARTE, WENT INTO HIDING
AFTER A WARRANT FOR HIS ARREST WAS ISSUED SUBSEQUENTLY, CTM
SECGEN FIDEL VELASQUEZ DECIDED TO APPOINT CHIHUAHUA FORD
PLANT LEADER JUAN JOSE SOSA AS INTERIM FORD UNION CHIEF IN
URIARTE'S STEAD. UNION DISSIDENTS PROTESTED THIS ACTION AND
LED BY RAUL ESCOBAR [Briones], CONTINUE TO PRESS VELASQUEZ
WITH THEIR DEMAND THAT THE CTM ELECTIONS AT FORD PLANTS
IN CHIHUAHUA, HERMOSILLO AND CUAUTITLAN BE HELD TO ELECT
NEW FORD UNION LEADERSHIP AS A CONDITION FOR RETURNING
TO WORK. THEY HAVE ALSO DEMANDED THAT THE CTM RECOGNIZE
THE DISSIDENT LEADERSHIP AS THE UNION REPRESENTATIVE IN
ANY CONTRACT NEGOTIATIONS WITH FORD. IF THEIR DEMANDS
ARE NOT MET DISSIDENTS HAVE THREATENED TO SECEDE FROM THE
CTM AND JOIN THE CONFEDERATION OF REVOLUTIONARY WORKERS
(COR), AN APPROXIMATELY 30,000 MEMBER UNION...[32]

On the same day (January 31), the Embassy reported that between
500 and 600 protesters were demonstrating in front of CTM headquarters. The majority of workers had little interest in returning to
work until they recovered their lost wages and year-end bonuses,
Ford rehired the local Executive Committee, problems with the
CTM were addressed, and the suspected murderers punished.[33]

On February 6, a big march from Cuautitlán to Zócalo was held.
The march wound along the Quertétaro highway for 60 kilometers
(37 miles) and took six hours. Along the route, people turned out
to greet the marchers and gave them water and fruit. They rallied
at Zócalo, calling on Salinas to address their claims.[34] Ambassador
Negroponte reported to Washington that,

THE DISSIDENTS HAVE DEMONSTRATED UNEXPECTED TENACITY.
INCLUDING THE ORGANIZATION OF LARGE VISIBLE MARCH ON
FEB. 6 TO THE CITY TO PROTEST AT THE NATIONAL PALACE. THIS
COMBINATION HAS THE POTENTIAL FOR LABOR VIOLENCE WHEN

FORD ANNOUNCES ITS DISMISSALS THUS PUTTING THE QUESTION
OF LABOR UNREST ON CENTER STAGE...[35]

The struggle at Cuautitlán was now receiving international attention, and the Ford workers were getting letters from unions in the
U.S., Canada, Germany, Argentina, and Brazil.[36]
Ambassador Negroponte visited the Ford Hermosillo Assembly
plant on February 9, and though there were rumors of a possible
protest, it didn't materialize. When workers at the Ford Chihuahua
engine plant accepted a new contract that included a 27 percent
wage increase, the chance of a strike there was ended.[37]
The Ford Cuautitlán plant was only partially operational on
February 8, with about 1,000 workers (out of a pre-strike total
of 3,800) on the production lines.[38] Ford was determined to fire
between 600 and 1,000 workers. The Embassy reported that an end
to the month-long strike remained elusive. They expressed concerns
to Washington about the effects of the strike:

MORE WORRYING IS THE STRIKE'S IMPACT ON MEXICO'S IMAGE AS A
PLACE TO DO BUSINESS. A SENIOR FORD REPRESENTATIVE HAS TOLD
US THAT AS THE STRIKE DRAGGED ON, HIS COMPANY HAS BECOME
INCREASINGLY NERVOUS ABOUT PROPOSED EXPANSION PLANS FOR
ITS CHIHUAHUA PLANT. THE GOM [Government of Mexico] IS
ALSO CLEARLY CONCERNED AND IS SENDING COMMERCE SECRETARY
JAIME SERRA PUCHE TO THE U.S. NEXT WEEK TO REASSURE FORD
EXECUTIVES ABOUT DESIRABILITY OF FORD'S PROPOSED EXPANSION
PLANS IN MEXICO. END COMMENT NEGROPONTE.[39]

In April 1991, the Embassy would report:

BY EARLY 1990, DESPITE EXTENSIVE COMMUNICATION EFFORTS, ONLY
ONE THIRD OF THE WORK FORCE HAD RETURNED TO WORK. AFTER
CONSULTATION WITH THE GOVERNMENT, UNION AND COMPANY
MANAGEMENT, ALL ABSENT EMPLOYEES WERE TERMINATED AND THE
PROCESS OF HIRING/REHIRING REPLACEMENT WORKERS WAS BEGUN.
APPROXIMATELY 600 (OF 3,800) FORMER TERMINATED EMPLOYEES
WERE IDENTIFIED AS ACTIVE DISSIDENTS OR SYMPATHETIC TO THE

ACTIVIST MOVEMENT. ACCORDINGLY, THESE INDIVIDUALS WERE
NOT OFFERED REEMPLOYMENT.[40]

The court granted Ford's petition to end the collective bargaining
agreement, and the company sent out letters telling all the workers
that they would terminate them if they did not return to work. By
February 15, 1990, 2,500 of them had returned to work, but Ford
determined that they were not as submissive as had been expected
and still had unresolved grievances. It suspended the rehiring process
for ten days, leaving 1,500 still outside in the camp.

A cable from Ambassador Negroponte dated February 21, 1990,
informed Washington on the situation:

2. IT IS STILL UNCLEAR HOW MANY DISSIDENT FORD WORKERS
WILL FINALLY BE DISMISSED, BUT AT THIS POINT IT APPEARS THE
NUMBER MAY RANGE BETWEEN 600 TO 1000. UNION DISSIDENTS
(MAINLY THOSE WHO HAVE RECEIVED DISMISSAL NOTICES AND
HAVE NOT BEEN REHIRED) CONTINUE TO CARRY OUT PROTEST
ACTIVITIES, WITH MARCHES IN FRONT OF THE EMBASSY AS WELL
AS FORD AND CTM OFFICES ON FEB. 19/20. PROTESTORS ALSO
BLOCKED THE STREETS AROUND THE FORD PLANT, AS WELL AS
MAINTAINING AN AT TIMES RACOUS [sic] PRESENCE AT THE PLANT.
ON FEB. 20 WORKERS ALSO BLOCKED MEXICO-QUERETARO BOUND
TRAFFIC UNTIL ABOUT MIDDAY. IN THE LAST TWO DAYS, MEXICAN
RIOT POLICE WERE STATIONED (BUT NOT DEPLOYED) AT THE PLANT
TO AUGMENT REGULAR POLICE PRESENCE THERE. DESPITE MORE
WORKERS ON THE LINE, PRODUCTION IS STILL BEING AFFECTED,
WITH NEWLY RETURNED WORKERS WEARING BLACK ARMBANDS
IN SUPPORT OF DISSIDENT WORKERS SEEKING TO BE REHIRED.
FORD REPRESENTATIVES HAVE TOLD US THEY ARE WARY ABOUT THE
POSSIBILITY OF RENEWED VIOLENCE SINCE THEY ARE DETERMINED
TO STICK TO THEIR DECISION TO DISMISS BETWEEN 600 TO 1000
STRIKING WORKERS.[41]

Labor Secretary Farell announced he would mediate the dispute
between Ford and the workers. He called a meeting attended by
himself, Ford de Mexico President Scheele, newly appointed Ford
CTM official Juan Sosa (he had replaced Uriarte), CTM legal staffer

Juan Moisés Calleja, and Gabriel Abogado, who led a delegation of
Ford Cuautitlán workers. At the meeting, Scheele gave the workers
an ultimatum. Ford workers, but not all of them, would continue to
be rehired slowly with no reprisals. Ford would discharge those that
did not return to work. There would be no pay for lost wages during
the two-month work stoppage, and any other work stoppages would
nullify the agreement. Having no real option, the workers reluc-
tantly agreed.[42]

The Embassy gave the details of the agreement in a cable dated
March 5, 1990:

1. (LOU)...ON MARCH 1, FORD COMPANY OFFICIALS SIGNED A
WRITTEN "UNDERSTANDING" WITH THE WORKERS (AND THE
CTM) AFTER A SIX HOUR MEETING, ATTENDED BY FORD DIRECTOR
NICHOLAS SCHEELE, AND PRESIDED OVER BY MEXICAN SECRETARY OF
LABOR, ARSENIO FARELL. THE AGREEMENT CALLS FOR THE WORKERS
TO BE BACK AT WORK BY MARCH 6. THE UNDERSTANDING OUTLINED
STEPS TO: (A) REINSTATE A LARGE NUMBER OF RETRENCHED
WORKERS WHO HAVE NOT BEEN RECALLED BY FORD, (B) REHIRE ALL
WORKERS THROUGH THE CTM, (C) CARRY OUT THE REINSTATEMENT
PROCESS OVER THE NEXT FOUR WEEKS, AND (D) COMMITS FORD TO
CARRY OUT THE REINSTATEMENT PLAN, BUT ONLY IN THE ABSENCE
OF WORKER THREATS AND DISRUPTIONS TO PLANT OPERATIONS.[43]

By March 25, 600 hundred workers had still not been rehired. On
April 20, several hundred of them attempted to return to work *en
masse* but were blocked by a cordon of 1,500 policemen.[44]

On June 13, a group of activists went to the Federal Board of
Conciliation and Mediation office and stripped naked, symbolically
making the statement that they were totally without protection, and
they made it onto the front pages of the newspapers.[45] Getting such
prominent coverage in the print media was a significant accomplish-
ment. In 1990, the Mexican government maintained a monopoly
on newsprint, which they used to control the press. Embassy
cables inform Washington that the government has been successful in limiting press coverage of the events: "THE GOM HAS KEPT A
LID ON NEWS COVERAGE OF THE STRIKE"; "THE GOM HAS KEPT NEWS

COVERAGE OF THE FORD DISPUTE WELL UNDER WRAPS AND INVARI-
ABLY NEWSPAPER COVERAGE OF THE DISPUTE HAS BEEN MINIMAL AND
RELEGATED TO THE INSIDE PAGES OF THE PRESS."[46]

On July 26, with financial pressure mounting on the activists and their families, the fired workers finally settled with Ford, accepting four months' pay in return for terminating their contractual rights. A few did not take the agreement and continued their legal battle with the company.[47] Ambassador Negroponte described this final settlement in a cable dated August 3, 1990:

1. THE MEXICAN SUBSIDIARY OF THE FORD MOTOR COMPANY, PLAGUED
BY SEVERAL MONTHS OF LABOR PROBLEMS AT ITS ASSEMBLY PLANT
OUTSIDE MEXICO CITY, AGREED JULY 26 TO PROVIDE SEVERANCE PAY
TO 570 WORKERS DISMISSED DURING A STRIKE ACTION INITIATED
AGAINST THE FORD ASSEMBLY PLANT IN CUAUTITLAN EARLIER
THIS YEAR.... IT FIRED SOME 570 WORKERS; THE REST RETURNED
TO WORK. THE DISMISSED WORKERS HAVE CONTINUED TO HOLD
SPORADIC DEMONSTRATIONS. MOST RECENTLY, THEY OCCUPIED
THE COMPANY'S HEADQUARTERS FOR SEVERAL HOURS ON JULY 24
DEMANDING SEVERANCE COMPENSATION. ON JULY 26, FORD AND
THE WORKERS REACHED AN AGREEMENT, WORKERS WILL RECEIVE
THREE MONTHS' SALARY AND A PRO-RATED SUM BASED ON THE
LENGTH OF SERVICE WITH THE FIRM.[48]

A final chapter was still playing out. In February, the workers had decided that they needed to change their affiliation from the CTM to another legal labor federation affiliated with the PRI, the COR. The COR filed a petition demanding that they should be the collective bargaining representative of the Ford workers. On April 20, 1990 while workers were trying to return to Ford, the Mexican Supreme Court granted a writ of protection declaring that the Federal Board of Conciliation and Mediation would have to hear the COR claim to the Cuautitlán contract. José de Jesús Pérez, a COR leader, announced that the Ford workers at CAP were now members of the COR, and he hoped the workers at Hermosillo and Chihuahua would join them. On April 29, 1990, 3,000 Ford workers from Cuautitlán met and formally joined the COR. At a hearing on December 6, 1990, Ford demanded that the petition to change union affiliations be thrown out on technical grounds, but the board denied the demand. In late 1990, the Secretary of Labor and Federal Board of Conciliation and Mediation removed the leaders of COR and replaced them with leaders loyal to the PRI.[49]

On June 3, 1991, a court-ordered representation election between the CTM and the COR was held for the workers at the Ford facility at Cuautitlán. The election lasted from 6:00 a.m. until 11:00 p.m. Independent observers from human rights groups and labor education services monitored the voting. A report on the election found many cases of abuse, including the failure of authorities to conduct the voting by secret ballot. Instead, workers had to vote out loud in front of Ford management and a CTM representative. The government allowed the company to decide who was eligible to vote. The 600 that Ford had not called back to work were excluded from participating. Supervisors chose who could vote and then brought them to the voting area. Managers warned some workers that if they voted against the CTM, they could be fired. The company videotaped some workers while they were stating their vote. Even with all this cheating and intimidation, the CTM was able to win by only 126 votes.[50]

Ford and the DoS quickly adopted the explanation that the whole matter had been an internal CTM union dispute. The CTM did not embrace that interpretation. None of the DoS cables sent out under Ambassador Negroponte's name or Deputy Chief of Mission Pastorino's name mentioned the kidnapping of the local leaders on Friday, January 5, and the resulting work stoppage. Nor did any cable provide analysis of the attack of Monday, January 8. The DoS did not account for where the *golpeadores* got the Ford uniforms and ID badges or who financed the undertaking. They did not mention Walter de la Mancha in any DoS cables sent from January to August. However, a vital role in the attack was attributed to him by the press, the Mexican Congress, and by the CTM in a press conference. Perhaps the U.S. government officials sent information on Mancha via another communication channel to avoid public scrutiny. The Embassy discounted the role of the PRT, saying:

> 6. COMMENT: AS BECAME INCREASINGLY EVIDENT, THE LABOR DISPUTE PROVED TO BE AN INTERNAL UNION CONFLICT, ALBEIT EXACERBATED BY SEVERAL POOR MANAGEMENT DECISIONS ON THE PART OF FORD MANAGEMENT INVOLVING PAY ISSUES AND THE FISHING IN TROUBLED WATERS BY SOME UNION MEMBERS BELONGING TO LEFTIST POLITICAL PARTIES. THE INVOLVEMENT OF MORE RADICAL (BUT FEW IN NUMBER) UNION PLAYERS LIKE THE REVOLUTIONARY WORKERS PARTY (PRT) SYMPATHIZERS/MEMBERS WAS ANCILLARY TO RATHER THAN THE PROXIMATE CAUSE OF THE DISPUTE.[51]

And, in another cable:

> THE ACTIVITIES OF THE REVOLUTIONARY WORKERS PARTY (PRT) SYMPATHIZERS/MEMBERS WITHIN THE RANKS OF UNION DISSIDENTS APPEAR TO BE THAT OF "FISHING IN TROUBLED WATERS" RATHER THAN A DRIVING FORCE IN THE LABOR DISPUTE.[52]

The Embassy did not disclose the source of its intelligence for this analysis in the cable. It is an incorrect assessment of what happened. In the first cable sent on January 11, the Embassy reports that Ford blamed the attack on January 8 on the PRT.[53] Ford had told the Embassy they needed to discharge between 200 and 400 "dissidents" and would later terminate closer to 600 workers. In a cable of February 1, the Embassy reports that Ford said 300 militants had successfully pressured the remaining 2,500 union members to stay off the job.[54] Hector Uriarte blamed the entire incident on the PRT and the PRD.[55] PRT members controlled the local union Executive Committee from 1984 on.[56] It is likely that the information in the cable was designed to distract from the real motivation for the attack, an exercise intended to defeat leftist militants. Ambassador Negroponte was well aware that DoS cables were read by many people from his time in Honduras aiding the Contras:

The cables show that Negroponte enjoyed a close relationship with senior Washington policymakers, such as then-CIA Director William J. Casey, that was unusual for career diplomats. He used a back-channel system of communication through the CIA to send messages to Casey and others that he did not want widely distributed.[57]

The CIA station chief in Mexico, Vincent Shields, served in the same capacity with Negroponte in Honduras. In 1968, the CIA had between 15 and 20 officers working under cover of the Embassy in Mexico City.[58]

Rough Justice: The Fate of the *golpeadores*

A court convicted Guadalupe Uribe Guevara, his two sons Raul Uribe Soria and Rafael Uribe Soria, and seven others on a charge of manslaughter and weapons violations. They were sentenced to three years imprisonment for killing Cleto Nigmo Urbina and for assault on the others. Guadalupe Uribe would serve one year of that term.[59] In 1991, when he was released from prison, Uribe was rewarded. He obtained enough money to buy his first public transport vehicles and start the Transportation Credit Union of the State of Mexico. It may be that this was payment for what he had done at Cuautitlán. By 1998, Uribe had become a transportation union magnate and controlled over half the public transportation vehicles (taxis and microbuses) in the State of Mexico. His son Rafael, who had also served time for his role in the Cuautitlán affair, allegedly died in an auto accident in 1994, but the same day the autopsy took place, his body was cremated. Unofficial reports indicated that the car had two bullet holes in it. Uribe ended his affiliation with the CTM after his son's death. In an interview in 1998, Uribe said he was a Ford Motor Company employee and the transportation manager for Ford de Mexico. In 2012, he was living in La Montosa, an island in a lagoon.[60] In a 2018 interview, Raul Escobar Briones told Paula Cuellar Cuellar that Uribe had recently died.[61]

Hector Uriarte Martinez left Mexico City and avoided apprehension for the murder he had been accused of in January. On January

10, 1990, three Cuautitlán workers, Raul Escobar Briones, Jamie Flores Durán, and Alberto Martínez García, filed a complaint with the Mexican National Human Rights Commission concerning the attack on the workers at Cuautitlán. On February 22, 1992, the commission issued its findings.[62] They had no enforcement authority, but the report castigated government officials for making no effort to apprehend Uriarte. A few days after the report was released, the governor of the State of Mexico issued an arrest warrant for Uriarte. The attorney general promised to comply and arrest Uriarte, who was living in Hermosillo, Sonora, his hometown. "There is no justification for a nine month delay in the arrest," the commission said. Uriarte was wanted for murder, assault, burglary, and gun smuggling, *La Jornada* reported.

After four years of avoiding arrest Uriarte was finally arrested and placed under the jurisdiction of a state judge on October 31, 1994. He was apprehended in Hermosillo and detained on the charge of homicide and criminal association.[63] Uriarte denied participating in the violence at the Ford plant and claimed to have no role in the killing of Cleto Nigmo Urbina. There is no record of him ever being tried or sentenced. A man with the same name owned a restaurant in Hermosillo in 2017.

Wallace de la Mancha had attracted a great deal of attention with the attack on Ford Cuautitlán. Many witnesses identified him as being at the scene, and the newspapers reported that. This attention was so unwelcome that the mysterious figure wrote a letter to the editor of *La Jornada* denying he was involved. It was a high-risk undertaking, and it did not go well. Mancha must have been concerned that his employers would not be happy with all the scrutiny he was receiving. Mancha died the following year at age 59, supposedly of an undisclosed illness. Only two of his children and a CTM official attended the funeral. Rumors circulated that he was assassinated in Guadalajara. Along with Mancha, any direct evidence of CIA involvement in the storming of the Ford Cuautitlán plant may also have died.

The UAW has correctly received much credit over the years for its part in raising the living standards of American workers. The strike and occupation of several GM plants in Flint, Michigan, during 1936–7 resulted in the UAW winning union recognition and establishing itself as a viable institution. This event came to be known as the "Flint Sit-Down Strike." Local police and vigilantes met the seizing of the GM plants with a violent attempt to remove the workers. This led to the infamous "Battle of Bulls Run," in which workers beat back the attempt with many injuries on both sides. A group that included many communists and socialists, including Victor Reuther, planned, organized, and led the plant occupation and strike for union recognition. The strike was ultimately successful because of the intervention of Michigan Governor Frank Murphy. Murphy sent in the National Guard to surround the plant, but they did not evict the workers, forcing GM to settle with the UAW.

The union activists at Cuautitlán were every bit as capable, determined, and courageous as their counterparts at Flint had been in 1936, yet they failed to democratize the CTM and gain power for Mexican workers. Unlike the Flint workers, they were opposed by a conservative government that had come to power through election fraud. Another cause of their defeat was the intervention of the U.S., but precisely what its role had been would remain hidden for another quarter of a century.

PART III

Tracking the Assassins

9
Detroit

Of course, we cannot [sic] what happened to the materials before coming to our building, and cannot categorically guarantee that some external person may have [sic] tampered with the files. It just seems highly unlikely in my opinion that this is the case for a single folder worth of material...

Erik Nordberg, Director, Walter P. Reuther Library, February 2017

In the winter of 1990, while I was working at the Ford Twin Cities Assembly Plant (TCAP) in St. Paul, Minnesota, our UAW local union learned of an attack that took place on workers in the Ford Cuautitlán plant near Mexico City. These workers had been involved in a labor dispute and were injured by thugs. One died as a result of his injuries. This information appeared on a new thing called the World Wide Web.

The May 1990 issue of the *879 Autoworker*, the newsletter of the UAW local union at the TCAP, reported that Marco Antonio Jiménez, a newly elected leader of the Ford Cuautitlán Assembly Plant, said workers at the plant were attacked by thugs in Ford uniforms with Ford ID badges in January. The attack resulted in a 15-day occupation of the plant by 2,000 workers. Jiménez went on to say they had no union hall and that they needed hundreds of people to attend a union meeting to guarantee safety.

In December 1990, the UAW bargaining chairman for the St. Paul local, Ted LaValley, spoke at a public, quality award ceremony at the TCAP, which some Minneapolis/St. Paul area reporters attended. Referencing the Ford Cuautitlán situation, LaValley said, "There is blood on the floor in that plant." LaValley's comment would set off alarm bells for Ford, and they sent a spokesperson to St. Paul to meet with LaValley after he went public with these allegations. In the meeting with LaValley, Ford denied paying the attackers or providing them with uniforms and ID badges. They admitted they had given permission to enter the plant to a group who promised they would only "talk" to the workers.

During the ensuing months, local leaders learned more details about what had transpired, and invited two activists from the FWDM, Raul Escobar Briones and José Santos Martínez, to St. Paul, in January 1991. The St. Paul UAW union held a Cleto Nigmo Ford Workers' Justice Day on January 8, 1991, at the TCAP on the shooting's first anniversary. Many of the UAW workers wore black armbands and ribbons.

In a letter dated January 24, 1991, the UAW 879 recording secretary, Tom Laney, wrote Ambassador Negroponte to inform him that the local union had invited Escobar Briones and Santos Martinez to attend a conference on free trade to be held in the coming days at Macalester College in St. Paul. He asked for Negroponte's assistance with their visas. Escobar and Martinez were initially denied travel visas to the U.S. Laney was told by congressman Jim Oberstar's staff that the DoS had denied the Mexicans entrance into the country because they were communists.[1] With the intervention of Oberstar, the DoS finally gave visas to the Mexicans.

The UAW 879 letter raised apprehension in the U.S. Mexican Embassy. Negroponte cabled the Secretary of State, James Baker, about the UAW 879 letter. Negroponte sent the following cable on January 25, 1991:

LABOR: SENSITIVITIES OF FOREIGN INVOLVEMENT IN UNION RIVALRIES AT CUAUTITLAN FORD PLANT

2. WE THOUGHT IT WAS USEFUL TO BRING TO DEPARTMENT'S AND AIFLD'S ATTENTION THE INVITATION FROM UAW LOCAL 879 IN ST. PAUL, MN TO TWO LEADERS OF THE COR-AFFILIATED WORKERS' DISSIDENT GROUP TO COME TO THE TWIN CITIES TO ADDRESS VARIOUS UNION AND OTHER AUDIENCES TO GAIN THEIR SYMPATHETIC SUPPORT (REF FAX). WHILE THIS IS A LEGITIMATE ACTIVITY, IT HAS A POTENTIAL DOWNSIDE IN TERMS OF AFL-CIO AIFLD RELATIONS WITH CTM. WE UNDERSTAND THAT THIS SUPPORT FOR COR BY SOME UAW LOCALS DOES NOT NECESSARILY HAVE THE FULL SUPPORT OF UAW SOLIDARITY HOUSE AND AIFLD, SO

WE BELIEVE BILL DOHERTY MAY WISH TO REVIEW THE MEXICAN
SENSITIVTIES [sic].

3. MIKE VERDUE, RECENTLY RETURNED TO AIFLD FROM HIS
ORIT POST IN MEXICO CITY, OF COURSE IS WELL VERSED IN THE
COMPLEX LABOR RELATIONS PROBLEMS AT FORD, WHICH INVOLVE
THE STRUGGLE BETWEEN THE STILL LEGALLY RECOGNIZED CTM
UNION AND THE COR-AFFILIATED DISSIDENTS. THE MEASURES USED
BY THE GOM TO SUPPRESS THE UNAUTHORIZED 1989 STRIKE BY
THE DISSIDENTS, AND POLITICAL CONSIDERATIONS THAT INCLINED
LABOR SECRETARY FARELL AND CTM LEADER DON FIDEL VELAQUEZ
TOWARD A NEGATIVE ATTITUDE REGARDING THE DISSIDENTS. GIVEN
THIS POLITICAL CONTEXT, THEREFORE, IT CAME AS NO SURPRISE
THAT FARELL PRIVATELY TOLD THE AMBASSADOR AND LABATT ON
JANUARY 25, 1991, THAT HE WAS CONVINCED THAT THE UAW IS
BEHIND THE CONTINUING DISSIDENT ACTIVITIES AT THE FORD
PLANT. IN SUPPORT OF THIS VIEW, FARELL DISPLAYED COPIES OF
THE JANUARY 1991 EDITION OF THE DISSIDENTS' NEWSLETTER, "EN
LA LINEA," IN WHICH WERE REPRODUCED LETTERS OF SUPPORT
FROM UAW LOCALS 879 (ST. PAUL) AND 900 (WAYNE, MI).[2]

In addition to the cable, the ambassador faxed the UAW 879 letter
and a list of ten reference cables previously sent to the DoS on the
Ford Cuautitlán events to the Secretary of State. The fax was sent to
Tony Kern at the DoS with a request that he pass them on to Mike
Verdue at AIFLD.

Who was Mike Verdue, mentioned in the cable, and why would
Secretary Baker be reminded that "of course" Verdue knew about
events at the Mexico City Ford plant? Verdue's father, Angelo
Verdue, had been on the AIFLD staff. Angelo came as a child to
the U.S. from Alicante, Spain. He called himself a professional
anti-communist trade union organizer who had a bitter hatred of
communists based on the experience of having a communist organizer burn down his house, with his father inside, in the 1930s. By
the 1970s, the elder Verdue rose to the second tier of AIFLD management along with Samuel Haddad and Jesse Friedman. In 1974,
he was AIFLD Deputy Director.[3] Angelo was able to get his son,
Mike, hired at AIFLD.[4]

The cable highlights the direct links between the events at Ford Cuautitlán and AIFLD. Why did Negroponte feel the DoS needed to contact AIFLD and Bill Doherty about the activities of a U.S. domestic union (UAW 879)? AIFLD was officially not a government agency, but Negroponte believed contacting them through the DoS was the correct communication channel. The Government of Mexico and the CTM had been battling with the workers at Ford Cuautitlán since 1982. The PRI knew perfectly well that the UAW was not responsible for dissident activities there. Mexican government officials were aware of U.S. involvement in the attack on Cuautitlán and were very irritated that the U.S. was making no effort to reign in their dissidents contributing to the problems. Mexican awareness of events explains the cable's urgent tone.

In the fall of 1991, Raul Escobar Briones, whom Ford fired while he was the financial secretary of the Cuautitlán local, traveled to Minnesota and spoke to 850 delegates at the Minnesota State AFL-CIO convention in Minneapolis. Escobar said Mexican workers in the auto, brewery, rubber, and textile industries were already feeling the impact of free trade. He declared that Mexican authorities and government-influenced unions were eager to collaborate with foreign corporations and support the agreement [proposed NAFTA] to demonstrate that Mexico will supply cheap and cooperative labor. Briones told the group, "In our view the free trade agreement is not an opportunity for employment, but a strike against our collective bargaining gains." According to the St. Paul *Union Advocate*,

Escobar urged delegates to work in solidarity with Mexican and Canadian workers, "because we're all affected by the free trade agreement." He said Mexican workers "have little hope for change" without legal reforms in Mexico, and without international coordination by unions to defend labor gains in the face of "the global marketplace."[5]

Escobar's warnings about free trade would prove to be prophetic. In 1994, NAFTA was put into effect, and it resulted in both the loss of U.S. manufacturing jobs and an erosion of living standards in much of Mexico.

New Beginnings

As the years passed, the struggle at Cuautitlán began to fade in the U.S. as other issues moved to the forefront for labor. In 1995, John Sweeney and a union coalition called the "New Voice" forced Lane Kirkland to retire and instituted many reforms, resulting in a break with some of the policies of the Cold War AFL-CIO.[6] Although many of the CIA linked officials who had moved directly to the AFL-CIO from the DoS or CIA-linked training programs remained, the Federation made significant changes to its international relations, emphasizing worker solidarity.[7]

In the winter of 1996, as a vice-president of the St. Paul Ford UAW local, I attended a meeting of the Coalition for Justice in the Maquiladoras in Brownsville, Texas, and Matamoros, Tamaulipas, Mexico. The AFL-CIO now supported this organization, which was working to improve working conditions and wages on the border. After the two-day meeting, a staff person for the newly elected AFL-CIO President John Sweeney approached me. He introduced himself and told me he was aware that our local had done support work for the FWDM at Cuautitlán. He then said that the Sweeney administration had learned of AIFLD involvement in the events at the Ford Cuautitlán plant in 1989/1990. I knew vaguely that the CIA was associated with AIFLD and asked him if that meant the CIA was involved. He nodded his head in the affirmative. When I asked him what they had done there, he replied that Sweeney and his team didn't know, but were trying to find out. Sweeney's staff representative also reported on the entanglement of UAW President Owen Bieber, but he wasn't sure in what way he was connected. Bieber had retired in 1995. Within the next few months, the AFL-CIO closed down AIFLD, and William Doherty retired.

Upon returning to St. Paul, I met with the chief of staff for the Minnesota AFL-CIO President Bernie Brommer about my concerns with AIFLD involvement at Cuautitlán. Years later, this individual would only say that they knew they had a problem with the issue of AIFLD. Over the decade that followed, I talked with people who I thought might know something about what happened in Mexico in 1990. I did eventually locate a UAW staff person who had been involved in support work for the FWDM at the time, who had also heard, from a different but reliable source, that AIFLD had been engaged at Cuautitlán.

I would become our UAW local union president, and then, after Ford announced plans to close the St. Paul plant in 2006, I took a job on the UAW International Staff. From these vantage points, I watched the collapse of the manufacturing economy in the Midwest, as production fled to low-wage countries like Mexico. While watching the U.S. auto production shift to Mexico, I never forgot the events of January 8, 1990, and the struggle of Mexican auto workers to improve their conditions. Before my retirement in 2016, local historian Brian McMahon interviewed me for a book on the TCAP and Ford's history in Minnesota. While discussing, I told him about what I had heard about AIFLD. He questioned me as to why I had never tried to follow that up.

When I did retire, I began researching the events at Cuautitlán in 1989/1990. This would turn into a year's long effort, and result in battles with all the institutions who had information on the subject; the CIA, Ford Motor, the DoS, the AFL-CIO, the UAW, and the labor union archives. Union staff I had great respect for would refuse to respond to letters and emails, and others would battle over this in their own labor bodies. Unexpectedly, this undertaking would also lead me down the rabbit hole of CIA infiltration, manipulation, and control of the AFL-CIO and its foreign policy during the Cold War.

After learning that the AFL-CIO controlled the old AIFLD archives, my initial effort to research the Cuautitlán attack involved contacting an AFL-CIO staff person, Tom Allen (not his real name). I asked him for his guidance on gaining access to the AIFLD records on Mexico from the 1980s. In the process, I found out that a former UAW International Staff member had recently moved to the national AFL-CIO staff. This individual, Bob Martin (not his real name), had also been drawn into support efforts for the FWDM and had told me years earlier that AIFLD had been mixed up in the attack. In May 2016, he emailed me:

> AIFLD was indeed a problem at [Cu]Atitlan. It had a retired FBI guy working out of El Paso who used to muck around in labor politics in Mexico. AIFLD and its activities were a major reason the UAW left the AFL-CIO from 1968–1983. … There is a lot of material in the UAW archives in Detroit…

Tom and Bob had a meeting with the AFL-CIO Director of the International Department, Cathy Feingold, in Washington, DC, about the process of requesting AIFLD records. They told me I would need to send an official request to her.

Utterly inexperienced in the world of academic research, I began an effort to find an academic partner to work with. I finally located a professor from the University of California system who had researched the events at Ford Cuautitlán for his Ph.D. dissertation published in 1998. We talked on the phone, and I learned that he was interested in pursuing this project. The professor and I submitted a letter to Cathy Feingold requesting to view the AIFLD records on Cuautitlán in May 2016. On June 28, 2016, I received an email from Feingold in response, saying that she had received my letter and would process the request with the University of Maryland.

Although I would send Feingold several more emails and a letter, this would be the last communication I would ever receive from her. Both Bob and Tom stopped responding to my emails and texts, leaving me with the message, "This is a slow process." I submitted our request to view the AIFLD/Mexico records to the George Meany Memorial Archives (GMMA), the official repository of AFL-CIO records, at the University of Maryland, and got no direct reply. On their website, I noted that it could take up to a year for a request concerning viewing archives to be granted, so I was determined to give it that much time.

Supposing that the Ford Motor Company would also have information relevant to what happened in Mexico in 1990, I contacted a human-resources official at the Detroit-area-headquartered company. Bill (not his real name) emailed me back twice in the ensuing months, letting me know he had forwarded my inquiries to the appropriate person. After hearing nothing from them, I elected to send a letter to James Hackett, the CEO of Ford:

Dear Mr. Hackett,

When I retired from my job as a Regional Staff Rep for the UAW and a Ford Motor employee I began researching something that had long troubled me. In 1990 an armed group attacked workers at a Ford plant in Cuautitlán, Mexico. One worker was killed, and seven others were wounded, and it sparked a two-week occupation of the plant. At the time I didn't understand who had paid the three hundred attackers and provided them with Ford uniforms and ID badges. Ford denied doing this to my UAW local union leadership at the Ford Twin Cities Assembly Plant…

I have questions regarding this event and others related to it that I would like to have answered by Ford Motor. These answers would really help to clarify the events I have been researching. Some of the questions I am interested in getting answered include:

Did Ford give permission for the attackers to enter CAP on January 8, 1990?

Did Ford pay these attackers?

Did Ford provide the uniforms and ID badges for the attackers?

Why did Ford fire four members of the CAP local union Executive Committee in 1989?

A minor CTM official named Guadalupe Uribe served one year in prison for the murder of the Ford worker who was killed in the attack. In a 2002 interview Uribe claimed to be the transportation manager of Ford de Mexico. Was this true? … Thank you for your attention to my requests and questions.

Sincerely
Rob McKenzie

No response from Hackett or Ford would ever arrive.

While waiting for permission to see the AFL-CIO archives stored at the University of Maryland, I decided to pursue Bob's advice about UAW files in Detroit. Having just retired from the UAW International Staff a few months earlier, I assumed this would be less challenging than the AFL-CIO search, which was turning out to be slow and difficult. In June 2016, I emailed UAW International President Dennis Williams, whom I had known for 20 years, and who had hired me as an International Union staff.[8] Having received no answer from Williams by August, I drove to Ottawa, Illinois, to meet with UAW Region 4 Director Ron McInroy. I explained to Ron that I was looking for the old files about Ford and Mexico. He told me he would be seeing Dennis Williams in a few days and would speak with him about this and get back to me. When I hadn't heard from him in a month, I knew the UAW was going to be a problem too.

The UAW constitution allows any member to appeal any action or inaction of any UAW official using a procedure that concludes with an outside ethics committee, the UAW Public Review Board (PRB). I wrote Williams a letter asking for the minutes of the International Executive Board (IEB) meetings from 1988 to 1990 and the UAW files on the events at Cuautitlán. I asserted that I had a UAW constitutional right to these. It was clear that I had a right to the IEB minutes. The files were at best a gray area, but making the claim would send an appeal to the PRB. After hearing nothing from Williams in response to my first letter, I appealed to the IEB. After hearing nothing back from them, I contacted the PRB.

The PRB wrote me explaining they were an appellate body and perhaps the IEB needed more time, but stating that if the IEB didn't act on my appeal they would take it up. The PRB sent a copy of the letter to Rick Isaacson, an administrative assistant to UAW President Williams. Within a few days, I received a letter from Isaacson saying they wanted to discuss my appeal, but were considering it closed. By "closing" it instead of "denying" the appeal, the president's office seemingly hoped to circumvent the procedure, which would have required them to send the appeal to all the IEB members. Isaacson and I reached an agreement to drop my request for IEB minutes, if he would try and find the Cuautitlán files.

Isaacson made a determined effort to locate the files, and it resulted in a former UAW International staffer telling me their location. He emailed me:

Rob, sorry but the UAW archives I referred to are the official UAW archives at the Reuther Library at Wayne State, not UAW records at Solid House. The material is open to scholars and citizens at Wayne State. You want to look at International Dept and President's office files. They are indexed by box number. Here is Owen [Bieber node].

Working together with a friend who was a retired union staffer and a retired educator in the Detroit area, we found approximately a dozen references to Mexico in the Owen Bieber node in the Reuther Library at Wayne State University in Detroit. The most interesting folder was labeled "American Institute for Free Labor Development." When my friend and the other interested party got to the library, they found the records on Mexico except for the AIFLD file's contents. That file contained no documents concerning AIFLD and had only paperwork related to AFL-CIO meetings and Alaskan Oil Exports. The folders adjacent to the AIFLD folder in the box were labeled AFL-CIO meetings and Alaskan Oil Exports. Someone had removed the contents of the AIFLD folder and replaced it with material from the adjacent folders, perhaps so that they wouldn't return a box with an empty folder.

I contacted the senior archivist, William LeFevre, about the missing contents of the AIFLD folder. What followed was a bizarre series of emails concerning the AIFLD file:

Thanks again. Do you know why AIFLD would show up in the search but there are no files? Rob

LeFevre replied that he had no idea, as the folder heading was pretty clear.

When I continued to ask questions, the story changed to "there never was an American Institute for Free Labor Development" file and the folder name was actually "AFL-CIO meetings and Alaskan Oil Exports."

William,
The person who told me about Mexico related materials being in the collection was not really a friend, but they were correct. There were files concerning Cuautitlán that we found showing the Int'l was tracking events and knew the person who was eventually charged with murder.

Is it at all possible that someone viewing the box took out the documents on AIFLD, put them in another file or box then took papers out of 1.3 (Alaskan Oil Imports [sic]) and put them in 1.4 (AIFLD)? I don't know really how your system works but this seems more plausible than you or your staff made an error. There are others beside the UAW who know I am looking for this who wouldn't want me to find it. Thanks for your work on this. I have got more attention from you than I could have expected. Rob

Then the story takes a strange turn. LeFevre told me that there was no such file and that the file I had referenced was actually titled "Alaskan oil exports; AFL-CIO meeting." He goes on to say, "The AIFLD shows up in the index as being in 1.4 and that was obviously an error on the part of the processing archivist. Though relatively rare, mistakes are sometimes made by our processing archivists."

This was not consistent with what my fellow researchers had found. I had two witnesses who had seen the AIFLD folder in the box, and we had made a copy of the index. I appealed to the director of the Reuther Library, Erik Nordberg:

Dear Mr. Nordberg,
Here is a copy of the index on this: AFL-CIO meetings was 1.1.
Aging workforce, 13.24 AIFLD, American Institute for Free Labor Development, 1.4 Alaskan Oil Exports, 1.3
I find it totally implausible that the Field Archivist made up the AIFLD heading for documents that did not exist. He is also incorrect in his facts as the Alaskan Oil Exports (1.3) is the file

next to AIFLD (1.4). What is a more plausible explanation is that someone who did not want this file seen, viewed the box, took out the AIFLD documents and put them in another file or box and then filled the empty AIFLD folder with some documents in the file on Alaskan Oil next to it.

Is it possible to get a further investigation into this matter? ...

Rob McKenzie

Nordberg responded that it was much more plausible that it was simply a typographical error in labeling the folder with a wrong acronym. He elaborated saying,

Of course, we cannot [sic] what happened to the materials before coming to our building, and cannot categorically guarantee that some external person may have [sic] tampered with the files. It just seems highly unlikely in my opinion that this is the case for a single folder worth of material. ...

The header on the folder was not an acronym but the full name, American Institute for Free Labor Development. These records are indexed and labeled by trained and highly credentialed archivists. If the UAW had not wanted the material at the library in the first place, they would not have sent it over. If the UAW had changed their mind and wanted the material removed, they would have had an archivist do it in the same manner they did after my challenge. They would have changed the header and the index and left no trace of an AIFLD folder ever having been there, which happened following my search. If someone had removed the AIFLD documents, they had been careless and had no access to make "official" changes to the contents of the archive.

I later learned that Owen Bieber was a trustee on the board of AIFLD in 1985 and 1986 and probably from 1983 to 1995.[9] The organization would have regularly mailed him items like financial reports and newsletters, at a minimum. I believe these are the likely contents of folder 1.4, "American Institute for Free Labor Development," before the header was changed to make it consistent with the disappearance of the documents.

After discovering that the contents of the AIFLD file were missing from the Reuther Library, the University of California professor also withdrew his support for my research with no explanation. I wish him well and bear him no ill will. The Cuautitlán story was not only highly embarrassing to many participants, but it also involved a murder for which there is no legal statute of limitations. This was not going to be just another academic search for historical materials about Cuautitlán, but was also shaping up to be a struggle against gatekeepers who seemed to be actively opposing my research.

10

St. Paul

I would advise you to hold off in getting further involved personally and publicly on this issue and pushing it further within the labor movement and at *Labor Notes*. It would really help me out if you could back off a little bit and give me a chance to work behind the scenes to try and get these records open in the near future.

Ben Blake, Archivist, George Meany Memorial Archives,
November 2017

After waiting patiently for over a year for a response to my request to view the AIFLD files at the GMMA, I emailed Cathy Feingold, the AFL-CIO International Affairs Director, to update her on the progress I had made with the Cuautitlán research and renew my entreaty. After hearing nothing back from her, Tom, or Bob, I sent an email to the Meany archives at the University of Maryland. Surprisingly, I received an email back from Ben Blake, the labor collections archivist. Blake told me he had been working with the AFL-CIO to get permission to open AIFLD records for research and he hoped to have it very soon.

This email was surprising. I had assumed that the delay in granting my request rested with the UMD archives. The idea that the AFL-CIO was refusing to open the records on Cuautitlán had not seriously entered my mind. The project entered a new phase when I realized that the AFL-CIO may have been actively trying to prevent the details of AIFLD's activity in Mexico from coming to light. I emailed Bob to ask why the AFL-CIO had not approved my request to view the AIFLD archives.

I have recently been in communication with archivists at the University of Maryland. They have been seeking AFL-CIO approval to open new records from AIFLD for the last year. As of yesterday, the AFL-CIO had not granted permission.

Who has the authority to grant that approval? Do you know why it would be withheld? Is it unreasonable on my part to expect a straight answer on this request? Best, Rob

Bob replied that his understanding was that the delay was caused by the AFL-CIO being too short-handed due to layoffs to read through all the material I had requested, which was a necessary part of the procedure. Having worked on a national union staff, I found this to be an unconvincing explanation for several reasons. Feingold had not replied to my most recent email, and the archivist had not mentioned staff shortages as a reason that the Federation had denied them approval to open the files. A straight answer would not be forthcoming. The real reason for the AFL-CIO intransigence would seemingly become apparent in the coming months. Neither Bob nor Tom, both on the national staff of the AFL-CIO, had known that CIA involvement in AIFLD was a taboo subject. In the past, I had considered them to be kindred spirits on issues of international solidarity. Their jobs would potentially be endangered if they failed to follow directives from the leadership and they stopped responding to emails.

Back in 1990, AFL-CIO foreign policy was still in the grip of right-wing CIA-linked staff. But at the end of the second decade of the twenty-first century, revelations about an attack on a Mexican autoworker reform movement would be looked at very differently than it had been at the end of the Cold War. I guessed that the AFL-CIO leadership would be so embarrassed by their refusal to open records that if I started to go public in the labor movement, they would grant me permission to view the AIFLD archives and avoid the scrutiny on Ford Cuautitlán. I hoped that I would then be able to find out what happened in Mexico.

Since retiring, I was no longer a delegate to St. Paul Regional Labor Federation (SPRLF, AFL-CIO). I contacted an individual, Michael Madden, who was a delegate. Michael was willing to make a resolution at the September 2017 meeting in support of opening the

AIFLD files on Cuautitlán. At his suggestion, I contacted a person in the leadership of the North East Area Labor Council (northeastern Minnesota) who got me on the agenda of a constituent body, the Duluth Central Labor Council, to make a presentation on the issue of AIFLD and Cuautitlán in October.

My goal was to bring enough attention to the issue that the AFL-CIO would relent on opening the AIFLD files; it mattered little how that happened. I contacted the president of the St. Paul Labor Federation, Robert (Bobby) Kasper, whom I had known for many years due to serving on the SPRLF executive board in the recent past. I talked to him about the resolution Madden was going to present. After he spoke with national AFL-CIO leadership and advisors about the issue, he offered to meet with Madden and me to discuss the matter.

On August 31, 2017, Madden and I met with Kasper at a downtown St. Paul restaurant. In a long, rambling conversation, Kasper told us he had spoken with the AFL-CIO Midwest director and the SPRLF attorney. Kasper eventually read us an email off his phone that he received from the attorney on the subject that listed three reasons the AFL-CIO didn't want to open the AIFLD archives: 1) adverse publicity had hurt labor, and this would be more of that; 2) there might be criminal liability for the AFL-CIO resulting from the attack on Ford Cuautitlán workers; 3) Richard Trumka, the AFL-CIO president, was in a tough re-election battle which the delegates would settle at the October 2017 convention and the issue could harm his re-election chances. The St. Paul Federation lawyer advised Kasper not to pass the resolution.

I asked Kasper why there might be a legal liability. He said, "they [he was referring to the CIA] were involved, and AIFLD had condoned it." He added, "That is the rumor." Kasper asked us to hold off on the resolution at the September SPRLF meeting. A short time later, I received an email from Ben Blake, the UMD archivist, asking for the same thing and informing me he would be meeting with a representative of the AFL-CIO secretary-treasurer's office the following week. He anticipated getting their approval to open the great majority of the AIFLD/International Department records very soon. He went on to say, "In light [of] our ongoing progress on this issue, I would request that you hold off on your decision to introduce the resolution until October." Blake told me he would contact me immediately when he had approval to open the records.

Madden and I informed Blake and Kasper that we should hold off on the resolution until October. While someone from the AFL-CIO may have told Blake something they believed at the time to be true regarding opening the AIFLD files, it is more likely they were buying time and ensuring that a delegate wouldn't submit a resolution on this issue at the upcoming October AFL-CIO 2017 convention. After getting no response from emails or phone calls to Blake, I resumed the effort to take the issue public by the end of September. Madden, joined by a few others, would make the resolution at the SPRLF on October 11, and on October 12, I would present the resolution to the Duluth Central Labor Council. Labor federation delegates in Minnesota introduced this resolution at meetings that fall:

Whereas, workers in Ford Motor's Mexico City Assembly Plant were involved in a series of labor disputes in the late 1980s and early 1990s resisting efforts to bring their wages and benefits down to the level of the new plants on the U.S. border and demanding democratic elections in their union. Many were kidnapped, beaten, shot and fired. One died from wounds received in the plant.

Whereas, the American Institute for Free Labor Development (AIFLD), a now-defunct arm of the AFL-CIO was reputedly involved in these events, and the AFL-CIO has sent the old records from this group to the University of Maryland, the official repository for AFL-CIO records.

Whereas, the University of Maryland has requested permission for a year to open new AIFLD records and archive them for researchers and has not received approval from the National AFL-CIO to do so.

Therefore, be it resolved, That the National AFL-CIO take action necessary to allow archivists at the University of Maryland to open new American Institute for Free Labor Development records.

Following my presentation at the Duluth Central Labor Council, the delegates voted in favor of the resolution. It was controversial, and it hadn't been pre-approved by the national leadership. Most of the representatives did not know me and ended up voting with their conscience. Unions have refused to go away in a world where employers have few limits on their power to arbitrage labor in a global economy. Those opposed to unions have made determined and well-financed attacks on them, and despite often short-sighted and self-serving leadership, organized labor has persisted. Union bodies composed of workers like those of the Duluth CLC explain why unions have endured.

After the Duluth Central Labor Council meeting, an article on the resolution appeared in the October 25, 2017, issue of the Duluth *Labor World* and was republished with the title "AFL-CIO Must Shine Light on Past Foreign Policy, Activists Say" on the website of *Workday Minnesota*, an online publication of the Labor Education Service of the University of Minnesota. Then *Portside*, a national website, posted the piece. The article generated responses from a labor educator who had been active with the Mexican Ford workers and people who had been involved with attempts to open the AIFLD archives. I learned some of the previous histories of attempts to "clear the air" about the AFL-CIO and the Cold War.

The Solidarity Center

In 1995, a coalition of union presidents with roots in the National Labor Committee in Support of Democracy and Human Rights in El Salvador (NLC) and the foreign-policy debates of the 1980s forced Lane Kirkland from office.[1] The coalition was known as the New Voice slate. The new president, John Sweeney, a former member of the NLC, disbanded AIFLD, AAFLI, AALC, and the FTUC. He then transformed the FTUI into the American Center for International Labor Solidarity, now known as the Solidarity

Center.[2] William Doherty Jr. explained the foundation for the new organization in 1996:

> [The] new laissez-faire neo-colonial capitalism, or as they call it, neo-liberalism, was coming to the fore. The thesis was that trade unions were an anathema to the development of a strong private enterprise economy. So we not only had to take a defensive position, but in an effort to globalize the world for the free enterprise system, we had to make sure that we got involved in the globalization. ... So the AIFLD stopped in its tracks, regeared its whole efforts, and decided that its new education program, its training programs, would be in the area of human rights, workers' rights, trade policy.[3]

Some of the most hardened Cold War warriors, including William Doherty Jr. and Jesse Friedman, were retired in 1996. Paul Somogyi, the former AIFLD Mexico country director and assistant director of the International Affairs Department of the AFL-CIO, explained the Solidarity Center:

> While AIFLD no longer exists as a separate entity, John Sweeney completed a unification process that began under Lane Kirkland and Tom Donahue to merge all four regional labor Institutes into one, global entity for labor's work abroad (or at least that which may be carried out or sponsored by the AFL-CIO). As you probably well know, that single labor entity is the American Center for International Labor Solidarity, simply referred to as the Solidarity Center. It's very much alive and well, still receiving funding from the same entities [NED and AID] I mentioned above, and still working with labor unions around the world in their struggle for the workers they represent.[4]

Sweeney's first appointee to head the new Solidarity Center was Harry Kamberis. Kamberis took over the Solidarity Center after a long career as an international businessman and in the DoS, where he had been a political officer in Bangladesh, Pakistan, and Greece.

Kamberis was the South Korean country program director for the AAFLI and worked at the Institute between 1986 and 1997.[5] His father-in-law was Morris Paladino, former director of the AAFLI, who 20 years previously Agee had identified as a CIA agent. According to journalist Tim Shorrock, many insiders and activists believed Kamberis to have been an undercover officer for the CIA while at the DoS.[6]

The Solidarity Center, which in 2021 had a professional staff of 250 and operated in 60 plus countries, describes its vision as follows:

> We believe that economic and social injustice around the world are neither intractable problems nor acceptable byproducts of a global economy where some can win at the expense of many. Rather, we believe working women and men can collectively improve their wages and workplaces, call on their governments to uphold laws and protect human rights, and be a force for democracy, shared prosperity and inclusive economic development.[7]

In 2021, the chair of the Solidarity Center board of trustees was AFL-CIO President Richard Trumka, the secretary-treasurer was Elizabeth Shuler, who is also the Federation's secretary-treasurer, and Thomas Conway, the president of the Steelworkers Union, was a trustee.

After AIFLD and the other Institutes were disbanded, a movement developed on the west coast that called on the AFL-CIO to account for what had transpired during the Cold War years. In 2001 and 2002, the San Francisco and South Bay Labor Councils, the Washington State AFL-CIO, and then the California State Federation of Labor all passed resolutions calling on the AFL-CIO to renounce what it had done in Chile and other places and open its records to members and researchers so that a full accounting of the past could be made. The California Federation resolution called on the AFL-CIO to open a dialogue about its government-funded foreign affairs activities and "affirm a policy of genuine global solidarity in pursuit of economic and social justice."[8]

One of the activists involved in the California effort was Fred Hirsch, who had published the paper on Chile "An Analysis of Our AFL-CIO Role in Latin America", in 1974.[9] The California AFL-CIO leadership offered Hirsch and others a compromise resolution to replace the "Clear the Air" resolution they had been promoting. Hirsch and the foreign-policy activists accepted the new resolution in return for a group of national AFL-CIO leaders agreeing to come to California to meet with the advocates for openness about the past. Fifteen months after the Hirsch group had accepted the compromise resolution, Stanley Gacek (Assistant Director of the AFL-CIO International Affairs Department) and William Lucy (American Federation of State County and Municipal Employees [AFSCME]), both national AFL-CIO leaders on foreign policy, came to California to meet with over 50 activists.[10] Art Pulaski, the secretary-treasurer of the California AFL-CIO, reportedly chaired the meeting.

Gacek and Lucy told the California union activists that the AFL-CIO foreign policy had changed substantially under the Sweeney administration. The AFL-CIO was now working to support core international labor rights and to develop international labor solidarity. In response to the demand that they "come clean" on past AFL-CIO operations, however, the AFL-CIO national representatives argued that the past was past and that efforts to get them to come clean on these events would only give AFL-CIO opponents more ammunition to fight unions. The AFL-CIO was still conducting labor operations in several countries, and they did not explain why those countries and not others. They did admit to continuing to take money from the NED and AID and also stated that countries where the DoS had no interests, were "off limits."[11] Some of the activists described the meeting as a "dog and pony show" with no substantive discussion.[12] The group proceeded to take a resolution to July 2004 California State AFL-CIO convention.

Several labor bodies came together around a resolution called "Build Unity and Trust Among Workers Worldwide." The 400 delegates at the 2004 California State Convention passed this resolution unanimously. This west coast union body totaled 2.5 million workers and comprised about one-sixth of the total AFL-CIO membership of that time. Convention delegates sent the "Build Unity and Trust" resolution to the 2005 AFL-CIO National Convention in Chicago, where the Resolutions Committee, chaired by Gerald McEntee, President of AFSCME, seemingly changed it into one supporting the Solidarity Center. Then, to make matters worse, the convention chair prevented a real debate on the motion during the convention proceedings.[13]

In the run-up to the 2005 convention, the AFL-CIO was facing a declining union membership, and a leadership challenge developed from a coalition of unions that included the Service Employees International Union (SEIU), Unite-Here (UNITE), the Laborers (LIUNA), and the Carpenters (UBC) that called itself the New Unity Partnership. As a partial response, John Sweeney finally decided to eliminate the Federation's Cold War dinosaur, the International Affairs Department. On May 4, 2005, the *Washington Post* reported that the move would cut 167 jobs at the AFL-CIO. The entire Federation national staff was comprised of 450 people, and it is difficult to understand how the International Affairs Department was funded. Sixty-one of those laid off were offered an opportunity to apply for other jobs. A total of 105 positions were eliminated.[14] Those laid off included Stan Gacek, the assistant for Latin American affairs. According to an AFL-CIO spokesperson, some of the freed-up resources would be used for union organizing efforts.[15]

At an SPRLF meeting on October 12, 2017, the executive board voted to invite me to attend the November 8 meeting to make a presentation on opening the AIFLD records. Afterwards, a vote on the resolution would be conducted. The national AFL-CIO had used the time since September to mobilize union staff people against the resolution. After making a presentation at the November meeting, I was asked to leave. Following a contentious discussion, the executive board tabled the resolution. An international staff person from the United Steelworkers (USW) union, the appointed staff delegates from the AFSCME, and SPRLF AFL-CIO officers played a crucial role in its defeat. Throughout its existence, AIFLD had USW officers on its board of directors, and in 2019 the NED had a

USW vice-president, Fred Redmond, on its board of directors.[16] The NED had funded AIFLD, and it continued to finance the Solidarity Center, which had replaced AIFLD in 1997. AFSCME had a history with AIFLD, which it had reason to keep buried too. Its president according to the *New York Times* had taken money from the CIA in the 1960s and had allegedly been linked to the coup against Cheddi Jagan in British Guiana.[17] Virtually the sole argument made by opponents to the St. Paul resolution was that this was too much bad publicity for unions and so should not be made public.

On November 8, I received from Ben Blake a 44-page Excel spreadsheet with a list of all the AIFLD file titles in the UMD archives. The archives contained 3,700 files occupying over 400 boxes. There was no question Blake was working diligently and honestly to open the AFL-CIO records, but there was also no question in my mind that the national AFL-CIO was using him in an attempt to manage my attempts to access the archives. In a phone conversation with Ben, I made a vague threat to go to the *Labor Notes* conference with the Ford Cuautitlán/AIFLD story. *Labor Notes* is a reform labor journal with a history of taking controversial positions and challenging union leadership. They hold a well-attended annual conference. Blake responded to this quickly with an email: "I would advise you to hold off in getting further involved personally and publicly on this issue and pushing it further within the labor movement and at *Labor Notes*."

The GMMA archivist asked me to back off and give him a chance to work behind the scenes. He advised me if I waited until the *Labor Notes* conference was over in April, and if there was no movement by the AFL-CIO, I could return to the public campaign.

As I was not ready to go public with the Cuautitlán story yet, I agreed to hold off on public comment until April. Having spent a lifetime in organized labor, I was more skeptical of the national AFL-CIO than Ben was. He wrote on December 17 to tell me that he thought the AFL-CIO had moved past their Cold War attitudes. The people he was in contact with, "I do believe, operate in an ethical and principled way."

I committed to Blake that I would not comment publicly on the AIFLD archives, but I didn't believe that constrained me from privately pursuing research on AIFLD activity in Minnesota. On February 20, 2018, I emailed Bill McCarthy, the President of the Minnesota AFL-CIO, asking about a picture I had found of Danny Gustafson, the President of the Minnesota AFL-CIO, speaking at the 1985 national AFL-CIO convention. The photo caption identified him as having recently taken an AIFLD trip to Nicaragua.[18] Gustafson was speaking in opposition to the motion against aid for the Contras. I requested to see the executive board minutes from the period of Gustafson's trip and the transcript of the State conventions during the 1980s. I had known McCarthy for many years from my time on the Minnesota AFL-CIO executive board. He initially told me, "Danny speaks to this issue in detail at our 1987 MN AFL-CIO Convention. You're welcome to come in to review the minutes of the convention."

Fairly quickly, McCarthy reversed himself and emailed me that I would need to get permission from the national AFL-CIO to view the minutes from the Minnesota State convention. A letter to Richard Trumka, the President of the national AFL-CIO, to make this request went unanswered.

April came and went, and I heard nothing from Blake. He did not respond to emails or phone messages. Robert Kasper and McCarthy had been at a meeting with Trumka in Chicago on March 13, 2018, and they had taken a picture standing next to him along with the other attendees.[19] Kasper returned to St. Paul on March 14 and announced at the SPRLF executive board meeting he would pull out the resolution on AIFLD from the November meeting, which the board had voted to table, and hold another vote on it at the April meeting. This time the resolution was voted down. There was no particular reason to do this other than to send a message to the resolution supporters and to me that the national Federation was never going to open these files and that they could muster the votes to impose that decision. But other events were transpiring, which would change their minds.

11

Washington, DC

The AFL-CIO under presidents Meany and Kirkland enmeshed the organization with a large, mostly government funded foreign policy bureaucracy. A number of the people employed in this area including Jay Lovestone, Irving Brown, Serafino Romualdi, William Doherty and Andrew McClellan were allegedly CIA operatives for some if not much of their lives. Has the AFL-CIO ever made any public comments on this relationship with the CIA?

Rob McKenzie to Richard Trumka, November 2018

It appeared that the chances of viewing any labor archival files on AIFLD were small. I considered filing a Freedom of Information Act (FOIA) request with the CIA on Ford Cuautitlán and contacted an online organization called MuckRock. They describe themselves as "a non-profit, collaborative news site that brings together journalists, researchers, activists, and regular citizens to request, analyze, and share government documents, making politics more transparent and democracies more informed."

MuckRock advised me to forget about the CIA, since they weren't likely to release anything, but to try the DoS instead. On December 3, 2016, I sent a FOIA request to the DoS asking for records on, "An armed attack by several hundred men on striking Mexican workers at a Ford Assembly plant in Cuautitlán, Mexico in January of 1990." The DoS told me that the estimated completion date of my request was October 30, 2017, as they had a backlog of approximately 15,000 applications. The FOIA process would be another long slog, but I had good reasons to believe that relevant documents existed at the DoS.

While working on the project on Ford Cuautitlán, I came into possession of two documents. One was a letter U.S. Senator Paul

Wellstone had sent to President Salinas of Mexico on February 5, 1991:

Dear President Salinas:

As a member of the Committee on Labor and Human Resources of the United State Senate, it is my responsibility to evaluate the wisdom of allowing President Bush to negotiate a free trade agreement with Mexico under the "fast-track" procedure. In making this evaluation, I will be guided by the principle that any trade agreement must be designed to improve the living standards and security of working people in both countries, and to protect basic human rights.

At the invitation of several constituents, I recently had the opportunity to meet with leaders of the Ford Workers Democratic Movement from Cuautitlán and hear about their experiences. Their report has caused me great concern. I would appreciate it if you could provide me with answers to some of the questions they raised.

Is it true that Ford workers have not been allowed to have a representative election that was apparently ordered by a Mexican court? Is it true that charges have not been brought against company or union officials who workers believe must have approved of January 8, 1990 attack? Why have the most serious charges against those accused of the armed attack inside the plant been dropped? Can you verify that Ford decided not to take some 750 workers back to work after the events of January 8, 1990, despite an agreement to do so, which the Secretary of Labor was a party? Is it true that Ford has been permitted to fire elected local union leaders? Will the National Human Rights Commission, which you established last year, review the petition which the Ford workers presented, and, if so, when can a decision be expected?

I certainly respect the right of the Mexican people to handle their own affairs. At the same time, I consider it my responsibility not to cast votes in the United States Senate that would result in any harm coming to American or Mexican workers. I would appreciate your assistance in providing as much information as possible concerning this important Cuautitlán Ford plant case.

Thank you for your attention to these concerns. Your assistance is greatly appreciated.

Sincerely,

Paul David Wellstone United States Senator

The other was a fax sent to Wellstone by Assistant Secretary of State Janet G. Mullins on May 28, 1991:

Letter from the US Department of State to The Honorable Paul David Wellstone, United States Senate:

May 28, 1991

Dear Senator Wellstone:

Thank you for your inquiry of March 25, 1991 regarding the investigation and prosecution of those responsible for the violence at the Ford Plant in Cuautitlán , Mexico in January, 1990. The following is a summary of the Cuautitlán labor incident.

On January 8, 1990, a violent internal union confrontation over leadership of the national/local union took place outside the Cuautitlán assembly plant and resulted in eight people being shot. Mr. Cleto Nigmo, who was neither a CTM (Confederation of Mexican Workers) nor dissident union activist, later died of gunshot wounds. Immediately following this incident, the Cuautitlán complex was occupied by dissidents until January 22, 1990, when the facility was retaken by the police. By early February only one-third of the work force had returned to work. After consultation between the government, the union, and company management, all absent workers were terminated, and the process of hiring/rehiring replacement workers was begun. Approximately 600 (of 3,800) originally terminated were not offered reemployment.

Criminal charges stemming from the incident were sought on the day of the shootings when the workers detained three employees thought to be involved. The police subsequently released these employees for lack of evidence. Later, ten non-employees, including a Mexico City CTM official not associated with automotive industry and his two sons, were arrested and found guilty of manslaughter and weapons charges. The ten were fined and sentenced to three years in prison but remain free on bail pending appeal. Hector Uriarte, the then Ford CTM National Chairman, was subpoenaed for questioning but never appeared.

On July 26, 1990, the Ford Motor Company reached an agreement with dismissed workers over severance pay compensation, marking an end to the labor dispute.

Dissident activity increased significantly at the Cuautitlán plant during the week of January 7, 1991, which marked the anniversary of the union conflict and death of Cleto Nigmo.

Ford de Mexico's security measures and a strong police presence minimized the effect of the dissident activity that managed only to produce a single late start at Cuautitlán and a single lost shift at the LaVilla Parts Depot. On January 8, 1991, 25 people carrying a large banner and U.S. and Mexican flags picketed in remembrance of Mr. Nigmo. The group, purported to be tied to the UAW/CAW (Canadian Auto Workers) were orderly and left after one hour, without incident.

On January 14, 1991, the Mexican Federal Labor Court filed a ruling dismissing the dissident union (COR) petition to represent the Cuautitlán force.

The court has apparently accepted the CTM argument that COR's supporters are no longer Ford's employees and the petition is therefore invalid. A final COR appeal has been made to the Mexican Supreme Court.

I hope this has been of assistance.
Sincerely, [signed] Janet G. Mullins Assistant Secretary Legislative Affairs

The facts seem to differ from Mullins' characterization on some aspects of the events. For example, she tells Wellstone that the violent confrontation at Cuautitlán took place "outside" the assembly plant. The shootings happened inside the buildings at the Ford complex in

Cuautitlán. Mullins tells Wellstone that "dissidents" had occupied the plant following the attack. Two thousand Ford workers initially occupied the facility and went on strike. She failed to mention that Ford Motor had requested that Mexican police enter the plant in the early morning of January 8 to remove "non-Ford employees." Ford initially blamed the Revolutionary Workers Party for the attack, and Ford had requested that Ambassador Negroponte meet privately with Salinas on the matter. This was information readily available to her in DoS cables. Mullins is quite adamant that this was an internal Mexican union dispute even though the CTM never officially accepted responsibility for the attack and Ford CTM General Secretary Uriarte had not been detained in connection with it.

Janet G. Mullins began her career as a Republican Party staff person with Senator Bob Packwood of Oregon. In 1984, she was the campaign manager for Mitch McConnell in his successful election effort for the U.S. Senate in their home state of Kentucky that year. In 1987, she became the executive director of George H. W. Bush's political action committee and then joined his presidential campaign. When Bush won the 1988 election for president, he nominated her for assistant Secretary of State for legislative affairs. She served in this office from March 2, 1989, until August 23, 1992. In 1992, Mullins moved to the White House, where she became assistant to the president for political affairs. Mullins would become immersed in controversy in that job. She was accused of searching official records regarding Bill Clinton's draft status in violation of U.S. privacy laws. In 1995, after a four-year investigation by a Special Counsel, Mullins was exonerated of any wrongdoing. She was then immediately hired by Ford Motor Company as a vice-president for Washington affairs. She was the second woman to become a corporate officer at Ford in the 90-year history of the company and would work in that position until 2004.[1] There must have been something about Mullins that Ford really liked.

Ford's hiring of Mullins raised the specter of conflict of interest. As the assistant Secretary of State for legislative affairs, Mullins was in a position to know the details of what happened at Cuautitlán in 1989/1990. She faced the task of answering questions raised by a newly elected, progressive, populist U.S. senator who was advocating on behalf of the Mexican workers and his U.S. autoworker constituents. The DoS would have had some records on what happened at Cuautitlán, and the assistant Secretary of State would likely have had communications with Ambassador Negroponte. She may have had a security clearance that would have allowed her access to CIA files.

The Estimated Completion Date of the FOIA request to the DoS, October 30, 2017, came and went. The following day I called the DoS to inquire about the status of my request. The staff person on the phone told me (I believe inadvertently) that it was in "review status," which meant the DoS found documents, but they had not decided which would be released, if any. I called again in November, December, and January, but the information officers would only say that there was a big backlog of cases and the DoS hadn't completed mine yet. In March, I contacted the Madison, Wisconsin, office of U.S. Senator Tammy Baldwin and asked for help. One of Baldwin's staff people got in touch with the DoS in support of my FOIA request.

In late March, I received five cables comprising 24 pages concerning the Ford incident that the U.S. Embassy in Mexico City had sent to the Secretary of State in Washington and the U.S. consulates throughout Mexico in January 1990. They went out under the names of John Negroponte, the ambassador, and Robert Pastorino, the deputy chief of mission. They showed that events at Cuautitlán were being watched closely by the Embassy, which considered it a significant challenge to Salinas' economic policies. The cables portrayed the Salinas government, Ford, and the CTM as conspiring against the local union at Cuautitlán. The communications revealed that the Embassy had intelligence sources inside the PRI, the government of Mexico, and the CTM.

A great deal of information from the Embassy cables is missing from what was given to Wellstone by Mullins in 1991. I appealed the Agency's initial determination and argued there must have been more records based on Mullins' fax to Wellstone and possible conflict of interest. I also raised the fact that Escobar Briones and Santos Martinez had been initially denied visas in 1991 to visit the U.S.

ostensibly because they were communists.[2] The DoS had this information on Briones and Martinez from some source that they hadn't disclosed. Senator Baldwin wrote a letter in support of my appeal, and DoS granted it. In March 2019, an Office of Government Information Services agent, Lorraine Hartmann, began looking for records. I received 15 documents totaling over 100 pages soon after. The FOIA process produced a great quantity of information about the events I was researching. I don't believe this would have transpired in that way without the intervention of Senator Baldwin and her staff.

In April 2018, the SPRLF AFL-CIO leadership, with the assistance of several International Union staff people, pulled the motion on opening the AIFLD files off the table at the St. Paul Regional Labor Federation for the sole purpose of voting it down. Following this utterly unnecessary action, I emailed Ben Blake on April 16:

> Hi Ben,
> I hope things are going well for you. It is April and I have kept my promise I made in December to refrain from further public comment on the AFL-CIO and the AIFLD files. How goes your effort to get them opened? My guess is things aren't going smoothly. Best, Rob

It was five weeks later, at the end of May, long past the *Labor Notes* conference, when I received a return email from Blake who told me that the AFL-CIO had contacted him in relation to my request to access the AIFLD records related to Mexico. He believed I would have good news in the near future.

In August 2018, Blake notified me that the AFL-CIO had agreed to allow me to see the Mexico AIFLD files. I had been granted special permission to access the International Department/AIFLD records in the UMD archives. Blake had located 18 boxes of material relevant to Mexico, 1987–91. I could now schedule a visit to the GMMA in College Park, Maryland. Blake was also hoping to work out an agreement to open the currently closed records.

The only thing that had changed regarding my request to view the AIFLD files since the April beat down at the St. Paul Labor Federation meeting was the arrival of the five cables from the DoS on Cuautitlán. The AFL-CIO has close ties with the DoS through the Solidarity Center, and the FOIA grant had apparently been enough to convince the Federation that I now had documentation on U.S. government involvement at Ford Cuautitlán and their refusal to allow me to view the AIFLD files would be seen as the cover-up that I believed it to be.

The GMMA are adjacent to Washington, DC. The AFL-CIO material comprises the single largest donation to the UMD Libraries. The archive contains approximately 40 million documents, including the 3,700 AIFLD files.[3] I traveled to College Park on September 10, 2018. My first full day at the Hornblake Library, the location of the reading room for the Meany Archive, was September 11, the 45th anniversary of the 1973 coup against the Allende government in Chile. I met and had a brief discussion about AIFLD with a student from the University of Cambridge who was viewing the AIFLD archives on Chile. Patrick Dunne was working on his dissertation on AIFLD involvement in Chile.

Blake had located 44 boxes of AIFLD archives that might hold material on Mexico in the 1980s. This seemed to me to be a comprehensive selection of materials. I asked Ben if any researchers had viewed these boxes before. He responded, "Not that we know of." I photographed dozens of these records during the next few days.

I had now collected hundreds of documents, DoS cables, interviews, and records on AIFLD and read everything I could get my hands on about the subject. It became clear to me that the AFL-CIO was hiding more than just the involvement of AIFLD in the attack on Ford Cuautitlán in 1990. The evidence was overwhelming that the CIA was involved in developing and implementing AFL-CIO foreign policy directly with its own agents during the entire Cold War.

Jay Lovestone had been the Federation international affairs director from 1963 to 1974, and had developed a close personal relationship with the CIA's counterintelligence chief James Angleton during these years.[4] When George Meany found out the CIA was paying Lovestone, he forced him out of the organization in 1974.[5] By 1980, Irving Brown had been identified as having worked in counterintelligence for the CIA by at least five of the Agency's former agents, yet Lane Kirkland appointed Brown to be international affairs director in 1982.[6] Before that assignment, Brown had been in charge of the African American Labor Center (AALC). The very credible Philip Agee named Brown, William Doherty of AIFLD, and Morris Paladino of the AAFLI as having been CIA operatives.[7] These three institutes were primarily responsible for carrying out what they proclaimed to be AFL-CIO foreign policy during the Cold War.

These AFL-CIO/CIA relationships and the foreign policy they engendered had been contested in the U.S. labor movement. The Reuthers battled with Meany, Brown, and Lovestone over foreign policy for decades, and it may have cost Walter his life. When only a few national union leaders objected to the AFL-CIO-supported coup in Chile in the 1970s, local union activists protested AIFLD and the organization's foreign policy. In the 1980s, unions representing most of the AFL-CIO membership opposed Federation support for Reagan's policy in Central America. In 1995, Kirkland was forced out, and the institutes were disbanded. A new program of international relations finally began.

It was time to write to AFL-CIO President Trumka and ask questions about this history and the Federation's intransigence on opening up its files to researchers. On November 2, 2018, I wrote President Trumka:

When I retired from my job as an International Staff Rep for the UAW, I began researching something that had long troubled me. In 1990 an armed group attacked workers at a Ford plant near Mexico City, killing one, wounding eight and sparking an occupation of the plant. At the time I didn't understand who had paid the three hundred attackers and provided them with Ford uniforms and ID badges. Ford denied doing this to my UAW local leadership. The Ford I knew fairly well, would not have used violence against their own workers in their own plant (way too much bad publicity). The CTM that I was familiar with would never have gone into an employer's plant and shot the place up unless someone at least as powerful as Ford was behind it. In 1996 I was told by a staff rep for John Sweeney that the American Institute for Free Labor Development had been involved. When I asked him if this meant the CIA had been involved, he said "yes."

I have accumulated a large quantity of information regarding these events at this point including many hours of oral interviews done in Mexico City, Freedom of Information Act Requests from the Department of State and CIA, documents from the UAW archives at Wayne State and most recently documents from the AFL-CIO archives at the University of Maryland.

I have a question and requests concerning the debate in labor over AIFLD and foreign policy that now seem best to be directed to you.

I would like to view the minutes of the AFL-CIO national conventions from 1983, 1985 and 1987 pertaining to resolutions on El Salvador, Nicaragua and the murders of AIFLD employees Mark Pearlman and Michael Hammer…

I would also like to examine the minutes from the national Executive Council minutes from August 1966 as AIFLD was discussed in this meeting. In 1988 the International Affairs Department organized a cross border organizing conference with the CTM. I have documents concerning this from the UAW and would like to view the AFL-CIO archived records on this.

The AFL-CIO under presidents Meany and Kirkland enmeshed the organization with a large, mostly government-funded foreign policy bureaucracy. A number of the people employed in this area including Jay Lovestone, Irving Brown, Serafino Romualdi, William Doherty and Andrew McClellan allegedly were CIA operatives for some if not much of their lives. Has the AFL-CIO ever made any public comments on this relationship with the CIA? Thank you for your attention to my requests and question.

Solidarity Rob McKenzie

I never received a response to this letter from Trumka or anyone else from the AFL-CIO.

Having seen the DoS cables, I determined to file a FOIA request with the CIA. The attack on the Cuautitlán plant was a covert operation resulting in a murder for which there was no statute of limitation, and therefore it was unlikely the Agency would ever release documents. I did think it possible that I could force the CIA to take a national security exemption on the events of 1989 and 1990 at Ford Cuautitlán. Under Exemption 1 of the FOIA, information vital to national security can be withheld as exempt from disclosure if it meets the substantive and procedural requirements of the current executive order on national security classification. The Agency wouldn't have any trouble clearing that bar and, it would say a lot about what happened.

I sent a broad request for information to the CIA office of the information and privacy coordinator in March 2018 asking for records "On an armed attack on workers involved in a labor dispute at a Ford Assembly Plant in Cuautitlán, Mexico in January 1990 and events there that preceded this or followed." A couple of weeks later, I received a pleasant letter from an information and privacy coordinator asking me to clarify the scope with specific events. I gladly clarified it by adding the work stoppage of December 22, 1989, the kidnapping of the local leaders on January 5, 1990, and the police reoccupation of the plant on January 22. Six months later, I received a letter from the Agency telling me they did not locate any records responsive to my request and that it was "highly unlikely" that repeating those searches would change the result. "Nevertheless," I had the legal right to appeal. I filed an appeal.

Apparently, I needed to prove CIA involvement at Cuautitlán. I understood that the DoS contracted with the CIA to transmit cables from embassies, and this would mean that the Agency had the eleven cables I had at a minimum. One of the workers named in the cables as being a leader, Raul Escobar Briones, was briefly denied entry into the U.S. in 1991 apparently because he was a communist. The CIA would have collected this information... I had two declassified CIA documents that discussed the PRT. Both Ford and the Embassy reported the PRT as being involved in the events. I sent in my appeal in October 2018 and received a letter acknowledging the receipt dated October 15.

Having heard nothing by January 2019, I sent a letter asking for a status update. In response, the Agency sent a correspondence telling me my request was in process and that they had adopted the policy of handling appeals on a first-received, first-out basis. In April, I again sought an update. After receiving no response to that communication, in July, I sent a certified letter and copied the Office of Government Information Services (OGIS) at the National Archives and Records Administration. This is a government agency that does non-binding arbitration to settle FOIA request disputes, and they had played an essential role in the successful resolution of my FOIA appeal to the DoS. I was soon in possession of a letter from a new information and privacy coordinator telling me that my request was in process and providing me with an estimated completion date of March 23, 2020.

When March 23 came and went, and I still hadn't received anything, I sent a new letter to the OGIS, asking them to intercede in the dispute with the CIA. In addition to the basis for appeal I had previously given the Agency, I added some more reasons. Important information was absent from the DoS cables and must have been sent to Washington via another channel.

I argued to the OGIS that in July 1988, the PRI, which had governed Mexico since the late 1920s, lost an election to a candidate on the political left. The military seized the ballots, and the candidate of the PRI was declared the victor even though massive and widespread election fraud was apparently unquestionable.[8] Today, almost everyone agrees the PRI candidate lost. The U.S appointed John D. Negroponte as ambassador to Mexico a few weeks later. He had been ambassador in Honduras when the Contras were active. Negroponte was active in assistance for the Contras and this would have been a violation of an act of Congress if proven. The press reported that he allegedly used a CIA back channel to communicate with Washington and avoid detection by Congress.

Ambassador Negroponte could have used such a CIA back channel to communicate with Washington about events at Cuautitlán in 1990. The attack on the Ford plant on Monday January 8, was precipitated by an event on Friday, January 5. On that Friday, an unidentified group kidnapped local union leaders at Ford Cuautitlán. When workers in the plant learned of this, they halted work and engaged in a sit-down strike at the Ford assembly plant. The leaders were soon released. Ford had police come into the plant on Monday, January 8, and the attackers also entered the plant. There is no mention of the January 5 kidnapping and work stoppage anywhere in the DoS cables. It is not believable that the U.S. Mexican Embassy would have failed to notify Washington about an event like this concerning a large American employer, especially since it was important enough to generate eleven more cables. I believe the DoS informed Washington through a CIA channel.

The Mexican press reported that many witnesses saw the gangster Wallace de la Mancha at the Ford plant on January 8, and they believed him to be in command of the group of attackers. The CTM, the government-affiliated labor union, held a press conference and demanded an investigation of Mancha a few days later. Mancha died mysteriously, probably assassinated, within the year. The DoS cables never mention Mancha, nor do they provide any real explanation about who organized and financed the attack on the Ford plant on January 8. This information must have been sent to Washington through some other means.

Unfortunately, the CIA refused the OGIS offer to mediate. They also declined to give an estimated completion date, but they did assure the OGIS my appeal was still open and pending. The FOIA requires agencies to make a reasonable judgment as to when they will process requests. The Agency responded with an estimate of 2,594 days for "complex" requests, which mine appears to be.

Following the OGIS failure to resolve the matter, U.S. Senator Tammy Baldwin's staff began an attempt to get a resolution on the FOIA request. As a result of Senator Baldwin's staff query, the CIA wrote to me on June 24, 2020, saying that my case was in "active process" at the Agency. They were unable to estimate when the processing of my case would be completed:

> As you are aware, CIA provided an initial determination of **No Records Located** for your query, in response to which you subsequently exercised your right to an administrative appeal...dated 2 October 2018. Since that time, you have requested status updates. The estimated completion date we provided has obviously passed, and we wish to assure you that your case remains in active process, at the appellate level, and is in queue for Agency Release Panel (ARP) deliberation.... [I]t would be difficult for this office at this time to accurately estimate when the processing of your case will be completed.
>
> Mark Lilly Information and Privacy Coordinator

What took place at an auto assembly plant at the end of the twentieth century just outside of Mexico City had an meaningful impact on the lives of many people in Mexico and the U.S. Only the DoS has been willing to come forward with all the relevant documents. Other organizations with information persist in keeping it hidden. The events of January 8, 1990, will never be forgotten and someday the whole truth will come out. *La lucha continúa* (The struggle continues).

Conclusion
Putting Together the Pieces of the Puzzle

I began to research the events surrounding the attack on workers at the CAP because of an interest in answering questions that had lingered for decades. As I initiated the search for answers, I realized that the institutions that had information about this— i.e., the AFL-CIO, the UAW, the DoS, Ford Motor Company, and the CIA—may have been actively concealing evidence that might indicate their involvement in these affairs.[1] Their actions raised more questions about what had happened, and eventually, new avenues of research opened up. As the months and years passed, many individuals stepped forward to help with the project. Early on, a friend with excellent knowledge of the UAW's internal operations told me, "Don't give up. They are hiding something."

In the world of study into CIA covert operations, researchers can never completely prove Agency involvement in matters. Some speculation is required to reach a logical conclusion about events. However, I now know what happened at a Ford assembly plant near Mexico City in the late 1980s and early 1990s.

During a period of economic contraction and political instability, U.S. auto companies made substantial investments in export-oriented production facilities in Mexico. Militants aligned with a Marxist socialist party in a local union at a Ford facility began organizing opposition to the wages the employers wanted to pay and the work rules they demanded. These activists, who had won election to the Executive Committee, were also demanding democratic reforms from the corrupt, politically conservative, and pro-employer union federation, the CTM. The tactics the CTM had reportedly employed for over 50 years to subdue dissidents, like firings and physical intimidation, had been unsuccessful. The FWDM became a challenge to the political survival of the CTM leadership.

The movement also grew into a test of the Salinas government and its pro-business foreign investment policies, which the FWDM successes threatened. Salinas, the PRI candidate, had lost an election the previous year to a left-of-the-center candidate, whose coalition had included socialists and communists. The military seized the ballots, and the PRI claimed victory. The Cuautitlán union directly challenged the unpopular government's neoliberal policies. The U.S. responded to the political crisis by sending John Negroponte, an ambassador, and Vincent Shields, CIA station chief, to Mexico. They had gained experience working together on covert operations in a neighboring country. Individuals associated with the Reagan anti-communist offensive in Central America and national security posts were very much involved in initiating the NAFTA.

The Reagan administration had viewed Mexico as a very politically unstable country throughout its tenure. The near victory of the Cárdenas coalition in the July 1988 election had only confirmed that opinion. The CIA kept close tabs on leftist political parties in Mexico, including the PRT, whose members were very involved with organizing the workers at CAP. AIFLD, which had developed a close relationship with the CTM and occupied an office in their Mexico City headquarters, was likely quickly informed of events at Cuautitlán. AIFLD could have fulfilled its intelligence gathering function and alerted the CIA. AIFLD Executive Director William Doherty took part in meetings with the heads of the CTM auto unions in Washington, DC, in October/November 1988. The local union leaders at Cuautitlán were planning to run for the top post of the Ford CTM union in July. The CIA likely worked out a plan with the general secretary of the CTM, Hector Uriarte, to prevent them from winning this election, and someone may have approached Ford to coordinate the details. Ford fired four Executive Committee members from the Cuautitlán plant in June 1989, weeks before the CTM election. Instead of eliminating the opposition, the firings unleashed a new wave of protest. When a December work stoppage in protest of pay reductions took place at the CAP, the CIA decided to act.

In the 1980 documentary film about the CIA, *On Company Business,* Victor Marchetti, who was executive assistant to the deputy director of the CIA from 1955 to 1969, said about covert operations:

> In any dirty job such as paramilitary activity, assassinations, sabotage, and the like, what is known as special ops, almost invariably the direct agency involvement of the agency officer, the career officer, ends in the planning stage and sometimes even before that in the policy or decision-making stage. The dirty work will be carried out by either contract agents or one-time agents, gangsters, mercenaries, whoever happens to be available, whatever assets are available at that moment.

Wallace de la Mancha, a gangster, who had previously done violent work with the CTM, was contracted to work with Hector Uriarte, the general secretary of Ford CTM, on the project. Along with willing law enforcement officers, they would organize and arm a large force to assault the workers in the CAP and break the FWDM. On Friday, January 5, 1990, these forces kidnapped a group of local union leaders whom they were likely planning to murder. When the workers in the plant learned of the kidnapping, they halted production and occupied the CAP drawing Ford into the conflict. Faced with this unexpected action, Mancha ordered the union leaders to be released, although they resolved to act on an alternate plan.

Ford Motor appears to have decided to fire the leaders who had organized the January 5 work stoppage when they reported to work on Monday, January 8. They would have coordinated with the CTM and obtained their approval for this action. Ford must have known it should be prepared for a militant reaction this time and contacted the local police to have the fired leaders removed from the plant. Apparently, the company had locks changed and notices placed on these leader's coverall lockers on the night of January 7, telling them to report to the coverall storeroom and depot where the police would be waiting. Mancha ordered his little army of *golpeadores,* funded by the CIA and led by his lieutenant, Guadalupe Uribe, into the plant early that Monday morning to teach the workers a lesson and prevent another work stoppage. They entered the CAP with the police, and the thugs were wearing Ford uniforms and ID badges, which Uriarte had helped acquire.

Leaders of the Ford workers had heard about the strange activities in the CAP on the Sunday night. They met and developed a plan for the morning of January 8. When the *golpeadores* confronted and attempted to intimidate the workers, the workers picked up tools and scrap metal to oppose them. A fight occurred, with nine workers shot by the attackers. One worker, Cleto Nigmo, was shot twice at close range and died two days later. The workers went on strike and occupied the plant for two weeks in protest of the attack. Thousands of police eventually drove them out and retook the CAP.

The workers captured three of the *golpeadores* and turned them over to authorities. The three captured *golpeadores* told authorities that Uriarte and Uribe had hired them. The assault and violence had been successful in breaking the movement, but there would be a cost. In the press and the legislature, participants were being named, questions were being asked, and the public was aroused.

Uriarte was soon subpoenaed for questioning and fled Mexico City. Ten others, including Guadalupe Uribe, were eventually convicted of manslaughter and served six months in prison. The many public reports of his involvement in the attack at Ford on January 8 forced Wallace de la Mancha to write a letter to the editor of the newspaper *La Jornada* on January 10 to deny he was involved.

Victor Marchetti went on to say in the 1980 *On Company Business* interview:

> In the setup, the agency has where the dirty work is done by contract people or one-time hires and so forth, obviously if anything goes wrong they can be disavowed. If the person turns bad, turns sour and may want to speak out, and may possibly have some credibility and/or evidence well then, stronger action is called for, the ultimate termination of the agent.

Within the year, Wallace de la Mancha died mysteriously at the age of 59. There were reports he was ambushed in Guadalajara. With him died any potential direct evidence of CIA involvement.

The Cuautitlán local Ford union had many enemies, including the CTM leadership, the Salinas PRI, and Ford Motor management. The resources required to hire police agents on January 5 to kidnap the local union leaders and then to hire, arm, outfit in Ford uniforms, provide with ID badges, and transport 300 thugs willing to commit violence in the middle of the night on January 7/8 far exceeded the capacity of the CTM. On January 17, the head of the CTM autoworkers union held a press conference and called for the government to prosecute Wallace de la Mancha for criminal attacks on workers. Some individuals associated with the CTM, a notoriously compliant labor union, did participate in the action. They seemingly had no qualms about participating in a violent intrusion into an employer's factory, resulting in a large amount of production and profit loss. They believed someone more powerful than Ford was behind the attack and that there would be no retribution against them. They were correct in this assumption. Though having the motive to finance the operation, the Salinas PRI government was constrained by the many opposition party members in the legislature who supported the Cuautitlán local, as did much of the public. There was no known involvement by anyone associated with the Mexican military.

Arming a sizable paramilitary force to conduct illegal operations in a foreign country was nothing Ford Motor had ever done in its long history. The strike and occupation shut down the CAP for months. Ford suffered terrible publicity as a result of the attack, with many politicians blaming them. When Ford representatives met with the U.S. Embassy on January 13, they were confused about what had happened. While they had not approved the violent incursion in advance, from Embassy cables it appears that Ford may have quickly joined the cover-up, calling it an unfortunate inter-union conflict. Ford took no action against the CTM for their role in the assault. Ford later hired at least two individuals with knowledge about what had transpired to important corporate jobs.

The process of elimination leaves the CIA as an institution with the motive and the capability of sponsoring the attack. During the Cold War, perhaps hundreds of actions similar to the coup at Ford Motor in 1990 were instigated by the CIA in Latin America. Cuatitlán was different. That operation took place in the dying days of the Cold War. There was no justification based on national security or a Soviet menace. The causes of the worker rebellion at the CAP were created solely by the internal dynamics of Mexico. U.S. job losses to Mexico due to low wages were a greater danger to Americans than the Soviet threat from a previous generation. The defeat of the FWDM assured auto companies they would have a compliant workforce in Mexico and paved the way for the NAFTA. It is possible to conceive of a much different labor movement in Mexico today if the CAP activists had won the election to the general secretary of the CTM and had been allowed to promote the reforms they instituted at the Ford plant.

In 1944, an AFL-CIO convention passed a resolution, written by Jay Lovestone, creating the FTUC. For the first few years of its existence, the FTUC funded its operations in Europe from union dues and union contributions. By 1948, the forerunner of the CIA began funneling large amounts of money to the FTUC, and it became one of the most influential players in the Cold War. The FTUC leadership would clash with the Agency over how they would account for the money, the efforts by the CIA to recruit FTUC staff and tactics in the anti-communist struggle. Jay Lovestone thought he knew much more about fighting international communism than did the CIA, whom he referred to derisively as "Fizzkids" and "Fizzlanders." In 1958, the CIA–FTUC alliance ended.

As the main Cold War battleground moved to the developing world, the CIA, with the approval of the Kennedy administration, developed a new type of labor organization. The CIA had learned from its experience with Lovestone and the FTUC. AIFLD would be different. It would be entirely a government organization managed at the top by CIA agents operating under the auspices of the AFL-CIO and business leaders. Although an organized labor mask would be essential for the new organization, the labor federation would have no part in its day-to-day operations. The executive director would not need to contact the AFL-CIO president if they believed they worked within the Federation's very broad policy guidelines and objectives. Funding would be wholly independent of the AFL-CIO and its International Affairs Department.

The two executive directors of AIFLD, Serafino Romualdi and William Doherty Jr., were government intelligence agents their entire careers. CIA agents Morris Paladino and Irving Brown joined them in the Cold War labor struggle and enlisted close collaborators, like Joseph Beirne. George Meany finally forced Jay Lovestone out of his job as international affairs director in 1974 after learning the CIA was paying him. Other AIFLD/AFL-CIO employees may have been intelligence agents too, including Jesse Friedman and Michael Hammer. More questions need to be asked about exactly what AFL-CIO President Lane Kirkland's relationship to the CIA was. When he graduated from the Georgetown School of Foreign Service in 1948, he went directly to the AFL-CIO. After becoming a top aide to Meany, he falsely convinced Walter Reuther that AIFLD would not be a topic at the August 1966 AFL-CIO executive council meeting where a motion was passed condemning Victor Reuther for his exposure of the AIFLD–CIA link. Shortly after becoming AFL-CIO president, Kirkland appointed Irving Brown as international affairs director in 1982. Brown was more closely linked to the CIA than any other figure in labor. Kirkland seems to have focused primarily on the anti-communist struggle his whole career.

An article on the retirement and career of Lane Kirkland, which appeared in the *New York Times* in 1996, raised the question, "Is it too late for labor to revive itself?" In retrospect, the answer to that was likely "yes." Labor was unable to surmount the forces unleashed in the previous decades, and the relentless decrease in unionization rates continued. Today many older union activists ask another question, "Is there anything we could have done differently?"

The AFL-CIO enmeshed itself with a vast government-funded foreign-policy bureaucracy throughout the Cold War. Some of the government agents employed in the field collected intelligence information about American unionists. Others participated in labor's internal decision making and helped direct its policy. The irony of a labor organization, such as AIFLD, which defined itself in terms of the struggle for "free labor" in opposition to those labor organizations that were "government" controlled, being run by government agents was undoubtedly not lost on U.S. adversaries.

The Cold War led to a complete victory for the forces supporting neoliberal capitalism. In contrast, unionization rates in the U.S. as a percentage of the workforce peaked in 1955 at 33 percent. In 1962, the year AIFLD was founded, that figure stood at 29.3 percent. Union membership in terms of absolute numbers reached its zenith in 1979, the year Lane Kirkland became AFL-CIO President. By 2019, the unionization rate had plummeted to 10.3 percent, and that figure does not capture the full extent of the drop as it fails to account for workers who are covered by collective bargaining agreements but are not union members in the increased number of "Right-to-Work" states and sectors.[2] Organized labor was launched on a path of decline during the Cold War, resulting in it becoming a marginalized societal force in the twenty-first century. The full part that the AFL-CIO's collaboration with the CIA contributed to this deterioration, and the responsibility that the Agency's infiltration and manipulation of labor played in its demise, is still undetermined. It has been over 30 years since the Cold War ended, and the AFL-CIO has still never publicly addressed the issue of its collaboration with the CIA during that period. It is difficult to imagine a new labor movement emerging without coming to terms with this past.

Appendix
On the Home "Front"

In 1966, select groups of South American unionists, who could perhaps be spotted kicking a football among each other or enjoying an outdoor swim, began to enjoy their summers in a secluded, wooden-hutted, 74-acre campsite in the woods of Virginia.[1] This depiction of innocence contrasts sharply to the purpose underpinning the unionists' stay at the retreat. With a capacity of 40 residential students, Front Royal became home to AIFLD's "more advanced" education, providing a more secluded setting than the Institute's former training center at the heart of Washington's lobbying industry on K Street.

It was in these leafy confines that selected union leaders from different South American countries were invited to come and be trained in how to resist communism, both within their unions and in their countries more broadly. The Institute's first-ever course provides evidence for the centrality of anti-communism to AIFLD's academic program. Following two weeks of orientation, involving a history of the U.S. labor movement and a breakdown of the international labor movement, and then three weeks on techniques of trade union organization, students spent a whole two weeks on "dangers and safeguards for democratic labor."[2] There was no mistaking what the gravest "danger" was. After breaking down and scrutinizing communism's ideological formation, students were taught defense tactics against potential infiltration.

While the specific content of the classes is unlikely to ever be revealed, some transcripts of lectures that are available indicate that the message underpinning the courses remained constant. Romualdi's plea to the inaugural class on their induction day in 1962 revealed how it was "an essential part of our function...to share with you...our concern" over the dangers of communist infiltration into

the labor movement.³ Throughout the course of their stay, unionists would have this message continually drummed home, often
from prominent political figures in both the US and their home
countries. Dean Rusk, Secretary of State throughout the Kennedy
and Johnson administrations, was one such example, but he was
far more implicit in his anti-communist message, attempting in a
graduation day lecture "to demonstrate that social and economic
progress can be explained in a democratic society." Others, such as
the Chilean ambassador Sergio Gutiérrez-Olivos, lectured the graduates on how they "must answer to the Communist contention that
social progress can best be achieved in a non-democratic society."⁴
The graduates knew what the prime evil political force in the continent was, and they had it on good authority.

AIFLD's Effectiveness

The *Miami Herald*'s "David-and-Goliath picture," in describing the
first-ever U.S.-based AIFLD course, does not help in establishing
how effective AIFLD's educational and social programs were. Presented as "odds of 2,000 to 43," comparing an ongoing meeting of
communist unionists in Santiago to the 43 students in Washington
learning "how to fend off the Reds' clutches," the article depicted a
noble, uphill struggle that the Institute often wanted to convey, both
to the public and to its students.⁵ With no credible means established
of recording the Institute's effectiveness, coupled with the support
AIFLD received from the U.S. government, a simplistic portrayal
of a plucky effort that saved workers from "the clutches" of communism is unhelpful. As will become clear, AIFLD's education often
did strengthen anti-communist resolve among its pupils, although
social projects were often inadequate, or left unfinished. However, in
assessing the effectiveness of their overarching aim—the promotion
of tranquil labor–business relations in order to negate the attrac-
tiveness of communism—only case studies at a wider socio-political
level can provide the answer.

Gathered four or five times a year for a three-course luncheon,
members of the AIFLD board would hear proof of how their educa-

tion program had instilled fervent anti-communism into the hearts and minds of Latin American unionists. Graduation ceremonies at Front Royal, or previously at the Sheraton-Carlton Hotel in Washington, DC, provide the best available evidence of the immediate impact education had on pupils. Brazilian unionist Canuto Coelho Filho, for example, articulated this in April 1963 on behalf of his fellow graduates, assuring the AIFLD board and the teachers "of our willingness to fight against international communism" and demonstrating his commitment to "democracy" by claiming that "we are disposed to defend it, if necessary, with our lives."[6] A willingness to please the U.S. contingent does come through the sources, seen in the recognition of Romualdi's original message, with Colombian Carvajalino Lobo agreeing that "only by preparation in democratic leadership of the working masses will it be possible to prevent international communism." It might be that Lobo and his peers were genuinely grateful and in awe of what was a unique and presumably enjoyable experience. The select few workers enjoying cocktails and a "Breast of Capon" that day must have felt indebted in some way to the Institute.[7]

Statements reinforcing the Institute's educational message might not be sufficient evidence to argue that the classes had a transformative effect on their students' political beliefs. If a South American unionist had been deemed fit to study at Front Royal, their political conscience was by no means a *tabula rasa*. One of AIFLD's main functions of course was to collect detailed information on the political persuasions of unionists, so they were able to invite students who were sympathetic to their anti-communist message. There is evidence, however, to suggest that Latin American workers did not necessarily arrive at the Institute with the knowledge or ideology required to fulfill AIFLD's objectives. Trinidadian unionist Gaston Benjamin, for example, told of how learning about the American labor movement's achievements had been a "dazzling" experience, assuring that "we will aim at emulating your achievements."[8] Given that the Institute's message of cooperation between labor leaders and business was taught through a "history of US trade unionism," (the specifics of which are unknown), workers were not just having their own beliefs reiterated to them. Divergence in opinion over exactly how closely labor should align with private interests also suggests that AIFLD did have to convince workers of the legitimacy of their anti-communist front. Leader of Bolivian bank workers, Adolfo Antelo Añez, for example, warned that if "the powerful and respected North American [sic] trade union movement does not act to obtain a fairer treatment for our economies…the possibility of progress may well be restricted."[9] Being limited to the handful of graduation speeches that are available does not help in ascertaining whether AIFLD effectively conveyed their message to the unionists who were trained. But the repetition in the speeches of a committed anti-communism, combined with a recognition that trainees often arrived in the U.S. without a solid ideology or strategy toward the Red menace, suggests that in the leafy retreat just north of the Shenandoah River, AIFLD was effective in making its contribution to the Cold War.

Assessing the effectiveness of AIFLD's overseas programs is a more challenging task than when looking at the U.S.-based work. In part a problem of evaluation methods, the elusive nature of AIFLD's activities within countries compounds this difficulty in establishing both whether the recipient Latin American unions benefited from these projects, and whether they effectively served the Institute's primary objective of building an anti-communist front. The General Accounting Office recognized in their report of 1969 how "without established evaluation criteria" they failed to reach any conclusions on the effectiveness of the education programs. While a similar lack of clarity existed over the impact social projects were having on the unions involved, the report did not make for impressive reading for AIFLD. After looking at the 80 projects carried out in both Chile and Brazil between 1968 and 1969, the report denounced their effect as having a "very limited nature" which "in our opinion, would be insignificant." This was due to the relatively small scale of the projects when compared to the number of unionized workers in said countries (499,000 and 11 million respectively).[10] This damning revelation should not be too surprising given that AIFLD only sought to help unions whom they deemed to be sympathetic to their ideals, but it does undermine the effectiveness of their Projects Department in its quest to access more workers who could be used to fight communism. A report by the Institute's PR department, detailing efforts to promote their social projects by producing advertisements for 23 Latin American television stations, recognized the difficulty that AIFLD had in establishing the notoriety needed to succeed in its objectives.[11]

Despite their apparent inefficiency and lack of evaluation, AIFLD's social programs abroad did receive praise from government officials for their success in a subsidiary aim. Infiltrating workforces within individual countries was a key purpose of projects, in order to collect information about the political persuasion of unions and their members. It appears that it was actually AID rather than the AFL-CIO which set out the task of social surveillance, highlighted in the contractual agreement between AID and the Institute's Social Projects Department: "the Institute shall use its best efforts to develop projects...in line with US AID objectives."[12] Evidence for how exactly this was achieved is quite fragmentary, and necessitates crossing borders to piece together aspects of the Social Project Department's apparatus. In Chile, for example, when the maritime union COMACH applied for a housing grant in 1964, they had to answer a series of questions about their political orientation, the support they received, if internal frictions existed between leaders and members, and highly detailed biographical information regarding which member "stood out" or demonstrated "character." Surveillance continued after projects were completed, with AIFLD paying for a "small group of people" to see that one project, in this case housing in Mexico, "did not become a slum," as Meany put it. The close proximity established between U.S. personnel (such as retired navy captain Andrew Klay, who was in charge of the Mexican project) and Latin American workers through this system appeared to become the most useful and important aspect of AIFLD's in-country operations.[13] Arguing against attempts to phase AIFLD out of their Argentinian program in 1970, U.S. Ambassador John Davis Lodge pointed out to the DoS that "the program provides the United States with a special and favorable access to this most important sector of the Argentinian political scene," capturing how the most pertinent objective of AIFLD Social Projects was the infiltration into the everyday lives of Latin American workers.[14]

Photographs

1. A young Bill Doherty (tallest in the middle) on a PTTI study trip to Uruguay in October 1956. Doherty began working for the PTTI in Mexico in 1955. (Photo from the International Institute of Social History)

2. Cheddi Jagan (front, center) leads a protest march in British Guiana in the 1970s. Jagan was deposed as prime minister in an AIFLD assisted effort in 1962. When free elections were held again in 1992, he was reelected in the now independent Guyana and governed as a democratic socialist. (Photo courtesy of the Cheddi Jagan Research Centre. https://jagan.org/).

3. Left to right: Victor, Roy, and Walter Reuther at a UAW Convention in Long Beach, California, May 16–21, 1966. In an interview with the *LA Times* Victor linked AIFLD, the AFL-CIO, and the CIA. The interview was published during the convention. (Photo from the Walter Reuther Library)

4. Left to right: Joe Beirne, CWA President, Walter Reuther, and Bill Smallwood, CWA at a June 1963 CWA Convention in Kansas City, Missouri. In his 1976 book, former CIA agent Phillip Agee identified Beirne as a top CIA collaborator in labor. (Photo from the Walter Reuther Library)

5. Jay Lovestone at a rally in the 1930s. Lovestone was the general secretary of the U.S. Communist Party in the 1920s and then a leading anti-communist during the Cold War. He was appointed International Affairs Director of the AFL-CIO in 1963 and was forced out in 1974 when it was learned he was being paid by the CIA. Behind Lovestone is David Dubinsky the president of the Ladies Garment Workers Union. Dubinsky promoted the careers of Lovestone, Romualdi, and Morris Paladino. (Photo from the Marxist Internet Archive)

6. Jay Lovestone, AFL-CIO International Affairs Director. (Photo from the Rob McKenzie collection)

7. AIFLD activities in Mexico during the 1980s received funds from the National Endowment for Democracy (NED).

8. Ford Cuautitlán workers protest the attack on the plant after the Cleto Nigmo memorial service January 11, 1990. (Photo Courtesy of Jaime Flores Duran)

9. The workers occupied the plant before being driven out by police on January 22. (Photo Courtesy of Jaime Flores Duran)

10. The Ford banner is burnt at the end of the march. (Photo Courtesy of Jaime Flores Duran)

11. "January 8th is not forgotten. The struggle continues at Ford." Workers banner for the COR-CTM representation vote. June 1991. (Photo from Rob McKenzie collection)

Notes

Prologue

1. "Chinese wages higher than Brazil, Mexico," *China Economic Review*, February 27, 2017: "Average hourly wages in China's manufacturing sector trebled between 2005 and 2016 to $3.60, according to Euromonitor, while during the same period manufacturing wages fell from $2.90 an hour to $2.70 in Brazil, and from $2.20 to $2.10 in Mexico...."

Chapter 1

1. Quenby Olmsted Hughes, *In the Interest of Democracy. The Rise and Fall of the Early Cold War Alliance Between the American Federation of Labor and the Central Intelligence Agency.* Peter Lang (2011); Anthony Carew, *American Labour's Cold War Abroad from Deep Freeze to Détente, 1945–1970.* AU Press, Athabasca University (2018), pp. 9–147.
2. Serafino Romualdi, *Presidents and Peons. Recollections of a Labor Ambassador in Latin America.* Funk & Wagnalls (1967), p. 20.
3. Thomas C. Fields Jr., "Transnationalism Meets Empire: The AFL-CIO, Development, and the Private Origins of Kennedy's Latin American Labor Program," *Diplomatic History*, Vol. 42, No. 2 (2018), p. 311.
4. *Ibid.*, pp. 315–321.
5. Hughes, *In the Interest of Democracy*, pp. 58–63.
6. Hugh Wilford, *The Mighty Wurlitzer. How the CIA Played America.* Harvard University Press (2008), pp. 54–55.
7. Hughes, *In the Interest of Democracy*, p. 70.
8. James Barron, "William C. Doherty, Ex-President Of Letter Carriers' Union, Is Dead," *New York Times*, August 12, 1987.
9. *Ibid.*
10. "The Association for Diplomatic Studies and Training Foreign Affairs Oral History Project Labor Series WILLIAM DOHERTY" (interview conducted by James F. Shea and Don R. Kienzel), October 3,1996,p.1,https://adst.org/wp-content/uploads/2018/09/Doherty-William.pdf (accessed January 22, 2021).
11. Carew, *American Labour's Cold War*, pp. 18, 29, 57–58, 261; Wilford, *The Mighty Wurlitzer*, p. 69.

12. "The Association for Diplomatic Studies and Training WILLIAM DOHERTY," pp. 3–4; Barron, "William C. Doherty, Ex-President Of Letter Carriers' Union, Is Dead. "

13. Jonathan Kwitny, *Endless Enemies. The Making of an Unfriendly World*. Congdon & Weed, Inc./Methuen Publishing (1984), pp. 346–347.

14. *Ibid.*, p. 347.

15. "The Association for Diplomatic Studies and Training Foreign Affairs Oral History Project Labor Series LANE KIRKLAND" (interview conducted by James F. Shea and Don R. Kienzle), November 13, 1996, p. 12, www.adst.org/OH%20TOCs/Kirkland.Lane.1998.pdf (Accessed January 22, 2021).

16. Romualdi, *Presidents and Peons*, p. 415.

17. Fields Jr., "Transnationalism Meets Empire," p. 313.

18. Carew, *American Labour's Cold War Abroad*, p. 261.

19. "The Association for Diplomatic Studies and Training WILLIAM DOHERTY," pp. 8–10.

20. Romualdi, *Presidents and Peons*, p. 415.

21. "The Association for Diplomatic Studies and Training WILLIAM DOHERTY," p. 5.

22. Fields Jr., "Transnationalism Meets Empire," p. 318.

23. Jeff Schuhrke, "'Comradely Brainwashing': International Development, Labor Education, and Industrial Relations in the Cold War," *Labor. Studies in Working-Class History*, Volume 16, Issue 3 (September 2019), pp. 39–43, 49, DOI 10.1215/15476715-7569788.

24. Fields Jr., "Transnationalism Meets Empire."

25. Schuhrke, "Comradely Brainwashing," pp. 49–50.

26. *Ibid.*, p. 51.

27. Fields Jr., "Transnationalism Meets Empire," pp. 319–320.

28. Schuhrke, "Comradely Brainwashing," pp. 51–52.

29. Fields Jr., "Transnationalism Meets Empire," p. 323.

30. Romualdi, *Presidents and Peons*, pp. 419–420.

31. Carew, *American Labour's Cold War Abroad*, p. 260.

32. Cliff Welch, "Labor Internationalism: U.S. Involvement in Brazilian Unions 1945–1965," *Latin American Research Review*, Vol. 30, No. 2 (1995), p. 83.

33. Romualdi, *Presidents and Peons*, p. 420; Schuhrke, "Comradely Brainwashing," p. 52.

34. Romualdi, *Presidents and Peons*, p. 417.

35. Fields Jr., "Transnationalism Meets Empire," p. 323.

36. Ruth Needleman, "AFL-CIA" (typed notes from interviews conducted in both Chile and the United States between October 1972 to April 1974). Unpublished. Provided by the author.

37. Schuhrke, "Comradely Brainwashing," p. 53.

38. Romualdi, *Presidents and Peons*, pp. 432–433.

39. *Ibid.*, pp. 417–418, 426.

40. Needleman, "AFL-CIA."

41. "Biographic Sketch of Mr. William C. Doherty Jr.," AR2004-0016 Box 26, George Meany Memorial Archives, University of Maryland (hereafter GMMA, UMD).

42. *Ibid.*; "William Charles Doherty Jr.," obituary, *Washington Post*, August 30, 2011.

43. Kwitny, *Endless Enemies*, p. 347.

44. Robert Waters and Gordon Daniels, "The World's Longest General Strike: The AFL-CIO, the CIA, and British Guiana," *Diplomatic History*, Vol. 29, No. 2 (April 2005), p. 282.

45. *Ibid.*, p. 283.

46. *Ibid.*, p. 282.

47. Tim Weiner, "A Kennedy-C.I.A. Plot Returns to Haunt Clinton," *New York Times*, October 30, 1994.

48. Neil Sheehan, "C.I.A. MEN AIDED STRIKES IN GUIANA AGAINST DR. JAGAN; Worked Under the Cover of U.S. Union in 1962 Drive on Marxist Premier AGENTS PROVIDED FUND Public Employes Group in Washington Got Agency Money for 4 Years C.I.A. MEN AIDED STRIKES IN GUIANA," *New York Times*, February 22, 1967; Victor Reuther, *The Brothers Reuther and the Story of the UAW. A Memoir*. Houghton Mifflin Company/UAW Special Edition (1976), p. 416. AFSCME President Jerry Wurf severed the relationship with the CIA in 1964.

49. Waters and Daniels, "The World's Longest General Strike," p. 302.

50. Sheehan, "C.I.A. MEN AIDED STRIKES IN GUIANA AGAINST DR. JAGAN"; Reuther, *The Brothers Reuther and the Story of the UAW*, p. 416.

51. Romualdi, *Presidents and Peons*, pp. 345–346.

52. Waters and Daniels, "The World's Longest General Strike," p. 307.

53. *Ibid.*, p. 280.

54. Weiner, "A Kennedy-C.I.A. Plot Returns to Haunt Clinton."

55. Waters and Daniels, "The World's Longest General Strike," p. 303.

56. "The Association for Diplomatic Studies and Training WILLIAM DOHERTY," p. 23.

57. *Ibid.*, p. 14.

58. *Ibid.*, pp. 7, 22.

59. Schuhrke, "Comradely Brainwashing," p. 54.
60. Daniel Cantor and Juliet Schor, *Tunnel Vision*. South End Press (1987), p. 44.
61. Romualdi, *Presidents and Peons*, p. 422.
62. David Shamus McCarthy, "The CIA and the Cult of Secrecy." Dissertations, W&M ScholarWorks (2008), paper 1539623335, p. 28.
63. Philip Agee, *Inside the Company. CIA Diary*. Bantam Books (February 1976), Appendix 1, pp. 619, 620, 623, 624, 639, 641.
64. *Ibid.*, pp. 137–138.
65. Central Intelligence Agency, "Memorandum for the Record," September 7, 1978, CIA-RDP81M00980R000600300055-3, General CIA Records. Freedom of Information Act. Electronic Reading Room.
66. Kwitny, *Endless Enemies*, p. 347.
67. Raymond Bonner, *Weakness and Deceit America and El Salvador's Dirty War*, p. 159.
68. "Biographic Sketch of Mr. William C. Doherty Jr."
69. *Ibid.*
70. "The Association for Diplomatic Studies and Training WILLIAM DOHERTY," p. 6.
71. Ted Morgan, *A Covert Life: Jay Lovestone—Communist, Anti-Communist, and Spymaster*. Random House (1999), pp. 338–340.

Chapter 2

1. Wilford, *The Mighty Wurlitzer*, pp. 237–243.
2. "CIA Linked to AFL-CIO Foreign Unit," *LA Times–Washington Post News Service*, May 23, 1966.
3. Nelson Lichtenstein, *The Most Dangerous Man in Detroit*. BasicBooks, a division of HarperCollins (1995), pp. 1–73; I have been a member of the UAW since 1977. I was the president of local union UAW 879 for eight years and a regional service representative on the UAW International Staff for ten years.
4. Lichtenstein, *The Most Dangerous Man in Detroit*, pp. 248–270.
5. Reuther, *The Brothers Reuther and the Story of the UAW*, p. 412.
6. *Ibid.*, pp. 411–416.
7. Minchin, Timothy J., *Labor under Fire. A History of the AFL-CIO since 1979*. University of North Carolina Press (2017), p. 38.
8. Reuther, *The Brothers Reuther*, pp. 364–377.
9. *Ibid.*, pp. 420–424.
10. Carew, *American Labour's Cold War Abroad*, pp. 257–264.
11. Schuhrke, "Comradely Brainwashing," p. 54.
12. Carew, *American Labour's Cold War Abroad*, pp. 257–264.

13. Welch, "Labor Internationalism," p. 84.
14. Carew, *American Labour's Cold War Abroad*, p. 264.
15. Reuther, *The Brothers Reuther and the Story of the UAW*, p. 419.
16. Schuhrke, "Comradely Brainwashing," pp. 60–62.
17. Paulo Fontes and Larrissa R. Corrêa, "Labor and Dictatorship in Brazil: A Historiographical Review." Published online by Cambridge University Press, May 3, 2018, p. 27.
18. Schuhrke, "Comradely Brainwashing," pp. 60–62.
19. Welch, "Labor Internationalism," pp. 84–85.
20. Lloyd, Jojol, "Tom E. Robles: Labor Leader, EEOC Official Fought for Workers," *Albuquerque Journal*, December 18, 2010.
21. Kwitny, *Endless Enemies*, p. 348.
22. Alan Francovich, *On Company Business*. Documentary film (1980), www.youtube.com/watch?v=ZyRUlnSayQE> (Accessed January 22, 2021).
23. Reuther, *The Brothers Reuther*, p. 419.
24. Carew, *American Labour's Cold War Abroad*, p. 264.
25. Reuther, *The Brothers Reuther*, p. 423.
26. Carew, *American Labour's Cold War Abroad*, p. 265.
27. *Ibid.*, p. 267; Harry Bernstein. "V. Reuther Links CIA, AFL-CIO," *Washington Post*, May 23, 1966.
28. Reuther, *The Brothers Reuther*, p. 423.
29. Lichtenstein, *The Most Dangerous Man in Detroit*, p. 408.
30. Carew, *American Labour's Cold War Abroad*, p. 271.
31. *Ibid.*, p. 270.
32. Lichtenstein, *The Most Dangerous Man in Detroit*, p 408.
33. Romualdi, *Presidents and Peons*, p. 431.
34. Agee, *Inside the Company*, Appendix 1, pp. 623–624.
35. Carew, *American Labour's Cold War Abroad*, pp. 273–276.
36. Lichtenstein, *The Most Dangerous Man in Detroit*, p. 409.
37. Thomas W. Braden, "Why I'm Glad the CIA Is 'Immoral,'" *Saturday Evening Post*, May 20, 1967, pp. 10–14; Reuther, *The Brothers Reuther*, p. 423.
38. Wilford, *The Mighty Wurlitzer*, pp. 244–247.
39. Harry Bernstein, "CIA Linked to AFL-CIO Foreign Unit," *LA Times–Washington Post News Service*, May 23, 1966.
40. Morgan, *A Covert Life*, pp. 48–66.
41. *Ibid.*, pp. 84–103. About this time in Russia, Lovestone later wrote, "When I was detained in Moscow and everybody was allowed to leave and I was not, I had the feeling of being in a locked trunk… the last sound of life you hear from the outside is the snapping of the lock."

42. *Ibid.*, pp. 105–112.

43. *Ibid.*, pp. 110–124.

44. *Ibid.*, p. 124.

45. *Ibid.*, pp. 125–126.

46. *Ibid.*, pp. 130–132.

47. *Ibid.*, p. 144.

48. *Ibid.*, p. 286.

49. *Ibid.*, p. 288.

50. *Ibid.*, p. 246.

51. *Ibid.*, pp. 251–252; John M. Crewdson, "C.I.A. MEN OPENED 3 SENATORS' MAIL AND NOTE TO NIXON," *New York Times*, September 25, 1975.

52. Jefferson Morley, *The Ghost. The Secret Life of CIA Spymaster James Jesus Angleton*. St. Martin's Press, First Edition (2017), pp. 188, 218, 219.

53. *Ibid.*, p. 87.

54. *Ibid.*, p. 56.

55. Morgan, *A Covert Life*, pp. 244–258.

56. *Ibid.*, p. 349.

57. Fred Hirsch, "An Analysis of Our AFL-CIO Role in Latin America in Chile or Under the Covers with the CIA," January 25, 1974. The Nettie Lee Benson Latin American Collection General Libraries, University of Texas at Austin, p. 7.

58. "Union Aide Renews Charge CIA Intervened in AFL-CIO," *Baltimore Sun*, February 16, 1967.

59. Carew, *American Labour's Cold War Abroad*, p. 270.

60. Reuther, *The Brothers Reuther*, p. 458.

61. "National Transportation Safety Board Aircraft Accident Report, File No. 3-0125, Executive Jet Aviation Inc., Lear Jet L23A, N434EJ, Near the Emmet County Airport, Pellston, Michigan, May 9, 1970, Adopted: December 22, 1970, Report Number NTSB-AAR-71-3," p. 10, http://libraryonline.erau.edu/online-full-text/ntsb/aircraft-accident-reports/AAR71-03.pdf (Accessed January 22, 2021).

62. Michael Parenti and Peggy Noton, "The Wonderful Life and Strange Death of Walter Reuther," *CovertAction*, No. 54 (Fall 1995), p. 42, https://covertactionmagazine.com/wp-content/uploads/2020/01/CAQ54-1995-3.pdf (Accessed May 3, 2021).

63. Reuther, *The Brothers Reuther*, p. 464.

64. "National Transportation Safety Board Aircraft Accident Report, File No. 3-0125," pp. 13–14.

65. A TSO is a minimum performance standard for specified materials, parts, and appliances used on civil aircraft. Federal Aviation Admin-

istration website: www.faa.gov/aircraft/air_cert/design_approvals/
tso/ (Accessed January 22, 2021).

66. A.J. Weberman, "Was Joe Biden the Target of a Botched Assassination
Attempt by CIA'S Domestic Operation Phoenix Component?"
http://educationforum.ipbhost.com/topic/15078-was-joe-biden-
the-target-of-a-botched-assassination-attempt-by-cia's-domestic-
operation-phoenix-component/?tab=comments#comment-175317
(Accessed January 22, 2021). Kollsman was not found liable in any
way for the crash.

67. *Ibid.*

68. *Ibid.*

69. *Ibid.*

70. Parenti and Noton, "The Wonderful Life and Strange Death of
Walter Reuther," p. 43.

71. John Barnard, *American Vanguard. The United Auto Workers During
the Reuther Years 1935–1970.* Wayne State University Press (2004),
p. 446.

72. Central Intelligence Agency, "1973-03-07. Air America, Inc. Vientiane, Laos Facilities And Operations," 197307 pdf. General CIA
Records. Freedom of Information Act. Electronic Reading Room.

73. Weberman, "Was Joe Biden the Target of a Botched Assassination
Attempt?"

74. FOIA-2018-00306: "In response to your FOIA request regarding
an aviation accident on 05/09/1970 in Pellston, Michigan. The
only information available is the final report on NTSB.GOV. Here
is the web address to access the report": www.ntsb.gov/_layouts/
ntsb.aviation/brief.aspx?ev_id=2646&key=0 (Accessed January 22,
2021). No. FOIA-2021-00253 and FOIA-2021-00254. The NTSB
did not begin keeping records on microfiche until 1978.

75. Parenti and Noton, "The Wonderful Life and Strange Death of
Walter Reuther," p. 43.

76. Elisabeth Reuther Dickmeyer, *Putting the World Together. My Father
Walter Reuther. The Liberal Warrior.* LivingForce Publishing (2004),
p. 356.

77. Neal E. Boudette and Noam Scheiber, "Dennis Williams, Former
U.A.W. Leader, Is Accused of Conspiracy," *New York Times*, August
27, 2020.

78. Robert Snell and Daniel Howes, "UAW Offers Unprecedented
Meeting with Feds amid Corruption Scandal," *Detroit News*, March
26, 2020.

Chapter 3

1. Argentina Independent, *Salvador Allende's Last Speech with English Subtitles* (September 11, 2013). Available at: www.youtube.com/watch?v=HC8UirZLCZQ (Accessed January 7, 2019). Also referenced in a Noam Chomsky translation available at: www.youtube.com/watch?v=BA8W3bnTeNc&ab_channel=DanielBasilio (Accessed September 14, 2021).

2. Peter Kornbluh, *The Pinochet File. A Declassified Dossier on Atrocity and Accountability*. New York: The New Press (2003), p. 115.

3. U.S. Senate (December 18, 1975), *Covert Action in Chile. 1963–1973* (94th Congress, 1st Session).

4. Jonathan Haslam, *The Nixon Administration and the Death of Allende's Chile. A Case of Assisted Suicide*. London; New York: Verso Books (2005), pp. 130–132.

5. Edy Kaufman, *Crisis in Allende's Chile. New Perspectives*. Praeger Publishers (1988), p. 82.

6. Hal Brands, *Latin America's Cold War*. Harvard University Press (2010), pp. 2, 118, 119.

7. Tanya Harmer, *Allende's Chile and the Inter-American Cold War*. University of North Carolina Press (2011), p. 197.

8. Kristian Gustafson, *Hostile Intent. US Covert Operations in Chile, 1964–1974*. Potomac Books (2007), p. 205.

9. National Security Council, "Memorandum for Dr Kissinger," November 17, 1970. Library of Congress. Freedom of Information Act. Electronic Reading Room.

10. Letter from Robert O'Neill to Andy McLellan. November 3, 1972. International Affairs Department (hereafter IAD in notes). Country Files, 1969–1981. Box 5, File 16. GMMA, UMD.

11. AIFLD Memorandum, From William Doherty to Andrew McLellan, Joseph Beirne, Jay Lovestone, Ernest Lee. September 16, 1971; AIFLD Memorandum, From William Doherty to McLellan, Beirne, Lovestone, Lee. September 9, 1971. IAD. International Labor Organizations Activities, 1946–1985. 17/9. GMMA, UMD.

12. Central Intelligence Agency, Intelligence Memorandum. "Communist Influence in Latin American Labor." February 1, 1967. General CIA Records. Freedom of Information Act. Electronic Reading Room.

13. Letter from Serafino Romualdi to Thomas Walsh. August 17, 1962. IAD. Country Files, 1945–1971. 018/2. GMMA, UMD.

14. AIFLD Memorandum. Robert O'Neill to Jesse Friedman. June 6, 1972. IAD. Country Files, 1969–1981. 5/16. GMMA, UMD.

15. Hortensia Allende Bussi, quoted in Fred Hirsch, "The Labor Movement: Penetration Point for US Intelligence and Transnationals," in Fred Hirsch and Richard Fletcher, *The CIA and the Labor Movement*. Nottingham: Spokesman Books (1977), p. 37.

16. AIFLD Report. "Statement on Free Trade Union Situation in Chile." Circa 1966. IAD. Country Files, 1945–1971. 018/8. GMMA, UMD.

17. "Minutes of the Annual Meeting of the Board of Trustees of the American Institute for Free Labor Development." May 19, 1969. Office of the President. George Meany Files, 1940–1980. 58/1. GMMA, UMD.

18. "Labor Organization Cancels Its Boycott of Chilean Cargoes," *The Washington Post*, January 17, 1979.

19. Intelligence Meeting. June 11, 1973. General CIA Records. Freedom of Information Act. Electronic Reading Room.

20. AIFLD Social Projects Department, "Report on Activities." March 1965. Office of the President. George Meany Files, 1940–1980. 57/6. GMMA, UMD.

21. Hirsch, "The Labor Movement," p. 31.

22. Letter (in Spanish) from O'Neill to McLellan, April 14, 1971; Letter from Deak & Co. Manager Otto J. Ruesch to AIFLD. April 8, 1971. IAD. Country Files, 1969–1981. 5/15. GMMA, UMD; "Was CIA Financier-turned Wall Street Banker Assassinated by the Bearded Bag Lady?" *The Daily Mail*, December 10, 2012.

23. Patricio Guzman, *The Battle of Chile—Part 2, The Coup D'état* (1976). Uploaded to YouTube by Radio Stocolmania (June 13, 2017), *The Battle of Chile Part 2 SUB INGLES*. Available at: www.youtube.com/watch?v=mR8xNnHQq-M&t=271s (Accessed January 9, 2019).

24. Hirsch, "The Labor Movement," p. 31.

25. Patricio Guzman, *The Battle of Chile—Part 1* (1975). Uploaded to YouTube by Ronaldo Entler (January 18, 2011), *La Batali de Chile*. Available at: www.youtube.com/watch?v=5kFPGxl3fMk&t=13s (Accessed January 9, 2019).

26. Theodore H. Moran, *Multinational Corporations and the Politics of Dependence. Copper in Chile*. Princeton; Cambridge: Princeton University Press (1975), p. 6.

27. AIFLD Memorandum, O'Neill to Jesse Friedman. June 6, 1972. IAD. Country Files, 1969–1981. 5/16. GMMA, UMD.

28. Letter from McLellan to O'Neill. August 31, 1971. IAD. Country Files, 1969–1981. 5/16. GMMA, UMD.

29. Letter from O'Neill to McLellan. November 3, 1972. IAD. Country Files, 1969–1981. 5/16. GMMA, UMD.

30. Guzman, *The Battle of Chile—Part 1*.
31. Report from McLellan to Jay Lovestone, "Chilean Strike Picture." May 22, 1973. IAD. Country Files, 1969–1981. 5/17. GMMA, UMD.
32. Guzman, *The Battle of Chile—Part 1*; Haslam, *A Case of Assisted Suicide*, p. 175.
33. Kornbluh, *The Pinochet File*, pp. 3–17.
34. "Under the Covers." Draft of text, probably written by Fred Hirsch, in AIFLD Archives. IAD. International Labor Organizations Activities, 1946–1985. 17/14. GMMA, UMD.
35. Haslam, *A Case of Assisted Suicide*, p. 171.
36. Needleman, "AFL-CIA."
37. Needleman, "AFL-CIA"; Haslam, *A Case of Assisted Suicide*, p. 140.
38. Chile Government Workers Trade Union Team, "Final Summary Report. Period of Visit 13 November–7 December 1972." IAD. Country Files, 1969–1981. 5/16. GMMA, UMD.
39. Hirsch, "The Labor Movement," pp. 26–29.
40. Haslam, *A Case of Assisted Suicide*, p. 144.
41. Guzman, *The Battle of Chile—Part 2*.
42. Augusto Pinochet, quoted in Kornbluh, *The Pinochet File*, p. 113.
43. *El Mercurio*, June 27, 1974, quoted Fred Hirsch and Richard Fletcher, *The CIA and the Labor Movement*. Nottingham: Spokesman Books (1977), p. 5.
44. Kornbluh, *The Pinochet File*, p. 161–163.
45. U.S. Department of Labor, *Labor Rights Report. Chile*. Washington, DC: Government Printing Office (2003).
46. Cable from George Meany to Augusto Pinochet, April 9, 1974. IAD. Country Files, 1969–1981. 5/17. GMMA, UMD.
47. Joseph Beirne to Jay Lovestone, Report. "Current Problems and Prospects of the Latin American Free Trade Union Movement," April 19, 1971. 64/11. GMMA, UMD, p. 10.
48. Stephen G. Rabe, *The Killing Zone. The United States Wages Cold War in Latin America*. New York: Oxford University Press (2011).
49. Fred Hirsch, "An Analysis of Our AFL-CIO Role in Latin America or Under the Covers with the CIA." Central Intelligence Agency. Freedom of Information Act. Electronic Reading Room. Library of Congress, pp. 1–2. Available at: www.cia.gov/library/readingroom/ (Accessed January 22, 2021).
50. *Ibid.*, p. 53.
51. "AFL-CIO Role in Latin America Quizzed," *Northern California Labor, Santa Clara edition*, April 12, 1974, p. 2.

52. Fred Hirsh and Virginia Muir, "A Plumber Gets Curious About Exporting McCarthyism," in *The Cold War Against Labor. Volume Two*, Ann Fagan Ginger and David Christiano (eds.). Meiklejohn Civil Liberties Institute (1987), p. 745.
53. Kim Scipes, *AFL-CIO's Secret War against Developing Country Workers*. Lexington Books (2011), p. 71.
54. "Labor Protests CIA Role in Chile," *National Guardian*, October 9, 1974.
55. Ted Morgan, *A Covert Life*, p. 351.
56. Tania Opazo, "The Boys Who Got to Remake an Economy," *Slate*, January 12, 2016.

Chapter 4

1. Raymond Bonner, *Weakness and Deceit. America and El Salvador's Dirty War*. OR Books (2016), p. 160.
2. *Ibid.*, pp. 37–38; Chris Norton, "Build and Destroy," Report on the Americas. *Shadow Play*. November/December 1985. North American Congress on Latin America, p. 29.
3. Norton, "Build and Destroy," p. 27.
4. Bonner, *Weakness and Deceit*, pp. 14–17.
5. Norton, "Build and Destroy," p. 27.
6. Bonner, *Weakness and Deceit*, p. 17.
7. Norton, "Build and Destroy," p. 27.
8. Norton, "Build and Destroy"; Bonner, *Weakness and Deceit*, p. 58.
9. Norton, "Build and Destroy," p. 27.
10. *Ibid.*
11. *Ibid.*
12. Bonner, *Weakness and Deceit*, pp. 24–26.
13. *Ibid.*, p. 27.
14. Norton, "Build and Destroy," p. 27.
15. Schuhrke, "Agrarian Reform and the AFL-CIO's Cold War in El Salvador," *Diplomatic History*, Vol. 44 (2020), p. 539.
16. *Ibid.*, p. 24.
17. "The Association for Diplomatic Studies and Training Foreign Affairs Oral History Project Labor Series JESSE A. FRIEDMAN" (interviewed conducted by James F. Shea and Don R. Kienzle), September 22, 1995, p. 12, www.adst.org/OH%20TOCs/Friedman,%20Jesse%20A.toc.pdf (Accessed January 22, 2021). Some sources say Hammer was sent to Venezuela.
18. Bonner, *Weakness and Deceit*, p. 28.
19. *Ibid.*, p. 73.
20. *Ibid.*, pp. 80–83.

21. *Ibid.*, p. xvii.
22. Bonner, *Weakness and Deceit*, pp. 121–134.
23. Norton "Build and Destroy," p. 27.
24. *Ibid.*
25. Schuhrke, "Agrarian Reform," p. 543.
26. Bonner, *Weakness and Deceit*, p. 161.
27. Norton, "Build and Destroy," p. 27.
28. Bonner, *Weakness and Deceit*, p. 160.
29. Schuhrke, "Agrarian Reform," p. 545.
30. Norton, "Build And Destroy," pp. 27–28.
31. *Ibid.*
32. Schuhrke, "Agrarian Reform," p. 547.
33. Bonner, *Weakness and Deceit*, p. 160.
34. *Ibid.*, pp. 161–168.
35. *Ibid.*, p. 43.
36. Interview and emails with Frank Hammer in 2019 and 2020.
37. Arch Puddington, *Lane Kirkland. Champion of American Labor.* John Wiley & Sons (2005), p. 191.
38. Mike Sager, "Slain U.S. Adviser Had an 'Obsession' to Distribute Land," *Washington Post*, January 5, 1981.
39. Schuhrke, "Agrarian Reform," p. 549.
40. Bonner, *Weakness and Deceit*, p. 159.
41. Sager, "Slain U.S. Adviser Had an 'Obsession' to Distribute Land."
42. Kate Rogers, "The CIA Is Hunting for Its Next Generation of Talent," *CNBC*, April 6, 2018, www.cnbc.com/2018/04/05/the-cia-is-hunting-for-its-next-generation-of-talent.html (Accessed January 22, 2021).
43. Central Intelligence Agency, "Special Bulletin," CIA-RDP78-03090A000100110028-pdf. General CIA Records. Freedom of Information Act. Electronic Reading Room.
44. John Hollister Hedley, "Twenty Years of Officers in Residence CIA in the Classroom," CIA Historical Document, April 15, 2007. General CIA Records. Freedom of Information Act. Electronic Reading Room.
45. *Ibid.*
46. "The Association for Diplomatic Studies and Training JESSE FRIEDMAN," p. 11; *Ibid.*, p. 1.
47. Reed Irvine, "Anti-CIA Publication Targeted El Salvador," *Accuracy in Media*, January 17, 1981, p. 21.
48. "El Salvador Murders Linked to Far-Left 'CounterSpy,'" *Human Events*, February 14, 1981, p. 13.
49. Bonner, *Weakness and Deceit*, p. 159.

50. *Ibid.*
51. Frank Hammer email.
52. Bonner, *Weakness and Deceit*, p. 159.
53. Sager, "Slain U.S. Adviser Had an 'Obsession' to Distribute Land."
54. Norton, "Build and Destroy," p. 28.
55. *Ibid.*, pp. 29–31.
56. "The Association for Diplomatic Studies and Training WILLIAM DOHERTY," pp. 5–6.
57. Andrew Battista, "Unions and Cold War Policy in the 1980s. The National Labor Committee, the AFL-CIO, and Central America," *Diplomatic History*, Vol. 26, No. 3 (Summer 2002), Oxford University Press, p. 446.
58. *Ibid.*, pp. 422–423.
59. *Ibid.*, pp. 426, 430.
60. Bonner, *Weakness and Deceit*, pp. 37–38.
61. Schuhrke, "Agrarian Reform," p. 550.
62. *Ibid.*, p. 160.
63. Bonner, *Weakness and Deceit*, p. 10.
64. Norton, "Build and Destroy," p. 29.
65. *Ibid.*
66. *Ibid.*
67. *Ibid.*, p. 30.
68. Bonner, *Weakness and Deceit*, p. 250.
69. Battista, "Unions and Cold War Policy," p. 428.
70. Norton, "Build and Destroy," p. 30.
71. *Ibid.*, p. 31.
72. *Ibid.*, pp. 31–33.
73. Al Weinrub and William Bollinger, *The AFL-CIO in Central America*. Labor Network on Central America (1987), p. 21.
74. Norton, "Build and Destroy," p. 31.
75. *Ibid.*
76. Battista, "Unions and Cold War Policy," p. 422.
77. Frank Hammer, "Not Really Big Deal Killing in El Salvador," *New York Times*, December 11, 1984.
78. Interview and email with Frank Hammer.
79. *Ibid.*,
80. Battista, "Unions and Cold War Policy," p. 422.
81. Puddington, *Lane Kirkland*, pp. 205–206.
82. International Affairs Conference, "Memo," May 6, 1985, AIFLD/AFL-CIO, AR2004-0016 Box 40. GMMA, UMD.
83. *Ibid.*

84. Fred Hirsch, "The AIFLD, International Trade Secretariats and Fascism in Chile: An Open Letter to the Labor Movement," Northern California Chile Coalition (1975), p. 8.

85. Morris Paladino, "Bio," AR2004-0016 Box 40. GMMA, UMD.

86. Agee, *Inside the Company*, p. 638.

87. Puddington, *Lane Kirkland*, p. 12.

88. William Serrin, "Lane Kirkland, Who Led Labor In Difficult Times, Is Dead at 77," *New York Times*, August 15, 1999.

89. Puddington, *Lane Kirkland*, p. 21.

90. Minchin, *Labor under Fire*, pp. 51–52.

91. Puddington, *Lane Kirkland*, p. 30.

92. *Ibid.*

93. A.H. Raskin, "Lane Kirkland: New Style," *New York Times*, October 28, 1979.

94. Serrin, "Lane Kirkland, Who Led Labor In Difficult Times, Is Dead at 77."

95. *Ibid.*

96. *Ibid.*

97. Wilford, *The Mighty Wurlitzer*, p. 69: Following the breakup of the FTUC in December 1957, "Irving Brown, however, remained as active as ever, carrying out operations for the Agency on a freelance basis"; *AIFLD In Central America Agents as Organizers Tom Barry and Deb Preusch*, Hornblake AR20040016 Box 40: Former CIA agent John Stockwell is quoted as calling Brown, "Mr. CIA in the labor movement"; Jonathan Kwitny, *Endless Enemies*, pp. 340, 345: "At least five former intelligence officers say that while overseas Brown has done undercover work for the CIA—this was when he was ostensibly championing the cause of independent trade unionism." Kwitny also reported that in an interview with Thomas Braden, a former CIA officer, Braden said Brown used the pseudonym Norris A. Grambo for undercover work. Paul Sakwa said he was Brown's CIA case officer between 1951–1954; Hughes, *In the Interest of Democracy*, p. 3: In an interview with Hughes, Franklin Lindsay who worked for the CIA between 1949 and 1953 "...remembered Irving Brown as a 'tremendous operator' who managed the FTUC with AFL money before accepting CIA aid"; Francovich, *On Company Business*: Paul Sakwa was interviewed and said he was a CIA case officer for labor operations in France in 1952. He said Irving Brown received CIA money which he was passing around in France; Agee, *Inside the* Company, p. 624: "BROWN, IRVING. European representative of the American Federation of Labor and principal CIA agent for control of the International Confederation of Free Trade

Unions (ICFTU)"; Carew, *American Labour's Cold War*, pp. 24–27: "…there appears to be enough smoke to indicate a certain amount of fire and that Brown was indeed inducted into the world of secret intelligence in the closing stages of the war [World War II]. Why he should have been selected for such work—making contact with French trade unionists when he spoke no French, discussing sabotage with Norwegian partisans when he knew nothing of sabotage, and generally having no international experience—is puzzling. All that is certain is that Irving Brown was close to Jay Lovestone and that the latter was beginning to make his own contacts with U.S. intelligence. Brown, however, remained as active as ever, carrying out operations for the Agency on a freelance basis."

98. Carew, *American Labour's Cold War*, p. 4.

99. "Irving Brown Bio," AR 2004-0031 Box No. 18. GMMA, UMD.

100. Interview and email with Anderson June 2020.

101. Weinrub and Bollinger, *The AFL-CIO in Central America*, p. 16.

102. International Affairs Conference, "Memo."

103. Jane Slaughter, "AFL-CIO Leaders Defend Central America Policy," *Labor Notes* October 1985, p. 16.

104. *Ibid.*, p. 13.

105. Lynda Gorov, "AFL-CIO Split on Latin America," *Boston Globe*, May 12, 1985.

106. Cantor and Schor, *Tunnel Vision*, p. 1.

107. *Ibid.*, p. 3.

108. Battista, "Unions and Cold War Policy," p. 438.

109. *Ibid.*

110. "AFL-CIO Resolution Backs Central American Peace Plan," *Union Advocate*, November 9, 1987.

111. Haddad, Samuel, "Labor Groups Working Against AFL-CIO Labor Policy," February 15, 1985, AR2004-0016 Box No. 40. GMMA, UMD.

112. Jim Shannon, "Minnesota Unionists for Peace Oppose Contra Aid," *Union Advocate*, September 21, 1987.

113. Jim Smoger, "CLUW Member Knocks Contra Aid after Nicaragua Trip," *Union Advocate*, July 28, 1986.

114. Puddington, *Lane Kirkland*, p. 206.

115. Drew Mendelson, "Impressions: The State of Labor in Central America," *Union Advocate*, November 4, 1985.

116. Weinrub and Bollinger, *The AFL-CIO in Central America*, p. 34.

117. "Contra Issue Draws Sharp Debate," *Union Advocate*, September 28, 1987.

118. "Contra Issue Draws Sharp Debate."

119. AFL-CIO President Richard Trumka died of natural causes at the age of 72 in August 2021. He was elected federation president.

Chapter 5

1. Shifra M. Goldman, *Dimensions of the Americas*. University of Chicago Press (1994), pp. 294–295.
2. "Armed Americans at Greene's Mine," *New York Times*, June 3, 1906.
3. Agee, *Inside the Company*, p. 531.
4. *Ibid.*, p. 538.
5. Eric Pace, "William Casey, Ex-C.I.A. Head, Is Dead at 74," *New York Times*, May 7, 1987.
6. Edgar Chamorro and Jefferson Morley, "Confessions of a 'Contra.'" *New Republic*, August 4, 1985.
7. Woodward, *Veil. The Secret Wars of the CIA 1981–1987*. Simon and Schuster, pp. 341–344; Philip Taubman, "Analyst Reported To Leave C.I.A. in a Clash with Casey on Mexico," *New York Times*, September 28, 1984.
8. Woodward, *Veil*, pp. 340–345; *Ibid.*, pp. 137–138.
9. *Ibid.*, pp. 339–340.
10. "The Outlook for Mexico." The Central Intelligence Agency (April 1984), p. 1.
11. Woodward, *Veil*, pp. 341–344; "The Outlook for Mexico," p. 1.
12. "The Outlook for Mexico," p. 1.
13. CIA, "Mexico Public Debt by Country" (1985), CIA-RD-P91B00874R000100190019-2, General CIA Records. Freedom of Information Act. Electronic Reading Room. The 1984 NIE said Mexico was paying interest on $85 billion of foreign debt; *Ibid.*, p. 7.
14. "The Outlook for Mexico," p. 27.
15. "The Outlook for Mexico," p. 30.
16. Central Intelligence Agency, "The Opposition Left in Mexico," CIA-RDP83B00225R000100300002-6. June 1982. General CIA Records. Freedom of Information Act. Electronic Reading Room, pp. 1–12.
17. *Ibid.*, p. 2.
18. *Ibid.*, p. 22; Hector de la Cueva interview conducted by Paula Cuellar Cuellar in Mexico City, summer 2018. Translated by Paula Cuellar Cuellar.
19. *Ibid.*, p. 22.
20. Central Intelligence Agency, "Mexico: Labor–Government Relations," December 1983. General CIA Records. Freedom of Information Act. Electronic Reading Room, pp. iii.
21. *Ibid.*, p. 1.

22. *Ibid.*, p. 9.

23. *Ibid.*, pp. 12–13.

24. Burton Kirkwood, *The History of Mexico*. Palgrave Macmillan (2005), p. 203.

25. Julia Preston and Samuel Dillon, *Opening Mexico. The Making of a Democracy*. Farrar, Straus and Giroux (2004), pp. 103–105.

26. *Ibid.*, p. 99.

27. Kirkwood, *The History of Mexico*, p. 203.

28. Preston and Dillon, *Opening Mexico*, p. 113.

29. *Ibid.*, pp. 97–103.

30. *Ibid.*, pp. 105–109.

31. Central Intelligence Agency, "Mexico: Political Implications of the 1985 Earthquake—A Comparison with Nicaragua and Guatemala," CIA-RDP88T00768R0002001160001-7, General CIA Records. Freedom of Information Act. Electronic Reading Room, p. iii.

32. *Ibid.*, p. 11.

33. *Ibid.*

34. Preston and Dillon, *Opening Mexico*, pp. 113–115.

35. Kirkwood, *The History of Mexico*, p. 202.

36. Preston and Dillon, *Opening Mexico*, pp. 148–152.

37. "Socialist Mexican Party," Wikipedia, https://en.wikipedia.org/wiki/Socialist_Mexican_Party (Accessed January 22, 2021).

38. Jaime Flores Durán interview conducted by Paula Cuellar Cuellar in Mexico City, summer 2018. Translated by Paula Cuellar Cuellar.

39. Larry Rother, "A Killing Inflames Mexican Campaign," *New York Times*, July 5, 1988; Preston and Dillon, *Opening Mexico*, p. 158.

40. Preston and Dillon, *Opening Mexico*, p. 158.

41. *Ibid.*, p. 170.

42. *Ibid.*, pp. 159–167.

43. *Ibid.*, p. 171.

44. *Ibid.*

45. Jaime Flores Durán interview.

46. Preston and Dillon, *Opening Mexico*, p. 175.

47. *Ibid.*, p. 177. Vincente Fox was elected president of Mexico in 2000. Kirkwood, *The History of Mexico*, p. 205.

48. Preston and Dillon, *Opening Mexico*, pp. 176–179.

49. Central Intelligence Agency, "Mexico: Assessing the Potential for Short-Term Instability," August 10, 1988, CIA-RDP04T00990 R000200010001. General CIA Records. Freedom of Information Act. Electronic Reading Room.

50. Negroponte would be appointed U.S. ambassador to the U.N. and serve in that position between 2001 and 2003. Following the invasion

of Iraq, Negroponte became U.S. ambassador to that country during 2004–2005. He served as director of national intelligence from 2005 to 2007.

51. "The Association for Diplomatic Studies and Training Foreign Affairs Oral History Project AMBASSADOR JOHN D. NEGRO-PONTE" (interviewed conducted by Charles Kennedy), February 11, 2000 (Copyright 2017), p. 102.

52. Carla Anne Robbins, "Billions in U.S. Aid to Honduras Saw Little Long-Term Success," *Wall Street Journal*, July 2, 1997; "Negroponte's Time in Honduras at Issue," *Washington Post*, March 21, 2005.

53. Michael Dobbs, "Papers Illustrate Negroponte's Contra Role," *Washington Post*, April 12, 2005.

54. James Lemoyne, "CIA Accused of Tolerating Killings in Honduras," *New York Times*, February 14, 1986.

55. "The Association for Diplomatic Studies and Training Foreign Affairs Oral History Project AMBASSADOR JOHN D. NEGRO-PONTE," p. 102.

56. Walter Pincus, "In Clandestine Service, Not So Secret Strains," *Washington Post*, May 1, 1997.

57. Nickolas Marinelli, "Ambassador Robert Pastorino Dies at 73," *L'Italo-Americano*, June 11, 2013.

58. Larry Rother, "Uproar Over Envoy Strains Ties with Mexico," *New York Times*, February 14, 1989.

59. "The Association for Diplomatic Studies and Training Foreign Affairs Oral History Project AMBASSADOR JOHN D. NEGRO-PONTE," p. 102.

60. Sergio Munoz, "Mexico Steels Itself for Hard-Liner U.S. Envoy," *LA Times*, February 10, 1989.

Chapter 6

1. Ma. Isabel Studer, "Regionalism in the Ford Motor Company's Global Strategies," in *Confronting Change*, Huberto Juarez Núñez and Steve Babson (eds.). M.E. Sharpe (2002), p. 73.

2. David Halberstam, *The Reckoning*. A Thomas Congdon Book, First Edition (1986), pp. 111–172.

3. *Ibid.*, pp. 174–187. I traveled to Japan as part of a four-member UAW delegation as guests of the Japanese Institute for Labor in the summer of 1999 to study the Japanese auto industry and culture.

4. *Ibid.*, pp. 690–693. Shaiken would go on to be a professor at the University of California, Berkeley.

5. Studer, "Regionalism in the Ford Motor Company's Global Strategies," p. 81.

6. James M. Cypher, "Mexico since NAFTA: Elite Delusions and the Reality of Decline," *New Labor Forum*, Vol. 20, No. 3 (Fall 2011), p. 61.

7. Steve Babson, "Free Trade and Worker Solidarity in the North American Auto Industry," in *Unions in a Globalized Environment: Changing Borders, Organizational Boundaries, and Social Roles*. M.E. Sharpe (2002), p. 26.

8. *Ibid.*, pp. 26–27.

9. Studer, "Regionalism in the Ford Motor Company's Global Strategies," pp. 74–78. I was president of UAW 879 at the Ford Twin Cities Assembly Plant (St. Paul, Minnesota) between 1998 and 2006. It was the last Ford assembly plant in the U.S. to begin the transition to lean production in 2000. I was secretary-treasurer of UAW–Ford Sub Council #2, the National Collective Bargaining Council for Ford U. S. assembly plants, between 2002 and 2006.

10. Studer, "Regionalism in the Ford Motor Company's Global Strategies," p. 79.

11. *Ibid.*, p. 79.

12. Timothy Minchin, *Labor under Fire*, p. 262.

13. Babson, *Unions in a Globalized Environment*, pp. 21–22.

14. Cypher, "Mexico since NAFTA," p. 62.

15. *Ibid.*, pp. 80–81.

16. P. Roberto Garcia and Stephen Hill, "Meeting 'Lean' Competitors: Ford De Mexico's Industrial Relations Strategy," in *Confronting Change*, Huberto Juarez Núñez and Steve Babson (eds.). M.E. Sharpe (2002), p. 143.

17. Raul Escobar Briones interview conducted by Paula Cuellar Cuellar in Mexico City, summer 2018.

18. *Ibid.*; Hector de la Cueva interview.

19. Garcia and Hills, "Meeting 'Lean' Competitors," pp. 147–150.

20. Raul Escobar Briones interview.

21. *Ibid.*; "Ford Dismisses 3,200 Mexicans," *New York Times*, September 22, 1987; Dan La Botz, *Mask of Democracy. Labor Suppression in Mexico Today*. South End Press (1992), p. 143.

22. *Ibid.*

23. Garcia and Hills, "Meeting 'Lean' Competitors," p. 147. Hector de la Cueva interview: Cueva had been working at the Cuautitlán plant since 1982 but was discharged in the 1987 group. The PRT assigned him to continue working with others at the Cuautitlán plant.

24. *Ibid.*; Hector de la Cueva interview.

25. Preston and Dillon, *Opening Mexico*, pp. 63–67.

26. *Ibid.*, p. 69.

27. *Ibid.*, p. 70.

28. Central Intelligence Agency, "Latin America Review Mexico: Trends in Student Activism," October 11, 1985, CIA-RDP87T00 289R000200910001-7. General CIA Records. Freedom of Information Act. Electronic Reading Room, pp. 9.

29. *Ibid.*, pp. 68–73.

30. Agee, *Inside the Company*, pp. 573–575. Three weeks after the Tlatelolco massacre, Agee writes, "My resignation will be effective early next year.... The difficult admission is that I became the servant of the capitalism I rejected [as a student]. I became one of its secret policemen. The CIA, after all, is nothing more than the secret police of American capitalism...so that shareholders of U.S. companies operating in poor countries can continue enjoying the rip-off."

31. Preston and Dillon, *Opening Mexico*, p. 85.

32. *Ibid.*, pp. 87, 188.

33. Central Intelligence Agency, "The Opposition Left in Mexico," p. 2. The CIA considered them to be a divisive force on the left that year.

34. Hector de la Cueva interview; "1982 Mexican general election," Wikipedia, https://en.wikipedia.org/wiki/1982_Mexican_general_election (Accessed January 22, 2021). In 1994, Ibarra de Piedra became a federal deputy of the Party of the Democratic Revolution (PRD). In 2006, she earned a seat in the Senate representing the PRD. In 2005, Carlos Solana Macias was apprehended for the abduction of her son. "Rosario Ibarra de Piedra," Wikipedia, https://en.wikipedia.org/wiki/Rosario_Ibarra (Accessed January 22, 2021).

35. Hector de la Cueva interview.

36. *Ibid.*

37. Central Intelligence Agency, "Mexico: Labor–Government Relations," p. 2.

38. "The Association for Diplomatic Studies and Training WILLIAM DOHERTY"; Romualdi, *Presidents and Peons*, p. 426; "Biographic Sketch of Mr. William C. Doherty Jr."

39. "The Association for Diplomatic Studies and Training JESSE FRIEDMAN."

40. In the aftermath of World War II, faced with threats to our democratic allies and without any mechanism to channel political assistance, U.S. policymakers resorted to covert means, secretly sending advisers, equipment, and funds to support newspapers and parties under siege in Europe. When it was revealed in the late 1960s that some American PVO's were receiving covert funding from the CIA to wage the battle of ideas at international forums, the Johnson Administration concluded that such funding should cease,

recommending the establishment of "a public-private mechanism" to fund overseas activities openly. The bill spelled out the procedures by which the funding would flow from USIA to NED and the mechanisms for ensuring financial accountability. Included in the legislation were earmarks of $13.8 million for the Free Trade Union Institute, an affiliate of the AFL-CIO incorporated in 1978 that would serve as an umbrella for labor's regional bodies operating in Africa, Asia, Latin America, and Eastern Europe. NED website: www.ned.org/about/history/ (Accessed January 22, 2021)

41. Branko Marcetic, "Don't Mourn Democracy Promotion," *Jacobin*, March 7, 2018; "Institution Building International Trade Secretariates," AR2004-0016 Box 40. GMMA, UMD.
42. "Request for Funds for the FTUI from the NED," 1984, AR 2003-0076 Box 16. GMMA, UMD, p. 8.
43. *Ibid.*
44. Email from Paul Somogyi, May 2020.
45. "National Endowment for Democracy (NED) Reporting from the Field," memo from Doherty, 1985 AR 2004-0031 Box 26. GMMA, UMD.
46. "Memo from Kimble to Somogyi," 1993. AR 2003-0076 Box 26. GMMA, UMD.
47. AR20040016 Box 40. GMMA, UMD.
48. Chapter 7 will provide more details on the office.

Chapter 7

1. "U.S.-Mexico Automobile Committee," 1988, Bieber Node 7.23, Reuther Library, Wayne State University.
2. *Ibid.*; "AIFLD Letter Head Memo from Torres to Donovan Concerning Somogyi," AR2003-0076 Box No. 16. GMMA, UMD.
3. *Ibid.*; AR2004-0016 Box No. 16. GMMA, UMD.
4. AR 2003-0076 Box 16. GMMA, UMD.
5. Agee, *Inside the Company*, p. 632.
6. AR 2003-0076 Box No.16. GMMA, UMD.
7. Email from Paul Somogyi, May 2020.
8. AR 2003-0076 Box No. 16. GMMA, UMD.
9. "U.S.-Mexico Automobile Committee."
10. Interview with Steve Beckman, January 2020.
11. Steve Beckman email, January 2020.
12. "U.S.-Mexico Automobile Committee."
13. *Ibid.*
14. Phone interview with Anderson, May 27, 2020.
15. *Ibid.*

16. *Ibid.*
17. *Ibid.*
18. *Ibid.*
19. Email from Steve Beckman, January 2020.
20. John Holusha, "Union Rebel. Jerry Tucker—The Man Who Is Fighting the U.A.W. from Inside," *New York Times*, October 23, 1988. I was active in New Directions and was elected on a New Directions platform as a convention delegate from UAW 879 to the 1989 national convention. I met Jerry Tucker and Victor Reuther in this context.
21. "Cable from the U.S. Mexican Embassy to the Sec. of State afternoon of January 11, 1990," DoS F-2016-16693 Doc No. C06337075.
22. Dan La Botz, *Mask of Democracy*, p. 148.
23. Raul Escobar Briones interview.
24. Hector De La Cueva interview.
25. Raul Escobar Briones interview.
26. Lichtenstein, *The Most Dangerous Man in Detroit*, pp. 107–108.
27. *Ibid.*; La Botz, *Mask of Democracy*, p. 148.
28. Raul Escobar Briones interview.
29. *Ibid.*; Central Intelligence Agency, "Mexico. Labor–Government Relations," p. 1.
30. Angela Mulholland, "How Long Can One Survive on a Hunger Strike?" *CTVNews.ca*, December 27, 2012.
31. "Cable from the U.S. Mexican Embassy to the Sec. of State January 13, 1990," DoS F-2016-16693 Doc No. C06337074.
32. Raul Escobar Briones interview.
33. *Ibid.*; Dan La Botz, *Mask of Democracy*, p. 149.
34. Email from Jaime Flores Durán, May 2020.
35. La Botz, *Mask of Democracy*, p. 149.
36. *Ibid.*, pp. 149–150. Raul Escobar Briones interview.
37. La Botz, *Mask of Democracy*, p. 150. In 1992, La Botz believed Ford and the CTM were responsible for the kidnappings.
38. Raul Escobar Briones interview.
39. *Ibid.*
40. Human Rights Watch, "Human Rights in Mexico. A policy of Impunity" (An Americas Watch Report), June 1990, p. 68, www.hrw.org/report/1990/06/01/human-rights-mexico-policy-impunity (Accessed January 22, 2012).
41. National Commission on Human Rights Mexico, "Recommendation 22/1992. Subject: The Case of Workers of the Ford Motor Company Mexico," Federal District, February 19, 1992; Alberto Dogart, "Wallace de la Mancha: Un Producto 'Hecho en México'"

["Wallace de la Mancha: A Product 'Made in Mexico'"]. Tratado de Libre Comercio, March–April 1991, www.elcotidianoenlinea.com. mx/pdf/4011.doc (Accessed January 22, 2021); "Ford Union Leader Wanted for Murder," UPI Archives, February 27, 1992.

42. Human Rights Watch, "Human Rights in Mexico," p. 69; Dogart, "Wallace de la Mancha."

43. "¡Ya llegó Wallace de la Mancha…!" ["Wallace de la Mancha Has Arrived!"], *Proceso*, November 12, 1988.

44. *Ibid.*

45. Alberto Nájar, "Historias Del Pais Que Ya Cambio" ["Stories of the Country That Already Changed"], *Masiosare*, November 22, 1998.

46. "¡Ya llegó Wallace de la Mancha…!"

47. *Ibid.*

48. Dogart, "Wallace de la Mancha."

49. *Ibid.*

50. Nájar, "Historias Del País Que Ya Cambió."

51. National Commission on Human Rights Mexico, "Recommendation 22/1992. Subject: The Case of Workers of the Ford Motor Company Mexico."

52. Dan La Botz, *Mask of Democracy*, pp. 151, 207; Wallace de la Mancha, "Wallace de la Mancha no participó en la agresión a trabajadores de la Ford" [letter to editor], *La Jornada*, January 10, 1990, p. 2.

53. Dogart, "Wallace de la Mancha"; La Botz, *Mask of Democracy*, p. 157.

54. *Ibid.*, p. 153.

55. Dogart, "Wallace de la Mancha."

56. Interview with Professor Patrick McNamara, University of Minnesota.

57. Raul Escobar Briones interview; La Botz, *Mask of Democracy*, p. 150.

58. La Botz, *Mask of Democracy*, p. 150.

59. Raul Escobar Briones interview.

60. Nájar, "Historias Del País Que Ya Cambió."

61. Raul Escobar Briones interview.

62. La Botz, *Mask of Democracy*, p. 151.

63. *Ibid.*

64. "Cable from the U.S. Mexican Embassy to the Sec. of State early morning January 13, 1990," DoS F-2016-16693 Doc No. C06337075.

65. Conversation with Ted LaValley in 1991.

66. Raul Escobar Briones interview.

Chapter 8

1. Tamara Kay, *NAFTA and the Politics of Labor Transnationalism*. Cambridge University Press (2011), p. 72.
2. La Botz, *Mask of Democracy*, p. 151.
3. Raul Escobar Briones interview.
4. La Botz, *Mask of Democracy*, p. 152.
5. Raul Escobar Briones interview.
6. Human Rights Watch, "Human Rights in Mexico," pp. 68–69.
7. "Ford of Mexico Worker Killed in Union Dispute," *Automotive News*, January 15, 1990.
8. Raul Escobar Briones interview; La Botz, *Mask of Democracy*, pp. 151–152; Department of State FOIA Case No. F-2016-16693 C06337074 Doc. No. C06337074.
9. Department of State FOIA Case No. FM-2018-03406 Doc. No. C06714181.
10. Raul Escobar Briones interview.
11. Department of State FOIA Case No. F-2016-16693 C06337074 Doc. No. C06337074.
12. *Ibid.*
13. La Botz, *Mask of Democracy*, p. 151.
14. *Ibid.*, p. 151.
15. *Ibid.*, p. 152.
16. La Botz, *Mask of Democracy*, pp. 151, 207; Wallace de la Mancha, "Wallace de la Mancha no participó en la agresión a trabajadores de la Ford," p. 2.
17. Department of State FOIA Case No. F-2016-16693 Doc. No. C06337073.
18. Department of State FOIA Case No. F-2016-16693 C06337074.
19. Department of State FOIA Case No. F-2016-16693 Doc. No. C06337072; Department of State FOIA Case No F-2016-16693 Doc. No. C06337073; La Botz, *Mask of Democracy*, p. 156.
20. Department of State FOIA Case No. F-2016-16693 Doc. No. C06337072.
21. Raul Escobar Briones interview.
22. Briones and Durán estimated the police numbers at 5,000. La Botz reported 2,000 in *Mask of Democracy*. Embassy cables said 1,800.
23. Raul Escobar Briones interview.
24. *Ibid.*
25. Department of State FOIA Case No. F-2016-16693 Doc. No. C06337073.
26. U.S. Department of State Case No. FM-2018-03406. Doc. No. C06714181.

27. La Botz, *Mask of Democracy*, p. 151.
28. Department of State FOIA Case No. F-2016-16693 Doc. No. C06337072
29. U.S. Department of State Case No. FM-2018-03406-03406. Doc. No. C06714181.
30. La Botz, *Mask of Democracy*, p. 154.
31. Department of State FOIA Case No. F-2016-16693 Doc. No. C06337072; Dan La Botz, *Mask of Democracy*, p. 153.
32. Department of State FOIA Case No. F-2016-16693 Doc. No. C06337071.
33. *Ibid.*; Raul Escobar Briones interview.
34. *Ibid.*
35. U.S. Department of State Case No. FM-2018-03406. Doc. No. C06337069.
36. Raul Escobar Briones interview.
37. Department of State FOIA Case FM-2018-03406 Doc. No. C06337070.
38. Department of State FOIA Case No F-2016-16693 Doc. No. C06337071.
39. Department of State FOIA Case FM-2018-03406 Doc. No. C06337070.
40. Department of State FOIA Case FM-2018-03406 No. C06714181.
41. Department of State FOIA Case FM-2018-03406 No. C06337068.
42. La Botz, *Mask of Democracy*, p. 156.
43. Department of State FOIA Case FM-2018-03406 No. C06337067.
44. La Botz, *Mask of Democracy*, p. 156.
45. Raul Escobar Briones interview.
46. Department of State FOIA Case No. F-2016-16693 Doc. No. C06337071.
47. *Ibid.*
48. Department of State FOIA Case FM-2018-03406 No. C06711037.
49. La Botz, *Mask of Democracy Labor*, p. 157.
50. *Ibid.*, pp. 157–158; Raul Escobar Briones interview.
51. Department of State FOIA Case F-2016-16693 Doc. No. C06337072.
52. Department of State FOIA Case F-2016-16693 Doc. No. C06337073.
53. "Cable from the U.S. Mexican Embassy to the Sec. of State early morning January 13, 1990."
54. Department of State F-2016-16693 Doc. No. C06337071.
55. La Botz, *Mask of Democracy Labor*, p. 151.
56. Hector de la Cueva interview.

57. Michael Dobbs, "Papers Illustrate Negroponte's Contra Role," *Washington Post*, April 12, 2005.

58. Agee, *Inside the Company*, p. 521.

59. Alberto Aguirre M., "*¿Quién era Ruth Uribe?*" [Who Was Ruth Uribe?], *El Economista*, October 12, 2012; National Commission on Human Rights Mexico, "Recommendation 22/1992. Subject: The Case of Workers of the Ford Motor Company Mexico"; Raul Escobar Briones interview.

60. Aguirre, "*¿Quién era Ruth Uribe?*"; Nájar, "Historias Del País Que Ya Cambió."

61. Raul Escobar Briones interview.

62. National Commission on Human Rights Mexico, "Recommendation 22/1992. Subject: The Case of Workers of the Ford Motor Company Mexico"; Raul Escobar Briones interview.

63. "Ford Union Leader Wanted for Murder," UPI Archives, February 27, 1992, https://groups.google.com/forum/#!topic/misc.activism.progressive/87J4hEzH_QY (Accessed January 22, 2021).

Chapter 9

1. Brian McMahon, *The Ford Century in Minnesota*. University of Minnesota Press (2016), p. 270.

2. Department of State FOIA Case FM-2018-03406 Doc. No. C06711041.

3. "State Department Cable from Henry Kissinger," Public Library of U.S. Diplomacy, WikiLeaks, https://search.wikileaks.org/plusd/cables/1974STATE049997_b.html (Accessed January 22, 2021).

4. Needleman, "AFL-CIA."

5. "AFL-CIO Convention Delegates Ponder Devastating Effects of Free Trade," *St. Paul Union Advocate*, October 7, 1991.

6. Battista, "Unions and Cold War Policy," pp. 450–451.

7. Tim Shorrock, "Labor's Cold War," *Nation*, May 1, 2003.

8. After retiring in 2018, Williams was charged with conspiring to embezzle union funds for personal expenses and luxury travel in 2020. He pleaded guilty to charges and was sentenced to 21 months in prison in 2021. Robert Snell, Jordyn Grzelewski, and Breana Noble, "Ex-UAW Boss Williams Charged in Embezzlement Scandal as Federal Probe Continues," *Detroit News*, August 27, 2020.

9. AR2004-0016 Box No. 16. GMMA, UMD; "AIFLD officers 1992," *Sourcewatch*, www.sourcewatch.org/index.php/American_Institute_for_Free_Labor_Development (Accessed January 22, 2021).

Chapter 10

1. Battista, "Unions and Cold War Policy," p. 422.
2. Branko Marcetic, "Don't Mourn Democracy Promotion," *Jacobin*, March 7, 2018.
3. "The Association for Diplomatic Studies and Training WILLIAM DOHERTY," p. 17.
4. Email from Somogyi, May 2020.
5. Susan Chira, "Koreans Ask, Is the Society Fair to Labor?" *New York Times*, December 26, 1986; Simon Rodberg, "The CIO without the CIA," American Prospect, December 19, 2001, https://prospect.org/features/cio-without-cia/ (Accessed January 22, 2021).
6. Tim Shorrock, "Money Doesn't Talk, It Swears...," an online blog, Wednesday May 4, 2005, http://timshorrock.blogspot.com/2005/05/afl-cio-eliminates-international.html (Accessed January 22, 2021).
7. Solidarity Center, "Our Mission and Vision," www.solidaritycenter.org/who-we-are/our-vision/ (Assessed January 22, 2021).
8. Shorrock, "Labor's Cold War," *Nation*, May 19, 2003.
9. Hirsch, "An Analysis of Our AFL-CIO Role in Latin America," pp. 1–2.
10. Kim Scipes, "AFL-CIO Refuses to 'Clear the Air' on Foreign Policy, Operations," *Labor Notes*, February 1, 2004.
11. *Ibid.*
12. Kim Scipes, *AFL-CIO's Secret War against Developing Country Workers. Solidarity or Sabotage?* Lexington Books (2011), p. 75.
13. *Ibid.*
14. Minchin, *Labor under Fire*, p. 276.
15. Shorrock, "Money Doesn't Talk, It Swears..."
16. NED website, www.ned.org/about/board-of-directors/ (Accessed January 22, 2021).
17. Sheehan, "C.I.A. MEN AIDED STRIKES IN GUIANA AGAINST DR. JAGAN."
18. Weinrub and Bollinger, *The AFL-CIO in Central America*, p. 34.
19. Midwest District Meeting AFL-CIO, March 15, 2018, https://aflcio.org/2018/3/15/local-union-leaders-midwest-strategize-win-2018-and-beyond?link_id=0&can_id=a833acf17cf5c555fceccc32b0d762b5&source=email-labor-update-139&email_referrer=email_319747&email_subject=labor-update (Accessed January 22, 2021).

Chapter 11

1. Janet G. Mullins Grissom, Wikipedia, https://en.wikipedia.org/wiki/Janet_G._Mullins_Grissom (Accessed January 22, 2021).

2. McMahon, *The Ford Century in Minnesota*, p. 270.
3. UMD Libraries, GMMA website, www.lib.umd.edu/special/collections/afl-cio (Accessed January 22, 2021).
4. Morgan, *A Covert Life*, p. 24.
5. *Ibid.*, pp. 350–351.
6. Kwitny, *Endless Enemies*, p. 340.
7. Agee, Inside the Company, Appendix 1, p. 619.
8. "1988 Mexican general election," Wikipedia, https://en.wikipedia.org/wiki/1988_Mexican_general_election (Accessed August 11, 2021).

Conclusion

1. Ford did not respond to four emails and a letter requesting information about these events. As far as I can determine, the company has never publicly commented on this episode.
2. Gerald Mayer, "Union Membership Trends in the United States." Congressional Research Service Report for Congress (2004).

Appendix

1. "Picture, trainees playing football at Front Royal." Undated. 33/10. GMMA, UMD.
2. "Academic Program of the Institute. First Course, June 18–Sept 14, 1962." 57/2. GMMA, UMD.
3. "'Opening Remarks' by Serafino Romualdi." June 19, 1962. 57/2. GMMA, UMD.
4. "CWA Response to Fulbright Committee Report." 57/17. GMMA, UMD; *AFL-CIO News*. July 11, 1964. 33/8. GMMA, UMD.
5. *Miami Herald*. August 11, 1962. 57/2. GMMA, UMD.
6. Canuto Coelho Filho, "Graduation Address." April 25, 1963. 57/6. GMMA, UMD.
7. "Graduation Luncheon, and Subsequent Graduate Address." August 8, 1963. 57/6. GMMA, UMD.
8. Gaston Benjamin, "Graduation Address." November 29, 1965. 57/12. GMMA, UMD.
9. "Speech for the Class by Adolfo Antelo Añez." 57/16. GMMA, UMD.
10. "GAO Report, 1969." 57/17. GMMA, UMD.
11. "Report on Activities." February 1965. 57/10. GMMA, UMD.
12. "Confidential: Relationship of US Government Agencies with the Social Projects Department of the American Institute for Free Labor

Development; and Host Country Participation in Social Projects."
57/5. GMMA, UMD.

13. Needleman, "AFL-CIA."
14. Letter from John Davis Lodge to Charles A. Meyer, Assistant Secretary for Interamerican Affairs, Department of State. June 26, 1970. 17/8. GMMA, UMD.

Index

Thanks to our Patreon subscriber:

Ciaran Kane

Who has shown generosity and comradeship in support of our publishing.

The Pluto Press Newsletter

Hello friend of Pluto!

Want to stay on top of the best radical books we publish?

Then sign up to be the first to hear about our new books, as well as special events, podcasts and videos.

You'll also get 50% off your first order with us when you sign up.

Come and join us!

Go to bit.ly/PlutoNewsletter